THE BEST TEST PREPARATION FOR THE

CLEP

COLLEGE-LEVEL EXAMINATION PROGRAM

FRESHMAN COLLEGE COMPOSITION

Staff of Research and Education Association
Dr. M. Fogiel, Director

Research & Education Association
61 Ethel Road West
Piscataway, New Jersey 08854

The Best Test Preparation for the
CLEP FRESHMAN COLLEGE COMPOSITION

Printed in the United States of America

Library of Congress Control Number 00-108853

International Standard Book Number 0-87891-899-X

Research & Education Association
61 Ethel Road West
Piscataway, New Jersey 08854

REA supports the effort to conserve and
protect environmental resources by
printing on recycled papers.

About Research & Education Association

Research & Education Association (REA) is an organization of educators, scientists, and engineers specializing in various academic fields. Founded in 1959 with the purpose of disseminating the most recently developed scientific information to groups in industry, government, high schools, and universities, REA has since become a successful and highly respected publisher of study aids, test preps, handbooks, and reference works.

REA's Test Preparation series includes study guides for all academic levels in almost all disciplines. Research & Education Association publishes test preps for students who have not yet completed high school, as well as high school students preparing to enter college. Students from countries around the world seeking to attend college in the United States will find the assistance they need in REA's publications. For college students seeking advanced degrees, REA publishes test preps for many major graduate school admission examinations in a wide variety of disciplines, including engineering, law, and medicine. Students at every level, in every field, with every ambition can find what they are looking for among REA's publications.

Unlike most test preparation books—which present only a few practice tests that bear little resemblance to the actual exams—REA's series presents tests that accurately depict the official exams in both degree of difficulty and types of questions. REA's practice tests are always based upon the most recently administered exams, and include every type of question that can be expected on the actual exams.

REA's publications and educational materials are highly regarded and continually receive an unprecedented amount of praise from professionals, instructors, librarians, parents, and students. Our authors are as diverse as the fields represented in the books we publish. They are well-known in their respective disciplines and serve on the faculties of prestigious high schools, colleges, and universities throughout the United States and Canada.

Acknowledgments

We would like to thank Dr. Max Fogiel, President, for his overall guidance, which brought this publication to completion; Larry B. Kling, Quality Control Manager of Books in Print, for his supervision of revisions; Melanie Seickel, Editorial Assistant, for her coordination of revisions; Michele DiBenedetto, Elizabeth Grout, and Sandra Nygaard for their editorial contributions; and Wende Solano for typesetting the manuscript.

CONTENTS

CLEP FRESHMAN COLLEGE COMPOSITION
INDEPENDENT STUDY SCHEDULE

The following study schedule allows for thorough preparation for the CLEP Freshman College Composition. Although it is designed for six weeks, it can be condensed into a three-week course by collapsing each two-week period into one. Be sure to set aside enough time—at least two hours each day—to study. But whichever study schedule works best for you, the more time you spend studying, the more prepared and relaxed you will be on the day of the exam.

Week	Activity
1	Read and study Chapter 1, which will introduce you to the CLEP Freshman College Composition. Then take Practice Test 1 to determine your strengths and weaknesses. Make sure to time yourself! Taking the test under time restrictions will allow you to focus more completely on your strengths and weaknesses. Score each section by using the score chart found in Chapter 1. You can then determine the areas in which you need to focus.
2	Carefully read and study Chapter 2, *Introduction to College Composition,* which will review all forms of writing that you will encounter on the CLEP Freshman College Composition. This section will help you understand how writers employ different techniques and styles to convey their messages, and it will serve as an aid in improving your own writing skills.
3	Carefully read Chapter 3, *English Language Skills Review,* to sharpen your knowledge of all the aspects of grammar that are critical to effective writing. Be sure to take all the drills and review the answers thoroughly.
4	Take Practice Test 2, and after scoring your exam, review carefully all incorrect answer explanations. If there are any types of questions or particular subjects that seem difficult to you, review those subjects by rereading the appropriate sections of the review chapters.

Week	Activity
5	Take Practice Test 3, and after scoring your exam, review carefully all incorrect answer explanations. If there are any types of questions or particular subjects that seem difficult to you, review those subjects by studying again the appropriate sections of the review chapters.
6	Retake each of the three practice tests. This will strengthen the areas you originally found troublesome. Go back and study the review chapters and the drills to be sure you are comfortable with all the material.

CHAPTER 1
ABOUT THE CLEP
FRESHMAN
COLLEGE
COMPOSITION

Chapter 1

ABOUT THE CLEP FRESHMAN COLLEGE COMPOSITION

ABOUT THIS BOOK

This book provides you with an accurate and complete representation of the CLEP Freshman College Composition exam. You will find a complete review of college composition, as well as tips and strategies for test-taking. We also provide three full-length practice tests, all based on the official CLEP Freshman College Composition. REA's practice tests contain every type of question that you can expect to encounter on the actual exam. Following each practice test you will find an answer key with detailed explanations designed to help you master the CLEP test material.

ABOUT THE EXAM

Who Takes the CLEP Freshman College Composition and What Is It Used for?

CLEP (College-Level Examination Program) examinations are usually taken by people who have acquired knowledge outside the classroom and wish to bypass certain college courses and earn college credit. The CLEP Program is designed to reward students for learning—no matter where or how that knowledge was acquired. The CLEP is the most widely accepted credit-by-examination program in the United States.

Although most CLEP examinees are adults returning to college, many graduating high school seniors, enrolled college students, and international students also take the exams to earn college credit or to demonstrate their ability to perform at the college level. There are no prerequisites, such as age or educational status, for taking CLEP examinations. However, you must meet any specific requirements of the particular institution from which you wish to receive CLEP credit.

There are two categories of CLEP examinations:

1. **CLEP General Examinations**, which are five separate tests that cover material usually taken as requirements during the first two years of college. CLEP General Examinations are available for English Composition (with or without essay), Humanities, Mathematics, Natural Sciences, and Social Sciences and History.

2. **CLEP Subject Examinations**, which include material usually covered in an undergraduate course with a similar title. The CLEP Freshman College Composition is one of 29 subject examinations.

Who Administers the Exam?

The CLEP is developed by the College Board, administered by the Educational Testing Service (ETS), and involves the assistance of educators throughout the United States. The test development process is designed and implemented to ensure that the content and difficulty level of the test are appropriate.

When and Where Is the Exam Given?

The CLEP Freshman College Composition is administered each month throughout the year at more than 1,200 test centers in the United States and can be arranged for candidates abroad on request. To find out the test center nearest you and to register for the exam, you must obtain a copy of the free booklets *CLEP Colleges* and *CLEP Information for Candidates and Registration Form*, which are available at most colleges where CLEP credit is granted, or by contacting:

College-Level Examination Program
P.O. Box 6600
Princeton, NJ 08541-6600
Phone: (609) 771-7865
E-mail: *clep@info.collegeboard.org*
Website: *http://www.collegeboard.org*

HOW TO USE THIS BOOK

What Do I Study First?

Read over the course review and the suggestions for test-taking, take the first practice test to determine your area(s) of weakness, and then go back and focus your study on those specific problems. Studying the reviews thoroughly will reinforce the basic skills you will need to do well on the exam. Make sure to take the practice tests to become familiar with the format and procedures involved with taking the actual exam.

To best utilize your study time, follow our Independent Study Schedule, which you'll find in the front of this book. The schedule is based on a six-week program, but can be condensed to three weeks if necessary by collapsing each two-week period into one week.

When Should I Start Studying?

It is never too early to start studying for the CLEP Freshman College Composition. The earlier you begin, the more time you will have to sharpen your skills. Do not procrastinate! Cramming is *not* an effective way to study, since it does not allow you the time needed to learn the test material. The sooner you learn the format of the exam, the more time you will have to familiarize yourself with it.

FORMAT OF THE CLEP FRESHMAN COLLEGE COMPOSITION

The CLEP Freshman College Composition covers the material one would find in most first-year English courses. It measures a student's understanding of both mechanics and style, with questions concerning the structure of sentences, the logical development of essays, and the ability to recognize a writer's purpose and strategies in prose and poetry.

There are approximately 100 multiple-choice questions, each with five possible answer choices, to be answered in two separately timed 45-minute sections.

Coverage is apportioned approximately as follows:

65%	Recognizing logical development in student drafts as well as published prose
20%	Recognizing and using standard written English
15%	Demonstrating the ability to use resource materials*

* These questions appear only in Section I.

There is also an optional free-response section to the CLEP Freshman College Composition that you would take only if your college required it. If you were required to complete this section, you would have to respond to two essay question topics in 90 minutes, the first of which would be mandatory, while the second would be a choice between two topics.

We have not included sample essay questions within our practice tests. Since the scoring is left to the college that requests this portion of the exam, it is impossible to determine what a satisfactory answer would be in every case. Below, however, are three topics similar to the ones you can expect to find on the exam.

Topic No. 1 Our use of language differs depending on the manner or conditions in which it used. Our language may differ in use of syntax, inflection, vocabulary, and pronunciation, dependent on circumstances.

Write an essay describing the differences in the language you would use in two different circumstances—a conversation with a friend and a job interview, for instance. Your essay should indicate what purposes the differences in your use of language serve.

Topic No. 2 Polls of American youth suggest that they want high-paying jobs, not necessarily satisfying careers. This reflects the current cultural value implied in the popular media that money is the key which opens the golden door to satisfaction, unlike the traditional value of work for its own reward.

Do you agree or disagree with this statement? Support your opinion with specific examples from history, current events, literature, or personal experience.

Topic No. 3 Because of increased crime involving teenagers at area malls and other places of recreational activity, local city councils and many concerned citizens have recently proposed curfews, hoping to stem the tide of teen crime.

Write an essay, to be read by the city council and concerned citizens, approving or disapproving of the proposed curfews for teenagers.

ABOUT COMPUTER-BASED TESTING AND OUR BOOK

As of July 2001, CLEP subject exams will be computerized. The CLEP CBT (computer-based testing) exams will continue to test the same materials and types of questions you will find in this book, but they will be administered on computer. The CLEP exams will also contain several trial questions (which will not be identified) that will not count towards your score. The purpose of the trial questions is to test new questions for future exams. The optional essay section will be typed and then sent electronically to be scored. There will also be

RAW SCORE CONVERSION CHART

Raw Score	Scaled Score	Course Grade	Raw Score	Scaled Score	Course Grade
100	80	A	48	54	B
99	80	A	47	53	B
98	80	A	46	52	B
97	80	A	45	51	B
96	79	A	44	51	B
95	79	A	43	50	B
94	78	A	42	50	B
93	77	A	41	50	B
92	77	A	40	49	B
91	76	A	39	49	B
90	75	A	38	48	C
89	74	A	37	48	C
88	73	A	36	47	C
87	73	A	35	47	C
86	72	A	34	46	C
85	72	A	33	46	C
84	71	A	32	45	C
83	70	A	31	45	C
82	70	A	30	44	C
81	69	A	29	43	D
80	69	A	28	43	D
79	68	A	27	42	D
78	68	A	26	42	D
77	67	A	25	41	D
76	67	A	24	41	D
75	66	A	23	40	D
74	66	A	22	40	D
73	65	A	21	39	D
72	65	A	20	38	D
71	64	A	19	37	D
70	64	A	18	37	F
69	64	A	17	36	F
68	63	A	16	36	F
67	63	A	15	35	F
66	62	A	14	35	F
65	62	A	13	34	F
64	61	A	12	34	F
63	61	A	11	33	F
62	60	A	10	32	F
61	60	A	9	31	F
60	60	A	8	30	F
59	59	A	7	29	F
58	58	A	6	28	F
57	58	A	5	27	F
56	57	A	4	25	F
55	57	A	3	23	F
54	56	A	2	21	F
53	56	A	1	20	F
52	55	A	0	20	F
51	55	A	−1	20	F
50	55	A	−2	20	F
49	54	B	and below	20	F

Although colleges and universities often use their own standards for granting credit, the American Council on Education (ACE) usually recommends a minimum scaled score of 50. This score is believed to be the score you would receive if you had taken the corresponding class and attained a C average.

a tutorial at the beginning of the exams to familiarize you with the computerized format of the exam.

ABOUT OUR REVIEWS

Our review for the CLEP Freshman College Composition is divided into two areas. The first is an introduction that covers all the major styles of college writing, the tools used by effective writers, and useful techniques for handling a college research paper. This portion of the review will prove to be effective in scoring well in Section II of the exam and will serve as a good preparation tool for college-level work in general.

The skills review in this book provides a comprehensive study of the mechanics of writing, including diction, grammar, punctuation, and sentence structure. The drills in this section will sharpen your knowledge of all aspects of grammar, enabling you to score well in Section I of the exam and to hone your own writing skills.

SCORING THE EXAM

How Do I Score My Practice Test?

The CLEP Freshman College Composition is scored on a scale of 20 to 80. To score your practice tests, count up the number of correct answers and enter it in the scoring worksheet below. Next, total your incorrect answers, multiply this number by one-fourth and enter the number in the scoring worksheet. Subtract the two numbers—this will yield your total raw score. Finally, convert your raw score to a scaled score using the conversion chart on the next page. As of July 2001, the CLEP exams will adopt a new method of scoring. The CLEP exams will be scored only according to correct answers; no credit will be lost for incorrectly answered items. *(Note: The conversion chart provides only an estimate of your scaled score. Since scaled scores vary from one form of a test to another, your score on the actual exam may be somewhat higher or lower than what is derived here.)*

SCORING WORKSHEET (Effective until 7/01)

Raw   Score: _____ $-$ (1/4 x _____) = _____
                  # correct   *# incorrect*

Scaled   Score: _____

SCORING WORKSHEET (Effective 7/01)

Raw Score: _____   Scaled Score: _____

When Will I Receive My Score Report and What Will it Look Like?

Your score report will arrive about three weeks after you take the test. The CLEP CBT exam will enable you to receive your unofficial scores on the day of your test. Scores for the essay section of the CLEP CBT will be available two weeks after the day of your test. Your scores are reported only to you, unless you ask to have them sent elsewhere. If you want your scores reported to a college or other institution, you must fill in the correct code number on your answer sheet at the time you take the examination. Since your scores are kept on file for 20 years, you may also request transcripts from ETS at a later date.

STUDYING FOR THE CLEP FRESHMAN COLLEGE COMPOSITION

It is very important for you to choose the time and place for studying that works best for you. Some students may set aside a certain number of hours every morning, while others may choose to study at night before going to sleep. Other students may study during the day, while waiting on a line, or even while eating lunch. Only you can determine when and where your study time will be most effective. However, be consistent and use your time wisely. Work out a study routine and stick to it!

When you take the practice tests, try to make your testing conditions as much like the actual test as possible. Turn your television and radio off, and sit down at a quiet table free from distraction. Make sure to time yourself. Start off by setting a timer for the time that is allotted for each section, and be sure to reset the timer for the appropriate amount of time when you start a new section.

As you complete each practice test, score your test and thoroughly review the explanations to the questions you answered incorrectly; however, do not review too much at one time. Concentrate on one problem area at a time by reviewing the question and explanation, and by studying our review until you are confident that you completely understand the material.

Keep track of your scores and mark them on the Scoring Worksheet. By doing so, you will be able to gauge your progress and discover general weaknesses in particular sections. You should carefully study the reviews that cover your areas of difficulty, as this will build your skills in those areas.

TEST-TAKING TIPS

Although you may not be familiar with standardized tests such as the CLEP Freshman College Composition, there are many ways to acquaint yourself with this type of examination and help alleviate your test-taking anxieties. Listed below are ways to help you become accustomed to the CLEP, some of which may be applied to other standardized tests as well.

Become comfortable with the format of the exam. When you are practicing, simulate the conditions under which you will be taking the actual test. Stay calm and pace yourself. After simulating the test only a couple of times, you will boost your chances of doing well, and you will be able to sit down for the actual exam with much more confidence.

Read all of the possible answers. Just because you think you have found the correct response, do not automatically assume that it is the best answer. Read through each choice to be sure that you are not making a mistake by jumping to conclusions.

Use the process of elimination. Go through each answer to a question and eliminate as many of the answer choices as possible. By eliminating just two answer choices, you give yourself a better chance of getting the item correct, since there will only be three choices left from which to make your guess.

Work quickly and steadily. You will have only 45 minutes to work on 60 questions in each section, so work quickly and steadily to avoid focusing on any one question too long. Taking the practice tests in this book will help you learn to budget your time.

Learn the directions and format for each section of the test. Familiarizing yourself with the directions and format of the exam will save you valuable time on the day of the actual test.

Be sure that the answer oval you are marking corresponds to the number of the question in the test booklet. Since the exam is graded by machine, marking one wrong answer can throw off your answer key and your score. Be extremely careful when filling in your answer sheet.

THE DAY OF THE EXAM

Before the Exam

On the day of the test, you should wake up early (hopefully after a decent night's rest) and have a good breakfast. Make sure to dress comfortably so that you are not distracted by being too hot or too cold while taking the test. Also plan to arrive at the test center early. This will allow you to collect your thoughts and relax before the test, and will also spare you the anxiety that comes with being late. As an added incentive to make sure you arrive early, keep in mind that NO ONE WILL BE ALLOWED INTO THE TEST SESSION AFTER THE TEST HAS BEGUN.

Before you leave for the test center, make sure that you have your admission form and another form of identification, which must contain a recent photograph, your name, and signature (i.e., driver's license, student identification card, or current alien registration card). You will not be admitted to the test center if you do not have proper identification.

YOU MUST ALSO BRING SEVERAL SHARPENED NO. 2 PENCILS WITH ERASERS, AS NONE WILL BE PROVIDED AT THE TEST CENTER.

If you would like, you may wear a watch to the test center. However, you may not wear one that makes noise, because it may disturb the other test-takers. No dictionaries, textbooks, notebooks, briefcases, or packages will be permitted and drinking, smoking, and eating are prohibited.

During the Exam

Once you enter the test center, follow all of the rules and instructions given by the test supervisor. If you do not, you risk being dismissed from the test and having your scores canceled.

When all of the test materials have been passed out, the test supervisor will give you directions for filling out your answer sheet. You must fill out this sheet carefully since this information will be printed on your score report. Fill in your name exactly as it appears on your identification documents and admission ticket, unless otherwise instructed.

After the Test

Once your test materials have been collected, you will be dismissed. Then, go home and relax—you deserve it!

▼

CHAPTER 2
INTRODUCTION TO
COLLEGE
COMPOSITION

Chapter 2

INTRODUCTION TO COLLEGE COMPOSITION

THE CURRICULUM OF COLLEGE AND UNIVERSITY WRITING

Professors who teach courses that are specific to English departments—and not scientific, technical, or business disciplines—will demand that students write essays in response to the environment, society, or literature. *Literature*, broadly speaking, is anything written for the public to read—from newspaper articles to comic books, from encyclopedias to novels. However, most college curricula divide literature into two broad areas: *nonfiction writing* and *creative writing*.

Nonfiction writing includes essays and books which deal with any topic about which people want to know more. Nonfiction is literature about real people, places, and things, or important ideas, and speaks to the reader directly. Nonfiction forms, also called expository writing (from the verb "to espouse," or say), include books on history, philosophy, art, or religion and essays on politics, biology, or astronomy. Authors use nonfiction writing for four major purposes: *to describe, explain, inform, or persuade readers* to understand, believe, or agree about something. Nonfiction forms of literature are the most prevalent forms—ones people deal with every day—and they often have practical goals. Instruction manuals are an example of nonfiction writing.

Creative writing generally covers work done by writers to enlighten or move readers to either laughter or tears, or to the contemplation of a social (e.g., civil rights), philosophical (e.g., What does it mean to be good?), or aesthetic (e.g., What does it mean to be beautiful?) idea. Most college

English courses call for reading, criticizing, and analyzing of the relative beauty or effectiveness of creative works of literature. Students generally study creative literature in *genres*, or literary forms. These forms include *drama*, *fiction*, and *poetry*. The chart below, although not exhaustive, should put into perspective the different forms of literature created or generated by human beings.

LITERATURE

Nonfiction	Revelation	Creative
Essays or books on:	The Bible	Drama
Business		Tragedies
Science	The Koran and other	Comedies
Politics	religious writings attributed to or	Melodramas
Journalism	spoken by God	
Philosophy		Fiction
Religion		Novels and short stories
History		
Letters		Science fiction
Diaries		Mysteries
Autobiographical prose		Romances
Research studies		Poetry
Essays or books commenting on the arts		Epics and sagas
		Lyrical/ballads
Docudramas		Songs
		Docudramas

Writing and Reading as Forms of Learning

Professors know that students who write often and well learn more quickly and remember more than those who write infrequently and poorly. A number of modern scholars, such as Janet Emig and Robert Parker of Rutgers University, have done important research to show that using writing enables an individual to learn about the nature of the world and to gain self-knowledge, as well as to take in and master knowledge in disciplines across the curriculum of college and university courses. Whether the field of study is biology, map-making, or computer programming, writing improves learning. To say so of reading goes without question.

Taking notes, recording impressions in a journal, using personal words to describe your experiences—all these will help any writer or person to remember and deal with complex experiences and knowledge better.

Writing and Language Skills Improve Your Reasoning Skills

Students often complain about having to take the time to know how to analyze a poem or novel, understand an essay in detail, or take the time to comprehend the false arguments of a demagogue or other political leader. However, reasoning and analytical skills are keys to controlling the way life is led. An inability to analyze the arguments of a politician may lead to victimization at the hands of a dictator. A failure to comprehend the point of a rule or regulation on the job, may lead to dismissal from that job.

The abilities to reason and analyze situations well are not just relevant to mysteries or the complicated plots of novels, but how to solve many of life's problems and how to overcome obstacles. For example, how does one write back to an insurance company that will not pay for earthquake damage in order to be justly compensated? Learn to write (and communicate) well. These are critical life skills that make for an intelligent, informed and rational human being.

READING SKILLS AND THE READING PROCESS

The Steps of the Active Reading Process

Any course of study in English will inevitably call upon a student to demonstrate and use reading skills successfully. Reading is essential in order to compete effectively in college or in a chosen career. Students must learn or be able to read quickly—often hundreds of pages per day—and retain and comprehend most of what they have read. Of course, reading well is important to all learning activities, but, in college English, it is especially important.

Reading, like writing, is a process that requires active participation during study. Reading for learning in college means reading with a view toward at least three results: (1) retaining relevant information, (2) increasing understanding of a discipline or subject, and (3) thinking critically about the truth or accuracy of what has been read.

Although experts vary on the particular terms, the active reading process may be broken down into five stages: (1) prereading, sometimes called previewing; (2) initial holistic reading; (3) reviewing 1: rereading for thesis, logical development, and content or supporting evidence; (4) reviewing 2: checking for unusual or new vocabulary; and (5) formulating a critical response (agree/disagree; like/dislike; pro/con, etc.).

Prereading/Previewing

During *prereading, the active reader looks for cues to begin.* Before the reader actually sits down to read the article or chapter in question from beginning to end, he or she takes the opportunity to get a perspective on what it is he or she is about to read. *Prereading* involves several steps: *deciding on purpose, deciding on the nature of the audience, and scanning, or looking for basic cues about organization from the format, or layout of the piece.*

Determining the Purpose

Before beginning to read something the reader should first decide on the purpose for reading. In most college cases, the purpose of reading will be to learn. While reading may be for fun, to gather support for a personal argument, or even just to pass the time, *always read with a purpose in mind*. Next, determine *the writer's purpose*. Look at the headline or title of the piece to be read. Ask if the writer is trying to *entertain, explain, describe, inform or report, or persuade* by using argumentation to prove his or her main point or thesis.

For example, a travel writer such as Henry James in the nineteenth century used explanation and description to tell the reader about some famous European city in an effort to reveal its beauty and flaws to the reader. Newspapers will use reporting techniques to tell of a plane crash, the events of a distant war, or a local crime. Editors often write *editorials*, or short articles of opinion, in which *the editors express their points of view about a problem or public issue* (e.g., voting for 18-year-olds) and attempt *to persuade the reader that their opinions are the correct ones by arguing with facts, statistics, and other evidence.*

Determining the Probable Audience

Next, in cases in which the audience is most likely not a college student, decide who the intended reader, or audience, is for the piece. Asking a series of questions about a given passage can determine the nature of the audience. While reading, keep in mind the writer's purpose. Using the answers generated by the questions below, *develop a mental "picture" of the audience reading this passage.*

1. What does the writer intend the readers of this passage to take away with them?

2. What is the writer's point of view?

3. How old are the readers?

4. What is their level of education?

5. What is their social or economic class?

6. What attitudes, prejudices, opinions, fears, experience, and concerns might the audience for this passage have?

Considerations of audience will directly affect the *tone* of a passage, and thus determine what *level of usage or meaning* is appropriate in a given paragraph or section of an essay. *Tone* in expository writing is that *combination of abstract v. concrete; denotation and connotation; jargon and figurative, literal, or plain speech; and simple or complex language that the writer uses to generate a felt response in the reader of some complex attitude the writer has toward a given subject.* To use a simple example, when writing to a 13-year-old, which is more appropriate: "Please peruse with comprehension the tome offered," or "Please be sure to read and understand what is in this book"? The latter sentence, with its simple vocabulary, is the appropriate choice.

Scanning for Basic Features

If the literature is a textbook, read the *introduction,* scan the *chapter titles,* and quickly review any *subheadings, charts, pictures, appendices,* and *indexes* that the book includes. If it is an article, read *the first and last paragraphs* of the article. These are the most likely places to find the writer's *main point* or *thesis.*

Note that there is a significant difference between a thesis and a main point. Here is an example of a *main point*:

The Rocky Mountains have three important geological features: abundant water, gold- and silver-bearing ore, and oil-bearing shale.

Notice that this statement is not a matter of the writer's opinion. It is a fact. Now, notice the following *thesis*:

The Rocky Mountains are the most important source of geological wealth in the U.S.A.

What is the difference? The second statement offers an arguable conclusion or informed opinion. It may be an informed opinion on the part of the writer, but it is still an opinion. A *thesis*, then, *is a statement offered by a writer as true or correct but is actually a matter of opinion.*

In the first statement, whether the author has an opinion about it or not, these features are an important part of the makeup of the Rocky Mountains. In the second statement, the author may have contrary evidence to offer about Alaska or the Everglades. The second statement bears proving; the first is self-evident, and the writer would go on to show the existence of these features, not—as in the second case—the quality or value of those features. The writer of a main point paper is reporting or informing his or her audience; the writer of a thesis is attempting to sway the audience to his or her point of view.

Initial Holistic Reading Response

This stage is probably the most enjoyable for the active reader. The student should read the article in it's entirety. During this reading, *underline or highlight* sentences in which the writer makes an important point about his or her thesis. Don't stop reading to ponder what the writer precisely meant.

Distinguishing Between Idea and Evidence

While reading, make a distinction between key ideas and the evidence for those ideas. *Evidence* is anything used to prove that an idea is true, real, correct, or probable. However, only a few forms of evidence are available to the writer. The kinds of evidence that a writer can summon to support his or her position or point are as follows: (1) facts and statistics, (2) the testimony of authority, (3) personal anecdote, (4) hypothetical illustrations, and (5) analogy. Strictly speaking, the last two in this list are not true evidence, but only offer common sense probability to the support of an argument. In fact, there is a hierarchy for evidence similar to that of purpose. The best evidence is fact, supported by statistics; the least powerful is analogy. The following table suggests the relationship:

HIERARCHY OF VALIDITY OF EVIDENCE

Most Valid	Documented Facts and Statistics
	Expert Testimony
	Personal Experience and Anecdote
	Hypothetical Illustrations
Least Valid	Analogies of Any Kind

Documented facts and statistics are the most powerful evidence a writer can bring to bear on proving an idea or supporting a main thesis. Documented facts and statistics must be used fairly and come from reliable sources. For example, *Funk and Wagnall's Encyclopedia* is a reliable source; but Joe the plumber's *Guide to Waterfowl in Hoboken,* is not. This is true because, first of all, Joe is a plumber, not an ornithologist (a bird scientist), and secondly, no one has ever heard of Joe the plumber as an expert. Reliable sources for facts and statistics are the best information that can be offered.

Expert testimony is the reported positions, theses, or studies of people who are recognized experts in the field under discussion in the literature. A writer may use books, articles, essays, interviews, and so on by trained scientists, and other professionals, may be used to support a thesis or position. Most often, this testimony takes the form of quotations from the expert or a paraphrasing of his or her important ideas or findings.

Personal anecdote is the evidence of a writer's own personal experience, or a "little story" about an event, person, or idea that exemplifies the point he or she is trying to make. It holds weight if the reader trusts the writer, and it is valuable; but it is not as powerful or as conclusive as documented facts or the testimony of experts (unless the writer is a recognized authority in the field about which he or she has written).

Hypothetical illustrations are examples that suggest probable circumstances in which something would be true. Strictly speaking, a hypothetical illustration is not "hard" evidence, but, rather evidence of probability. For example, to demonstrate that "people will do whatever they can get away with," a writer might bring up the hypothetical illustration of someone at a ticket counter who gets back more change than he or she paid for the ticket. The chances are, the writer might point out, that the person would pocket the extra money rather than be honest and return it. In this case, the writer is not naming anybody in particular or citing statistics to make the point, but rather is pointing to *a situation that is likely but that is not an actual documented case.* This situation has either the weight of common sense for the reader or none at all.

Analogy is the last and weakest form of evidence. It is not actually evidence at all. A writer can use an analogy to depict or illustrate deeper meanings and issues by showing a powerful comparison between or among ideas that carries the weight of correctness or aptness for the reader. Analogies are characterized by comparisons and the use of the term "like" to show the relationship of the ideas. (Metaphor and simile, special forms of analogy in literature, are discussed later in this text.) For example, the writer might say, "Life is like a tree: we start out struggling in the dirt, grow into the full bloom of youth, and become deeply rooted in our ways, until, in the autumn of our years, we lose our hair like leaves, and succumb ultimately to the bare winter of death."

While reading, determine what sort of evidence the writer is using and how effective it is in proving his or her point.

Underlining Unusual Words and Phrases

During this stage, unfamiliar words or phrases may appear. Don't stop to try to understand all the unusual words during this stage. Underline them, circle them, or note them in some useful way, and then, when finished with this stage of reading, look them up in a dictionary.

Reviewing 1: Re-reading for Thesis, Logical Development, and Content or Supporting Evidence

During this portion of the reading process, review both the underlinings/ highlightings for main ideas and for vocabulary and determine (1) what the author's main point, or *thesis*, is and where it is stated; (2) what logical patterns the writer uses to organize the article or document (see the list discussed in Chapter 7); and (3) what evidence the writer uses to support his or her position. Commit these findings to memory. Always review as needed; *sometimes several reviews of a difficult chapter or article may be needed, but it is worth doing to gain full comprehension of a text.* There are no shortcuts. The reader must follow this reading process in order to fully understand the text.

Reviewing 2: Checking for Unusual or New Vocabulary

In this next stage, it's the active reader's job to concentrate on the way the writer is using the language. Come to grips with *precise meanings, new terms, and nuances of tone—such as connotation, figurative use of language, and logic.* There is no substitute for accuracy. Often, retention at this stage is indicative of a student's understanding of the entire work.

Using the Dictionary Effectively

Always learn the vocabulary that is new. To learn a word effectively, an individual must engage in several operations.

1. Look up the word in a dictionary of standard English. Be careful not to depend upon a thesaurus, which tells you only the possible *synonyms*. Synonyms, words that denote the same meaning as the word in question, may have widely different connotations not appropriate to the way the writer is using the word in the article or book in question. (See below for an expanded discussion of *denotation* and *connotation*.)

    Good dictionaries also list the *etymology,* or historical source or sources, for the word being researched. Usually, the dictionary will list an abbreviation for the language (e.g., "Fr." for French) from which the word originally sprang. While not always relevant to the way the author has used the word, etymology will always contribute to the total understanding of the word in question.

2. Learn how to pronounce the word correctly. Learn which syllable is most stressed, and how the vowels and consonants are sounded together. In most cases, the dictionary has a *pronunciation guide* either at the beginning or the end of the main word entries. Learn where it is and use it.

3. Learn what part of speech the word is (e.g., noun or verb).

4. Read the meanings and look back at the reading assignment to discover from the context which meaning is the most relevant to the textbook or article; then construct a sentence using the word correctly.

These tasks nearly guarantee permanent knowledge of the word.

Connotation and Denotation

In English, words carry with them not only what they actually, *literally* mean (their *denotation*), but also what they bring to mind in the form of *emotional or cultural associations* (their *connotation*). When reading assignments, try to understand not only what the word literally means, but also how the author might be using it to evoke *a particular set of emotional, social, cultural, or historical associations*. For example, take the word "cheap." The dictionary definition, its denotation or literal meaning, is "not expensive." But the word "cheap" is often associated, or given the implication of being "of poor quality."

Not all connotations are negative. For example, for most people, "house" is literally a dwelling in which a related group of people live. But when the word is changed to "home," even though its actual definition is the same as house, it brings added connotations of warmth, safety, tenderness, kinship, and family values. This is an entire group of positive feelings and associations that are not themselves the "house" in which people may live. *When reading, take into account not just what the word means literally, but whether or not the writer is trying to evoke a certain feeling*, as in using "tardy" instead of "late," or "home" instead of "house."

While the connotations of words do come into play in nonfiction, expository writing and literature, connotations play an especially important role in creative literature. The ways in which special meanings of words are used by novelists, poets, and playwrights will be discussed in a later chapter.

Abstract v. Concrete Language

Apart from carrying literal and associative meanings, words can be of two basic types. They indicate something that is either *concrete*, something that can be observed directly in a world of space and time through senses, or *abstract*, something that is understood only indirectly as an idea by association or indirect evidence.

Concrete words embody both qualities. For example, because a pencil can be seen, used, and touched, it can be spoken about concretely. However, there is also the idea of the pencil as that writing tool with graphite, sharp at one end and an eraser at the other. In the second case, a particular pencil may not be indicated. It has been used to point out a type, class, or species of that thing: pencils in general, pencils in the abstract. So, concrete words carry both concrete and abstract possibilities, while abstractions can be understood only indirectly.

Feelings, ideas, and notions cannot be directly observed, but can be understood only indirectly. For example, a kiss may be evidence of love, but we can observe only the kiss directly, not the love. The love is assumed. A kiss is sometimes the equivalent of a greeting, not a sign of love—as it is among French men, where a kiss on both cheeks is the equivalent of an American handshake. English has many such abstractions: hate, truth, beauty, friendship, etc.

Formulating A Critical Response

Once the text has been preread, read, reviewed, and checked for vocabulary, a critical response may be formulated. Comprehension of text calls for assessment and evaluation of what has been read. To *assess* a piece of literature, read the piece with an understanding of what its purpose is and how it develops logically to make its point. To *evaluate* a piece of literature, make a case for a personal but informed judgment about its relative success or failure in terms of its logic, its adequate development, and its relative use of literary or writing skills.

Of course, everyone is entitled to his or her own opinion about any piece of writing or set of ideas. However, in a college setting, students are often held responsible for making a case for what they think about a piece of writing, not just what they feel or opine about it. It can be said, "The Earth is flat;" but merely saying so or *asserting an opinion* doesn't make it real, true, or even probable. In college, as elsewhere in life, use reasoning skills to determine the relative validity, aptness, or truth of what the author has presented.

Implications and Inferences

When writers present ideas, conclusions about what they are saying based on the *implications*, or possible related ideas or positions consistent with their central idea, can be made. Ideas suggest other ideas, and as long as the ideas are logically consistent with the author's central point, the reader may assume that the writer would probably go along with these related ideas.

Writers sometimes *imply* things that would be a logical extension of what they actually say. For example, it would be unreasonable to suggest that the writer in the passage below is implying that he wants to live in a well-serviced industrial, urban environment. It doesn't logically fit the examples (E's) he offers in his paragraph.

> (E) I want a house that has no plumbing. (E) I want a house that looks out at the mountains. (E) I want a house that has rough cut walls and woodstove heat. (E) I want a house that has a wilderness for a backyard and a lakeview for a front yard. (E) I want a house with no neighbors but the birds, the bears, and the wild creatures of the earth.

One of the implications of this is clearly that the writer wants to live in just the opposite environment. But a real implication based on this passage is that this writer would rather live near animals than near people. Notice that the paragraph lists examples as evidence for the writer's point of view. All of the sentences exemplify characteristics of the "house" this writer wants—but not one of them is conclusive. So, this writer **implies, without actually stating,** the kind of "home" he wants. Yet, the reader still gets a clear picture or idea of where this writer's home would be set.

Although he doesn't say it, the point of the paragraph is this:

[The writer] wants a home in the wilderness. **(T)**

This would be the thesis (T) sentence of this writer's paragraph or passage if he had not implied it, but had instead stated it. There is a sense that the writer hates people—but **be careful:** that's what the reader may feel, not what the writer is implying. *Don't confuse feelings with the writer's facts or illustrations.*

Professors will often require students to understand and recognize what they can *infer* from the passage once they have read it. Actually, implications and inferences are very similar; the only difference is who is making them: *Writers imply; readers infer.* For example, with the example used above, the reader could infer that the writer is a person who probably likes the outdoors, camping, and even hunting. That's an *inference*: a reader's *probable* and *reasonable* conclusion or interpretation of an idea based upon what the writer has written.

Logic: Induction, Deduction, and Fallacies

In formulating critical evaluations of a piece of writing, professors may wish students to understand the problems, if any, with the logic of the piece they have read. Does it make sense? If not, why doesn't it? It is up to the reader to find the errors in any piece of writing he or she reads. Of course, if the writer is effective, the reader won't find these fallacies however, be on the lookout for them, because it is often a good way to refute, criticize, or counterargue if called upon to respond critically to any author's central idea, thesis, or main point. Make sure the evidence proves the writer's point and not something else.

Pay special attention to conclusions. The writer may not have proved the point. An essay is essentially a *syllogism* that proves something by *induction* or *deduction*. The *syllogism* is that *basic form of deductive reasoning* that is the cornerstone of most logic. It consists of a *major premise*, a *minor premise*, and a *conclusion*. Note how they are used in the discussion below. *Induction* is the sort of reasoning which arrives at a general conclusion based on the relationship among the contributing elements of an idea.

For example, a writer may observe under experimental conditions that whenever a spider begins to spin a web, it first rubs its back legs over its silk gland. The author may have observed 100,000 different species of spiders display this behavior. He or she may have also observed that they never rub their hind legs over the gland at any other time, only when they are about to put out silk to start a web. He or she may then *induce* from these observations that spiders must rub their hind legs over their silk glands in order to begin the production of silk to spin a web. Another individual may prove this theory may be proven wrong later, because new evidence shows up to invalidate the induction, but until that happens, this will be the conclusion drawn from observations of the behavior of spiders.

Deduction, by way of contrast, reasons from the general to the particular. For example, an author may assert that all trees grow upward from the earth, not downward from the sky. Until someone finds a tree that grows from the sky to the earth, an individual will assume that every tree started growing out of the earth, and base all other conclusions about the growth and flowering of trees upon this *deduction* as well.

Occasionally, however, the *premises* of a deductive argument are false or unprovable. The *premises* of an argument are those *definitions* or *assumptions* that are given (concepts which do not stand in need of proof but are either self-evident, common knowledge, or agreed upon as terms between the writer and the reader). For example,

Major Premise: All goats have beards.

Minor Premise: Harry Jones has a beard.

Conclusion: Therefore, Harry is a goat.

The conclusion is correct and logical *based on the premises*, or definitions or assumptions offered in this case, but the premises are selective. What about the fact that Harry is a human being and that goats are not human beings? These are mutually exclusive. Thus, Harry cannot be a goat.

Typical Logical Fallacies

Below is a list of typical logical errors that weak writers commit. The list is not exhaustive. Know how they occur and practice finding them in others' arguments, either in conversation or in essays they may have written.

1. *Either/or:* The writer assumes only two opposing possibilities: "Either we abolish cars, or the environment is doomed." Other factors may contribute to the destruction of the environment.

2. *Oversimplification:* Here, the author might first state, "Only motivated athletes become champions." Perhaps not; though unfortunate, athletes who use enhancing steroids occasionally become champions, too.

3. *Begging the question:* The writer assumes he or she has proved something which has not been proven. "He is unintelligent because he is stupid." A lack of intelligence is almost synonymous with being stupid; it cannot be proven that he is stupid by saying he is unintelligent; that "he" is either or both of these is exactly what needs to be proved.

4. *Ignoring the issue:* An argument against the truth of a person's testimony in court shifts from what the witness observed to how the witness's testimony is inadmissible because the witness is obviously unkempt and homeless. One has nothing to do with the other.

5. *Arguing against a person, not an idea:* The writer argues that somebody's idea has no merit because he or she is immoral or unintelligent: "John can't prove anything about dogs being faithful; he can't even understand basic mathematics."

6. *"It does not follow..." or Non sequitur:* The writer leaps to a wrong conclusion: "John is tall; he must know a lot about mountains."

7. *Drawing the wrong conclusion from a sequence:* "He trained and then read and then trained some more and therefore won the match." It is quite possible that other factors led to his winning the match.

The Power and Types of Reading in College

Reading well and with control is essential to a successful college career. Not all students will need coursework in reading per se. However, during a college career, the student's ability to understand reading material will make an enormous difference in how well he or she performs, not to mention the degree to which the student can learn a fact or even a given discipline.

Reading creative literature, while essentially the same *process* as noncreative literature, takes on particular characteristics and a particular jargon—or special vocabulary—which students are required to work with and understand. Every time a new discipline is learned or a new field of study is entered, new vocabulary needs to be mastered. The study of creative literature in college English courses involves the mastery of a special vocabulary by the student. Ahead we will examine much more deeply the special vocabulary used for the study of creative literature and how to understand and apply it in college courses that deal with literature as a creative art, rather than those college courses that deal with literature principally as expository prose that conveys information or opinion. First, however, the student must understand and control the other major process in college English: the writing process.

WRITING ABOUT LITERATURE

Elements of the Work

When writing about literature, the professor requires not only that the student put forth a logical thesis, but that he or she analyze elements of the work in order to show an understanding of that work.

Usually the professor requires the student understands the time in which a piece of literature was written, not the time in which it is set. To that end, a professor may ask that some historical analysis be included in an essay. For example, a student would probably want to include the fact that George Orwell wrote *1984* during the Early Modern period in English literature in 1948, while the time of the novel itself is set in the then future of 1984. Other important periods include the Middle Ages, the Renaissance, the Romantic Period, the Victorian Age, the Modernist Movement, and Post-Modernism.

Genres, or literary forms, continue to be the most standard approach to the study of literature at the undergraduate level. The organization of an essay about literature will still be that of introduction, body or middle development, and conclusion, but the elements under study will change somewhat from genre to genre. For example, the elements under study in the analysis of a *fiction* will include: *plot, character (and characterization), dialogue, setting, symbolic language, style,* and *theme.* In *drama,* these elements are very much the same, with the exception of studying not just the structural elements of the play, but also *the elements of production or staging,* which will include the *quality of the set, type of stage (in-the-round or dividing curtain), lighting, choreography, timing or pace, and the quality or style of the acting.*

In *poetry,* however, the elements shift again to a focus of *language* and *intensive elements.* The student also examines how the writer uses these elements of *figurative language* and *rhyme and meter* to move the reader to an aesthetic, ethical, or political response—including tears, laughter, and the whole range of emotions of which people are capable. The elements that are key to the *analysis of poetry* include *the narrator and persona (his or her voice), setting, rhyme (if any), metrical or rhythmic scheme, figurative language (including images, metaphors, and symbols), and mythical content (if any).* The job of the student who analyzes or interprets a poem is to show how these elements work together to produce the response that the student feels is the correct one to the poem.

Of course, in the case of the poem, a wide range of interpretation is possible for any given poem. While the student cannot prove that a poem meant one thing rather than another, by demonstrating how a majority of the elements of its structure (rhyme scheme, figurative language, setting, and persona) work in concert to produce the same response, the student can *make a case that is probable* that his or her response to the poem is consistent with the language in the poem itself.

The student must be careful not to go on instinct alone, but have some proof backing up his or her ideas; analyzing poetry is not merely a matter of personal interpretation. While it is true that the understanding of a poem is a matter of interpretation, it is not a very useful one if the understanding of a poem is the result of some wild, personal impression alone. A strong interpretation of a poem, or any form of literature for that matter, would be an *informed* interpretation *based upon a careful critical reading and analysis of the structural elements which the author has used to create a certain effect or produce a given response in the reader.*

While everyone has a right to his or her opinion, that doesn't make an analysis of a poem true, real, or probable. For example, the opinion may be held that the world is flat, but there is a great deal of documented evidence to show that such an opinion is empty of truth. Professors will probably also speak about avoiding two other fallacies in criticizing, or analyzing literature: *the intentional fallacy* and *the pathetic fallacy.*

Critics consider the *intentional fallacy* a major error in analyzing literature. Simply put, the fallacy is in *reasoning about the purpose or theme of a work based on what is the author's own expressed intent, or what you believe to be the author's intent.* Of course, many of the best authors are dead, and therefore, an individual cannot ask what message or meaning an author intended by a given work. Critics reason, not from intent, but from the effects that the particular combination of structural elements in the work of literature seem to consistently produce in the readers. This has its pitfalls, too, but it is less vulnerable to sentimental or arbitrary interpretations than the critical argument for the meaning of a work based upon the author's supposed or expressed intent.

The *pathetic fallacy* is often discussed among critics in reference to Romantic literature, and is one in which the author holds that his or her feelings about nature are those of Nature itself. Much of Romantic poetry in English engages in this fallacy and leads to the *anthropomorphic* interpretation of nature and art. It is the notion that because someone is feeling something (for instance, pathos) in the presence of nature, it must be true of Nature itself.

Apart from a *plot summary*, a student may write several types of papers. These include a *character analysis*, a *study of the figurative language*, an *analysis of the use of narration or persona*, a *thematic analysis*, or a *structural analysis*. In each case, it is advisable to use the organizational patterns explained earlier to demonstrate your thesis (define or describe a character; compare and contrast metaphors or themes; or classify or categorize two or more works read in class).

The Structural Elements of Fiction, Drama, and Poetry

Just as a carpenter uses his chief tools to build the house he wants, so writers use the "tools" of their trade to "build" their drama, fiction, or poem to reach their audiences with an idea, feeling, or combination of ideas and feelings. In the section that follows, the *structural elements* of literature as drama and fiction, and later poetry will be examined for what they are: the tools of the writer's trade, craft, or art. The student's job is to become critical of a work of literature, not based alone upon the sentiment of liking or not liking a work, but based on an *analysis of the use of the structural elements, or some dominating combination of the structural elements, of any work so as to suggest the nature of or success of the presentation of its theme, idea, or overall effect.*

A persistent device used in literature is that of *irony. Irony is the phenomenon of things turning out to be not what they originally appeared to be.* Authors depend upon irony for certain kinds of effects that make readers think or reflect on how unpredictable life can be.

Irony can take many forms. Perhaps the most common form is that of *dramatic irony*. In this form, the plot of a play or fiction may take a sudden unexpected turn that the audience was not prepared for earlier in the drama. For example, in Dickens' *Great Expectations*, Pip, the chief protagonist, believes that the scheming Miss Havesham is his benefactor. He treats her with respect and deference all his young life only to discover later in life that she had not been his benefactor at all. Instead, she had attempted to ruin his life by making him fall hopelessly in love with her protege, Estella. Pip learns later through his lawyer that it was not Miss Havesham who had been his benefactor all those years, but a lowly, anonymous criminal whom Pip had helped hide and feed. The *irony* lies in the *unexpected turn of events* that led to Pip's finding out that he had been—along with the reader—laboring under the illusion that Miss Havesham was his benefactor and guardian.

Other elements of literature can be ironic: characters who appear as villains who turn out to be heroes, and vice-versa; poems that appear to be about one kind of theme, end up ridiculing the theme or showing its opposite. Read, for example, W.H. Auden's poem "The Unknown Citizen."

One of the common forms of dramatic irony is that of *poetic justice*. Poetic justice occurs when a character, usually evil, ends up getting what he or she wanted done to others—a kind of inverse of the golden rule: *"to have done unto oneself or the evil character what the evil character had hoped would be done unto his antagonist."* Thus, in the case of Miss Havesham, who hoped to have Pip, like all men, destroyed by love the way she had been (left on her wedding day by her prospective husband), she is destroyed by her own hatred, and she burns horribly in a fire that Pip tries in vain to save her from. Estella, raised by Miss Havesham to destroy men and Pip in particular with her charms, finds herself married to a fool and a bore, imprisoned forever in a loveless life of duty and boredom.

Irony can also be linguistic. In this case the writer uses particular images, metaphors, or symbols to demonstrate the opposite of that for which they seem to be symbols. For instance a writer could have a narrator attribute particular qualities to one character then depict that character engaged in actions that are contrary to the original assessment, thus changing the reader's perception of that character.

Point of View and the Narrator: Omniscient, Limited-Omniscient, Limited

In any fiction, there is always a *narrator*, or *someone or something who is telling the story to the reader.* Unlike the point of view that may be used in an essay (first person or third person, see Chapter 4), which is just the way the author chooses to talk about a given topic, the *point of view* in fiction greatly influences the understanding of the story by the reader. A writer may choose to use the *omniscient narrator* and use the third person form to tell the story as if the narrator were god-like, or omniscient: all-seeing, all-knowing, able to be everywhere at once. This omniscient narrator seems to see everything that happens, and often talks to the reader from the page as though he or she were speaking from inside all the characters' heads, thinking their thoughts even as they think them themselves.

Through the words of the omniscient narrator, the reader sees all of the characters' thoughts. This is impossible in life and is merely a device to help the story move along effectively. The narrator thus functions as a unifying principle, keeping the story coherent and interesting. In one of the most famous uses of a narrator, Gustave Flaubert, the French novelist, uses his all-seeing powers as a kind of linguistic "trick" to enable the reader to see into the title character's, or, Madame Bovary's, own thoughts.

Thus, although it is actually the writer Gustave Flaubert who is making Madame Bovary have these thoughts, it seems as though the reader is hearing Madame Bovary's thoughts as she thinks them. This special twist on the insight of the omniscient narrator is another literary device called *the internal monologue*. This device enables readers to hear or read, through the power of the omniscient narrator, the internal thoughts of the character in question. This is an illusion, but it is another useful device for moving a story forward.

The *limited-omniscient* narrator is one who tells the story from the vantage point of the first person ("I first met Strether Martin in the streets of Paris in 1832…") and who usually already knows the outcome. With the *limited-omniscient narrator*, readers know all of the narrator's thoughts, but not other characters' thoughts, at which the narrator sometimes guesses. The limited-omniscient narrator thus becomes a character in the story itself. He or she will often display prejudices and opinions about the conflict and other characters in the story that are contrary to or other than those displayed by the other characters about whom the narrator reports.

The *limited* or restricted narrator is one who tells the story, not only with limited insight into what will happen next, but from his or her own position of prejudice, opinion, or conviction. Thus, in Herman Melville's famous "Bartleby the Scrivener," the tragic story of Bartleby unfolds through the eyes of a narrator who becomes a major character in the story. In most cases, the limited narrator is a major character in the story and helps to move the plot forward.

In poetry, the author employs a special form of the narrator called a *persona*. The *persona* is the one who becomes a character and tells the poem. The persona may be a god, sometimes an animal, sometimes a character from history. The reader should not confuse the narrator of a poem with the writer of the poem. The poet, then, may often "tell" the poem in the voice of the imagined narrator, be it an animal, a god, or even an idea, and any understanding of the poem must take into account the nature of the *persona* of the narrator. In Robert Browning's "My Last Duchess," the comments the *persona* makes are as important as the painting about which the narrator/monk speaks. This particular way of using a narrator/persona is called a *dramatic monologue* and uses a "speaker" as a particular character to "tell" the poem. T.S. Eliot's *The Lovesong of J. Alfred Prufrock* is also a dramatic monologue.

Plot

The *plot* is the *storyline of the work in which one action after another occurs until the completion, end, or resolution of the conflict among the characters.* The elements in the plot include (1) *the introduction of the characters and opening of the action,* (2) *the complications of the action and the introduction of conflict,* (3) *the climax, and* (4) *the denouement or resolution of the conflict.*

At first, most students of English believe that to analyze a piece of fiction is merely to tell the story over again, or write what is called a *plot summary*. This doesn't serve much purpose except as a way to recap key events in the story. Sometimes, however, a professor may ask for a plot summary to see if material was read effectively.

Plot development begins with the introduction of a set of characters who embark upon a course of action that leads to some conflict between or among them. Most often, an author will present fiction or drama as a "second" universe. That is, it looks like the real world and universe, and it is peopled with characters who look and act like real people, but it is, of course, not the real universe in which actual people live but only a fictional representation of it. This phenomenon is often called *"slice of life."* Put simply, it means that each story read or drama watched is a "slice" taken out of the "pie" of real life. Because the writer has chosen to write about this particular time rather than some other, the reader can experience this "slice" as if present in it. This phenomenon of presenting in a story or drama a "look" at a universe that appears just like the real one is called *verisimilitude*, and most novels, television sitcoms, and police melodramas use this technique. Thus is born the phrase that [literature] is often an "imitation of life." This makes the drama being watched, or the fiction being read much easier to follow and to believe in.

Samuel Taylor Coleridge, a famous Romantic English writer and poet, once pointed out that in order to take part in a piece of literature, the reader or watcher must *"suspend [his or her] disbelief"* because he or she is not watching or reading about a substitute universe. The reader must act as if he or she is actually watching a real universe—that the stage isn't a room with an exposed fourth wall through which he or she views the action, but is actually a room. In other words, the reader has to pretend. Without this ability, a reader cannot watch or read a piece of fiction or a drama with any degree of comfort or acceptance. The illusion of a second, virtual universe—just like the real one—is what makes the enjoyment of literature possible at all. Readers and viewers must immerse themselves in this illusion in order to enjoy it.

Once having brought into play a series of characters involved in a situation, the writer then introduces or develops a major conflict. This conflict— sometimes love, sometimes war, sometimes the lust for gold and riches, among other possibilities—develops until it reaches a *climax,* or the moment when the conflict reaches its peak or the tables turn forever in favor of the protagonist or the antagonist. One of the most common forms of *plot development* is that (1) boy meets girl, (2) boy falls in love with girl, (3) boy loses girl, and (4) boy regains the love of the girl. *Resolution* comes when all the strands of the plot reach a solution: for example, the two lovers live "happily ever after" or the police get the criminals. Writers do not always resolve storylines, however, and some—as in the famous case of *Huckleberry Finn,* by Mark Twain—are left for the reader to determine. In that novel, the main character, the namesake of the title of the novel, tells the readers that he's going to "light out for the territory," and since he is only a boy, the reader must guess what will become of him and his life.

Paradigmatic v. Episodic

Plots in drama and fiction, while having the basic elements explained above, can be of two basic types: *episodic or paradigmatic.* The *episodic plot* is that in which one episode or event seems to happen after another in the logic of time unfolding as it normally does, but without any apparent logic other than that of time. *Huckleberry Finn* is an excellent example of just that. As Huck goes down the Mississippi with his pal, the escaped slave Jim, crazy things occur in rapid succession: they meet Huck's father; they meet two Shakespearean actors; they meet the Colonel, and so on. This is a plot often associated with the *picaresque novel,* so-called because it is about the adventures of a young man or woman, usually an orphan, or *picaro,* who by virtue of his or her wits, manages to overcome the many obstacles thrown in his or her path, as in the case of Huck, who overcame all to keep his freedom.

A *paradigmatic plot,* however, is one in which one thing happens after another as though designed by fate or "the gods" (as in Sophocles' *Oedi-*

pus Rex), or by a logic so compelling as to leave no doubt as to the links among the characters and the action (as in a mystery). *Paradigmatic plots* (so called because they are built on a model puzzle, or *paradigm*, of logical sequence of cause and effect) are those most often associated with mysteries and detective melodramas, or "who-done-it" movies.

Suspense, Flashback, and Foreshadowing

Writers use these common plot devices to create excitement and raise expectations in their audiences.

Writers generate *suspense* when they create an expectation in the plot between two or more of the characters in conflict, or between characters and impending events. The reader *expects something dangerous or critical* to happen at any moment, or in the very next "moment" of the drama or storyline. Sometimes, the event will happen as expected and sometimes it won't, with the writer giving false signals and expectations, hoping to surprise the reader.

One of the devices used to create suspense is that of *foreshadowing*, in which the author uses some prop, a bit of dialogue, or a reference to some imagery or symbol that suggests to the reader a possibility or mood of future action. The Russian playwright Chekhov, for example, said that if a pistol is over the fireplace in the first act, it should be used by the last act, or it shouldn't be in the play at all. One of Chekhov's characters might say in the first act to his rival, "You know, Markov, somebody could get killed with that pistol." By Act III, Markov and the speaker are in a duel and one gets killed with the pistol. A continual reference to some upcoming event, either through props, dialogue, or imagery, will build suspense and create an expectation within the reader, sometimes even without the readers themselves knowing why they are feeling anxious, expectant, or concerned.

Flashback is a plot device in which the narrator of a fiction, drama, or movie (as a voiceover, or a voice offstage) speaks in the present and relates a tale of an event that happened in the recent or distant past. Sometimes this technique takes the form of the reader meeting the narrator in the present; then the narrator begins to tell a tale of something that happened in the past, only to return to the present by the end of the story, drama, or movie. Suspense is thus created because the narrator knows the outcome of the story; so we hold on, waiting to know from the "story-teller" how the conflict will be resolved, how it will come to an end, and how it is that the narrator, or chief protagonist, came to be telling us this story in his or her present circumstances. *Revenge dramas*, for example, often start out with the chief protagonist remembering with pain the story of the murder of his family, friends, or other significant persons, and then lead forward to the climax of his or her revenge, usually bringing us to the climactic moment in which he or she is about to consummate his or her revenge in the "present." This is the sort of plot device that keeps the reader paying attention because he or she wants to know what happens next.

Characters/Methods of Characterization

Without characters, fictional plots in drama and fiction could not take place. Characters are the "people" of the virtual, or "second," universe in the "slice of life" that the author lets the reader see. Most fictions and dramas have *protagonists*—the main characters who are at the center of the action and the story—and *antagonists*—those who struggle against the protagonist in the conflict presented in the story or drama. Characters can be of many types, but there are some fundamental *methods of characterization* that writers use over and over again with great variations.

The writer uses two general methods for characterization. Characters can be either *flat, round*, or *three-dimensional characters*. Those who have a single overriding quality (such as the Hare in Aesop's fable) and never change or develop in the course of a story or drama are considered *flat characters. Flat characters* are also associated with fairy tales, romances, and allegories, where they are always representative of a quality or an idea and lack true individuality. In the "Grasshopper and the Ant," the ant represents patience, hard work, and industry, and the grasshopper represents frivolousness, fecklessness, and irresponsibility. Neither of them changes from the beginning of the fable until the end. Their purpose and their role is to remain just as they are.

Round or *three-dimensional characters* show a complex variety of qualities and attributes and are "human" through and through—full of failures and successes. *Round characters* change and develop in the course of the story or drama and demonstrate an individuality, sometimes within a type; thus, Huckleberry Finn is styled after the type of flat character called a picaro, or orphan, who makes it in the "school of hard knocks" and survives by his wits. But Huck, although he fits this type, also has his individuality and his own rough opinions of things, making him a much more interesting character than just the character of type.

In addition to depicting characters by type or individuality, writers who use *round* characters show them develop, from bad to worse, from good to bad, from bad to better, or from bad to good. Comedies usually show characters who develop from bad to good or from good to better, while tragedies usually depict characters who go from good to bad or from good to bad and back to good by having suffered some unchangeable and uncontrollable setback from which they cannot recover. Thus, Oedipus in *Oedipus Rex* finds out too late that he has killed his father, been lovers with and married to his mother, and brought a plague upon Thebes, the city that he thought he saved from the Sphinx by solving the famous riddle years before.

Usually, however, tragic characters show some degree of nobility in the face of overwhelming odds: for example, ethical strength, sometimes courage, sometimes unconditional love. Varieties are only as limited as the authors who create them. The tragic hero usually must overcome or deal with what the ancient Greeks called *hubris*, or overwhelming arrogance and pride in the face of the gods or fate. Usually, the gods or fate win and humble the arrogant hero in the course of time by the end of the play or fiction.

In addition to using individuals and types, writers use other more immediate methods to develop or reveal their characters, natures, and personality. Characters are revealed to the reader or viewer through several specific qualities and devices: *their looks* (their manner of dress; their height; their deformities, scars, or hairstyles; what kind of habits they reveal), *their words v. their deeds, and how other characters in the same story view them in the context of the story or play*. A "portrait" then emerges of the character in question, based on these ways of observing who or what they are.

Heroes and Antiheroes

A special form of protagonist, known as the *hero* or *heroine*, has changed greatly since the beginning of extant literature in the West. Aristotle's guidelines for the hero are as follows: a man of noble or high birth, a king or aristocrat; a man of noble intention and with high ethical and intellectual skills; a man of great courage and high purpose. This *heroic type* did not include women, except as adjuncts or relatives of the hero. Gradually, this concept of the hero began to change.

The chief change comes with the Renaissance in Europe, when heroes started to appear who had fewer of these qualities. In particular, in Spain, a chief protagonist appeared who had none of these qualities—they were all the opposite: *the picaro*. The Renaissance began to move away from accepted types in literature toward more individual and personable heroes. In fact, the *picaro* actually emerged as the direct opposite of the traditional hero and became the *antihero*. Since then, many changes have occurred.

What is important to remember is that a *chief protagonist could now have any of the qualities from the high noble to the low criminal and still be the main driving force behind the action and/or narrative of the story at hand.*

Stock Characters and Stereotypes

Over the course of time, a number of characters appear over and over again in literature. Some are so well known that they have become *stereotypes*, or stock characters, who have lost their individuality and are only important as minor, flat characters who support the main characters in moving the action forward. For example, in a western, the stock character, or stereotype, of the confiding bartender at the local saloon who lets the hero know where the "gang of bank robbers" is meeting to plan their deed.

Some of these characters have been mentioned previously in Chapter 2, but some deserve special mention because they appear over and over again. Some characters are used *ironically* as stereotypes who turn out not to be what they seem to be. For example, some writers use the hero as some form of "the knight in shining armor"—who looks good, talks a good story, comes from a good family, and even has intelligence and courage, but who turns out to be an evil, ugly, vicious criminal in his internal character and personality despite his outward trappings. Sometimes this is a cowboy in a western; sometimes it is a businessman, a doctor or the like. The reverse is also sometimes true—the character appears rough, of low birth, and even stupid (as with Benjy in Faulkner's *Sound and Fury*), but turns out to be deep in his or her soul, excellent, upright, and righteous.

Dialogue

Dialogue is the talk in which characters in a fiction or in a drama engage in with one another. Dialogue serves two main purposes: it helps to move the action of the play or fiction forward, and it characterizes the character by revealing his or her ways of thinking. Many writers use colloquial language, dialect, and other devices to indicate a character's education, ethical interest, and other ways of seeing the world. Some authors use a special form of dialogue known as *internal monologue*, which reveals the innermost thoughts of their characters. James Joyce, the Irish author, takes this technique to one of its limits when he uses *internal monologue* to show Molly Bloom, the main female character, thinking her thoughts in a freely associative way at the moment she is thinking them: this technique is called *stream of consciousness. Stream of consciousness* is a literary technique which creates the illusion of a character thinking thoughts without any logical or censoring control at the very moment that they occur in that character's mind. This device may or may not appear as dialogue.

Figurative Language and Tone: Image, Metaphor, Symbol, and Myth

Figurative language in fiction, drama, or poetry, not only uses connotations to evoke mood and help characterize an actor or character, but is often used to point to or suggest by implication larger themes to the reader. For example, Huck Finn visits many cities along the Mississippi, one of which is Goshen, by which Mark Twain may invoke a comparison or analogy between Huck's journey down the river and the Biblical journey to the City of Goshen. *Archetypal patterns*, or recurring literary themes, images, and plots, first noticed by the psychologist Carl Jung, are often used by writers to promote comparisons or analogies between the problems of the characters in the immediate work and all humanity. These patterns suggest connections with others. Some of these patterns, along with other standard forms, will be discussed below.

Images

Images are rarely used for their own sake in a good work of art. An *image* is sensory and tangible and may be any sight, sound, smell, taste, or physical feeling that a writer may use to generate a pervasive mood or tone. For example, to evoke the hot, busy mood of the New York City streets in summer, a writer may bring in the sounds of horns and other street noise, the smells of food, the actual temperature, the greasy feel of clothes or tools, the colors of objects in the environment, and so on.

One special form of image that writers have begun to use is an *intellectual image*, (not a sensory image), called a *literary or historical allusion*. The writer may allude or refer to anything in the public record—science, art, literature, music, and so on—in an effort to have the reader associate the character or situation with that history, knowledge, or idea. For example, in his famous poem, "The Love Song of J. Alfred Prufrock," T.S. Eliot alludes to the famous Italian Renaissance sculptor Michelangelo to heighten, by way of contrast, the genius sculptor with the sense of the superficial and petty world in which Prufrock exists: Prufrock says,

> In the rooms,
> The women come and go,
> Talking of Michelangelo...

Metaphors and Similes

Metaphors and similes are used by writers to show relationships between situations or characters in drama, fiction, and poetry that point to larger issues and themes and to create a mood. A *metaphor* is the linking together of two items not usually associated, the combination of which suggests an identity between them that does not exist in real life, but which has the force of truth or feeling. For example, "Life is a journey through a dark wood," suggests that going on in life is like taking a journey through a dark forest. This identity between the two unlike or otherwise unrelated ideas is a metaphor that evokes a mood of dread and of the unknown. The metaphoric comparison brings up fears of what lies ahead on "the path of life."

Metaphors can take many forms: *auditory* ("the fear sounded a bell in my heart"), evoking memories of sound linked to an emotion; *olfactory* ("death is a fermenting, rancid cheese…"), evoking a relationship between an idea and the sense of smell; *visual* ("death is a red sunset"), evoking something seen coupled with an idea; *tactile* ("the nails of his fear dug into his hands…"), coupling an idea with something touched; *savory* ("the warm bread of his feelings for her…); or *tensile* ("the responsibility was a stretched band in his gut"), evoking bodily muscular tension. In all cases, the author links an image to an idea which may be another image, thing, or person, to evoke a thought greater than the sum of its parts.

Metaphors sometimes take a special linguistic form known as a *simile* in which the writer compares two or more ideas and uses the words "like" or "as" to make the comparison or analogy. For example, here are two *similes*:

> "Jeannie was as worried *as a long-tailed cat* in a room full of rocking chairs."

> "George raised his hand *like a hammer* over the fallen gangster."

Symbols in literature are usually concrete objects that stand for or represent an abstraction. *Symbols* in literature are not always things. Sometimes characters become *symbolic*, especially in allegories, fables, and romances, where they may represent whole ideas such as Truth or Beauty. In some of the early "passion plays" of medieval Europe, characters were named for Christian figures. Christ might be called "the Lamb," for "the lamb of God," that is, Jesus. Or a character who stands for all humankind (in those days, mankind) might be called Everyman so that viewers would be sure to know that for which he stood. In Marjorie Kinnan Rawlings' *The Yearling*, it might be said that the yearling deer represents Innocence, so that when the animal has to die, the young male protagonist "loses" his "innocence."

Symbols, like metaphors and images, allow readers or viewers to understand a work of literature at a different level than the literal. Figurative language allows the reader or viewer to raise the story from merely a story to possible universal applications to the human condition. It is through figurative language that literature acquires its "deeper meanings." The student's job is to analyze the figurative language with a view to showing how those metaphors, symbols, and images support the theme or convey some deeper meaning than just the literal events of the story itself.

Myths and Mythologies

Myths and mythologies are the crowning combination of a story told through images, metaphors, and symbols of the deepest cultural beliefs of a people or civilization. *Myths* have, for some people, the negative connotation of being "untrue stories" or "unbelievable tales." But these are corrupt and superficial meanings of the term. *Myths* are the stories that a people or civilization holds dear, and they reflect the mores, norms, and other social values held by that civilization.

The Greek myths that often depicted the conflict between the gods and humans reflect much about the values that the ancient Greeks held sacred. Courage and knowledge were very important to the Greeks, for example in their mythology, there is the mythical story of a daring and proud young man named Prometheus. In Greek mythology, Prometheus is the man who gave humans the knowledge of how to use fire. He made a deal with Zeus (the God of all the gods), and acquired the knowledge of how to start and use fire, under the condition that he wouldn't give that knowledge to his fellow humans. However, he did give away this knowledge (showing great courage in defying the gods). For this, Zeus punished Prometheus and had him live forever chained to an exposed mountain rock where each day an eagle came and ate out his liver. Prometheus's liver was restored each day, only to have him suffer the pain of having it eaten again and again.

This "myth" is not a lie; it is a made-up story. It didn't actually happen in reality, but Prometheus's story is one with a thousand human analogies. How often have humans "defied the gods" only to "pay" some eternal "price" for the "knowledge"? For example, Oppenheimer and others learned to split the atom and unleash the enormous power of the atomic bomb (the knowledge from "the gods"), but the price of that knowledge was the need for a new "eternal" vigilance to prevent the possible wholesale destruction of the Earth and everyone in it.

The student's job is to see if a given author uses *literary or mythic allusions* with images, metaphors, and symbols to refer to or remind the audience of the similarity or contrast between his or her fiction or drama and a well-known cultural myth thereby enlarging the scope or deepening the meaning of what is happening in a given story or play.

Allegory and Romance

Allegory and romance are special forms of storytelling that deserve mention here. *Novels* are long works of fiction that can imitate real life and are set in the present (Updike's *Rabbit Run*, Styron's *Sophie's Choice*), the known historical past (Crane's *The Red Badge of Courage* set in the Civil War), or the imagined future (Clarke's *2001*). *Novels* began to take precedence over other forms of literature as the Industrial Revolution came about. The works of Dickens (*Oliver Twist, David Copperfield*), Jane Austin (*Pride and Prejudice*), and George Eliot/Mary Ann Evans (*Silas Marner, Middlemarch*) are exemplary. Novels are about realistic characters in realistic settings of time and place.

Allegories and *romances*, however, are set in timeless places and unreal or idealized settings (*Beauty and the Beast, King Arthur and the Knights of the Round Table, The 1001 Arabian Nights*), and tend to have an air of timelessness and distance. The hackneyed opening of a child's "fairy tale" is emblematic of how romances strike a tone: "Once upon a time in a land far, far away, there lived a…" In romances and allegories, the characters tend to be flat and do not develop much, except perhaps to overturn the villain. Characters in allegories are never ironic, they are always what they appear to be and are sometimes named as such. Consider the following common allegorical melodrama:

> Mr. Right meets Miss Innocence and they fall in love. The evil banker, named Mr. Greedyone, appears and tries to foreclose on Miss Innocence's mother's home, called HomeSweet. Mr. Greedyone says, however, that if Mrs. Goodmother will give Miss Innocence's hand in marriage to him, he will tear up the mortgage. But Mrs. Goodmother (Miss Innocence's mom), knowing this is not right, turns to Mr. Right for help. And sure enough, through hard work, Mr. Right finds the money in time to save Mrs. Goodmother's home and foil Mr. Greedyone's plan to get HomeSweet and Miss Innocence. Miss Innocence turns to Mr. Right with love in her eyes and says, "My hero!" And they all "live happily ever after."

Allegories are rarely subtle, and though the characters' names might not be this obvious, their deeds and their roles always match their allegorical names (Mr. Greedyone might instead, for example, be called Mr. Moneybags, but the effect would be the same). These stories and tales, since they are vehicles for the dramatic presentation of ideas, usually dramatically depict the working out of some moral. In this case, we might say the moral of the story is that *love conquers all.*

Aesop's fables are allegorical and demonstrate another device: *personification.* Personification is that device in which *a writer turns an idea, object, or feeling into a living being.* Personification is one of the most widely used literary devices. It is this device that makes dogs capable of speech and feeling as in *The Lady and the Tramp* cartoon or in one of the most famous personifications ever, that of the dog Buck in *The Call of the Wild,* a novel by Jack London that is told completely from Buck's point of view. Other examples include having trees with voices and faces (as in *The Wizard of Oz*), mirrors that can talk back to you, or where the young heroine is the *personification of beauty.* Allegories have largely lost their appeal to modern audiences except as children's stories or futuristic science fantasy.

Romances, which are often timeless, are nevertheless often set in a familiar setting, though no particular time is named. Romances are often, but not always, about thwarted or illicit love. The key to an effective romance are emotionally grand characters doing grand and daring deeds in exotic and turbulent settings, and these stories can be found on any drugstore bookstand in America (with a cover that usually shows a barely clothed woman being "swept off her feet" by an equally ill-clad youth in some violent storm on a ship at sea, on a faraway island, or in a grand castle or mansion). They are still a much-read and much-loved genre, though their contribution to the growth of the literary form has fundamentally ceased.

Archetypal Patterns and Common Themes in Literature

Literary works often show the recurrence of common themes and common situations. Some of these have been touched upon above. The psychologist Carl Jung, among others, has noted how these reappear in literature over and over. These *archetypal patterns,* when revealed in a work of literature, serve to frame the fiction on a mythic level or just help the student to understand the fundamental themes at play in the work in question. Psychologists and literary historians believe that these patterns appear because they are fundamental to the human condition and that literature brings them before us in a myriad of variations relevant to our time and place, and yet they are still the same patterns.

Person Against Person, Nature, Society, or God (or the gods)

Most literature depicts one or another of these classic conflicts and will resolve them or not, depending upon the intent of the author. Stories of rival kings (or queens) and man against man or woman v. woman; novels about one woman's attempt to escape from the emotional grip of a vicious and philandering husband (woman against man); science fiction novels about a woman defeating a grossly sociopathic organism never before encountered by science, as depicted by Sigourney Weaver against the Alien in the movie of that name (woman against Nature); epic poems about an uncommonly heroic warrior king overcoming the power of the gods to have his way (Odysseus in the ancient Greek poet Homer's epic poem *The Odyssey*); or myths about man against the gods which move the human spirit to new awareness of the struggle of human life in a difficult and hostile universe. The best works of literature seem to depict all of these conflicts happening at once, or at least to one life, that of the chief protagonist—hero or antihero—and we are kept wondering at how the conflict will be resolved.

Rites of Passage/Literature as the Imitation of Life's "Journey"

Literary critics such as Northrop Frye and others have observed that one way to view literature is not as a series of genres, but as a series of forms that reflect the *archetypal patterns of social and cultural rituals*. Literature, in their way of thinking, is a series of analogues for specific *rites of passage* in our culture. A rite of passage is that dramatic, social ritual that is performed in a culture and is used to mark the onset or change, or "passage," to the next major stage of a life. Typically, there are four major rites of passage in most cultures: rituals marking birth, entry into adulthood and the end of adolescence, fertility, and death, or "passage" to some heavenly afterlife. Awareness of such patterns as a student critic of literature will add weight to any thesis which might be brought forth about the meaning of a work of literature. A student may, of course, only be called upon to explain or describe the presence of such a pattern or symbolic use of a rite in a paper.

Birth and Rebirth

Authors will often write stories and poems showing that someone is "reborn" into a new and better life after a great struggle—either internal or external—to overcome difficult odds. For example, in Melville's epic novel

Moby Dick, Ishmael, the narrator, survives the harrowing voyage with Ahab in search of the white whale Moby Dick, and is cast into the sea, only to come back "reborn" as a man with greater insight into the dark workings of a dark universe. Writers often use images such as the sea, nearly drowning, or some other "transformation" to point to a "reborn" spirit or character.

From Adolescence to Adulthood

Some fictions, dramas, and poems are about growing up and becoming a fully successful man or woman. For example, Dickens' *David Copperfield* and *Oliver Twist* show just this sort of shift and growth. But, again, an author may use this archetypal pattern or ritual as a backdrop to the action shown. A character, while not really a boy or girl, may move symbolically from an "adolescent" frame of mind into that of a successful "adult" simply by developing from an irresponsible, deadbeat dad to one who pays his bills and shares in the raising of his own abandoned children.

The author might depict such a character in the beginning as concerned about "adolescent" things like looks, peer approval, and clothes to one who matures in concern for others, handling decisions on a personal basis, and nurturing the talents and skills of those around him or her not as fortunate as he or she in the end. The deadbeat dad will thus have symbolically gone through a rite of passage from "adolescence" to "adulthood" by taking a new course of action in his life.

Marriage and Fertility

This rite of passage is legion in literature. It can be used ironically, showing the destruction of a marriage and an "infertile" relationship. This rite is mostly celebrated in musicals, comedies, romances, and soap operas. But the rite may serve as a symbolic backdrop or undercurrent to a story in progress. Thus, a chief protagonist may be "married to his work," making him or her give "birth" to new ideas or a successful marriage, while ironically losing the love of his or her real flesh and blood wife or husband in the process. Sinclair Lewis's famous *Dodsworth* shows just such a situation, when the American businessman who has been "married to his work" takes his wife abroad to Europe and discovers what his false "marriage" has cost him in his real one.

In Shakespeare's *Macbeth*, the reader sees a marriage of real love destroyed by the lust for power, and Lady Macbeth and Macbeth himself complain of their "infertility"—a biological dysfunction symbolic of the "infertile" and "sterile" life to which they are damned by their murderous ways.

Death/Rebirth

Sometimes this rite dominates the literature of horror, as in Bram Stoker's *Dracula* where the ritual of death is overturned by the perverse ritual of vampirism and unholy love. The rite of death becomes ironically turned into the source of eternal life. Death, too, can be used in a symbolic pattern. Thus, novels of psychological horror might depict a man "losing his mind" and identity in a kind of psychological "death," only to recover and become "alive" again in a new and productive selfhood. This pattern is most often associated with literature about the transformation of the spirit and the soul.

SOME BASICS ABOUT GOOD STYLE

Format

Whether writing about literature or some other topic, professors will expect the students to write in standard English with control over style. The student will organize the paper in a logical and useful way that supports the purpose. When the student controls the appearance or format of the paper is controlled, the paper becomes more accessible to the reader. Students often complain that an English teacher will give them a poor grade with the student commenting, "Gee, my English teacher never even talks about my great ideas!"

Great ideas are not separate from the language with which the writer communicates them. That's what makes them great ideas: they are written in clear sentences, and they communicate to people quickly, accurately, and without grammatical flaws. Editing style is the key to communicating thoughts.

Papers should not only be well organized, but should also be attractive to the reader's eye. Some standards will be required, but sometimes formatting the paper with original design or graphics is a good idea. Many word-processing packages have programs to help format correctly, and some have interesting graphics to use to communicate ideas in a striking manner. Formatting a paper should be done during the revising stage of the composing process. Review the paper and make changes later, but formatting it should be set up before editing, i.e., to control sentence structure, tone, and punctuation.

Format is the way the paper looks to the reader. Usually professors want papers typed on $8\frac{1}{2}$" × 11" unlined paper. They should be typed on one side only, and all the pages should be numbered in the same place on each page. Names, titles, and class identification should be placed where the professor requests them. Typos, or minor typing mistakes, spelling errors, paragraph indentations, and other minor errors in the quality of your copy must be corrected before you hand in your paper.

Most papers are double-spaced, and the right-hand margins are best left naturally uneven, unless the professor directs you to do otherwise. Underlining and *italics* are used mostly for subheadings and to highlight important elements in the text. Be careful to use underlining, **boldface**, and *italics* sparingly; otherwise, they lose their effectiveness.

Paragraphs should be indented a standard five spaces from the left-hand margin. Paragraphs should be kept brief (three or four sentences on average), so as not to tire the reader's eyes with a busy or cluttered look to the page.

Sentences should be varied and relatively brief and should average about 10 to 15 words each. Of course, longer sentences will be written, but sentences that are over 25 words must be read slowly. Sentences that are 30 words or longer usually have to be read twice by the average reader. Make sure that sentences are correct in grammar as well.

Titles of long works, such as novels or histories, are written in *italics*. Titles may also appear underlined. Parts of large works, such as a chapter from a book, or an article in a journal, are cited using quotation marks rather than italics: e.g., "The Rising Cost of Living" might appear in *The Journal of American Economics*. For the formats of particular writing, such as business memos, follow the practices set by the business communications or English department.

Sentence Style

Too often, writers in college do not offer the reader an interesting and coherent flow among their sentences. Students often use the same sentence style repeatedly, making the writing sound disjointed, pedestrian, and choppy. Consider the passage that follows:

> "This outline is merely a tool of analysis. It is in the form of questions. It should remind its user of responsibility. It should remind the user that only he or she can provide the answers. We hope we can talk to one another about literature. We hope we can exchange information about it. A given work of fiction should mean something to us. A work of fiction should be felt completely. We must wrestle with the work. We must not use others as guides or informants."

Notice how choppy and unrelated the ideas seem. Notice how all the sentences have the form [subject] + [predicate], producing a monotonous tone and halting reading.

Now consider how the original writer, Robert W. Lewis, Jr., in his article from *College English*, actually wrote it:

> "This outline is merely a tool of analysis, and being put in the form of questions, it should constantly remind its user that only he or she can provide the answers. We hope we can talk to one another about literature and exchange informed and reasoned opinions about it, but if a given work of fiction is to mean anything to us, if we are to feel and know it completely, we must at one stage wrestle with the work bare-handed, without others as guides or informants."

This version has drive and energy, not just because the words are slightly different, but because it uses sentences of different types and different lengths to convey Mr. Lewis's thoughts and opinions. Notice how Mr. Lewis uses the "if" to lead a clause or phrase to build up energy in the middle of his statement, leading to the emphatic, "we must..." clause, which "pushes" on to the end. S*entence variety*, then, or *varying the kinds and lengths of sentences to reflect the emphasis and the flow of your ideas*, is a quality to bring into personal writing style.

In English, there are several basic ways to write sentences other than by just having a series of simple sentences with a subject and verb pattern. Writers may combine sentences in English to show relationships among ideas in time or in logic. Writers must be careful to show the relationship of one idea to another with the correct combining word or phrase. Below are three short, choppy sentences could be written to illustrate this point:

> Peter is the boss. He controls the office. He is very tyrannical.

But a writer *could* combine these three sentences to make one complex sentence (an independent and a dependent clause) in the following way:

> Peter is a tyrannical boss who controls the office.

Not only does the sentence get clearer and more interesting, but it becomes shorter. The sentences don't always get shorter when this is done, but the relationships among ideas do get clearer for the reader when a writer varies sentences effectively.

Writers may, however, *coordinate ideas* to show that ideas have equal value. Writers may combine sentences by using *and, but, nor, for, or, yet,* and *so* as logic demands. For example:

> Peter, the boss, controls the office, and he is tyrannical.

Writers may *subordinate ideas* to show the logical or temporal (timely) dependence of one idea upon another. In these cases writers use *since*, *although, because, even though, while, when*, and *if* to show clear relationships between **cause** and **effect**, **time**, or **conditional dependence**. For example:

> **Since** Peter is the boss in charge of the office, he is sometimes tyrannical. [cause…effect]

In the following example, notice how the connecting word **"although"** supports a *different* relationship among the ideas, suggesting contradiction:

> **Although** Peter is the boss in charge of the office, he often acts more like a clerk. [conditional dependence]

Here is an example of a temporal relationship:

> **When** Peter became the boss in charge of the office, he started to act like a tyrant.

Writers may show the relationship among ideas by using **transitions** such as *however, consequently, therefore,* or *thus*.

> Peter is the boss in charge of the office; **consequently**, he is very careful.

> Peter is the boss in charge of the office; **however**, he often acts like a clerk.

Notice how the different relationships among the sentences and their clauses generate different thoughtful responses and considerations for the reader even though the basic message, "Peter is the boss in the office," remains mostly the same.

Narrative Stance: "I" v. "It," "He," "She," or "They"

In writing effective essays, a writer must decide upon a *narrative stance*, or *point of view*. If an essay is personal and reflects personal memories, opinions, and ideas, then writing from the point of view of "I" or "we" may be appropriate. But in trying to keep the reader's focus on the subject at hand, and not the writer, it may be best to take the *third person point of view*. As mentioned above in a different context in Chapter 2, it may be preferable to talk not about "I" so much as "it" or "they," keeping the subject at a distance from a personal point of view, while focusing instead on the topic at hand.

Numbers

As a matter of style, the writer should use numbers in text in a few standard ways, depending upon whether following scientific, A.P.A., or M.L.A. guidelines. The writer must do as instructed by a professor, but use personal judgment otherwise and be consistent. As a final note, it is not considered good writing style to begin a sentence with a number written as a figure as in this sentence:

"42 people came to the meeting."

The difference between *cardinal* and *ordinal* numbers is also important to know. A cardinal number is simply the number itself or the number of anything: 1, 15, 400, 2368, and so on. An ordinal number is one that places the item or items referred to in a sequence: *first, second, third, fourth,* and so on. Spell out all ordinal numbers that can be expressed in one or two words. A hyphenated ordinal number counts as one word: *twenty-second, thirty-fifth.* For particular rules governing fractions, lists, and other special uses of numbers, consult your handbook.

HANDLING RESEARCH ASSIGNMENTS

Planning Time

During the course of a college career, research papers will be written, sometimes in a technical field, and sometimes about literature itself. Whatever the assignment is, the purpose of research papers is to develop skills in finding out information, evaluating what was found, and giving the reader either new information or a new insight into information already known. Research papers are generally longer than the average 500-word essay required in most composition courses, so plan more carefully for them. They vary in length from 3,000 to 5,000 words on average. In this section, we will discuss the special needs of the research paper.

Writing a research paper is a long-term project; consequently, time must be scheduled during a term so that the completed paper can be delivered on time. Since the research paper must go through the same stages as any essay, use the stages of the writing process to plan time. Whatever time you have, a paper should be scheduled in such a manner that it can be completed by your professor's deadline.

Your research paper, although longer term, is basically another paper that must be written using the writing process. During the *prewriting stage,* use the time to gather research at the library. Do not hesitate to seek the help of a *research librarian in the library at your college*. Research librarians can point out where to find the information sources the writer needs.

Basically, a student may find research material in either a *card catalog* or a *computer catalog*. Most libraries now have computer catalogs, so it is helpful to become computer literate to use them effectively. Sources that should be sought out in the library include, of course, *books relevant to the topic that can be found in the Library of Congress subject headings* or, in some libraries, in the *Dewey Decimal System*. These are the systems used to catalog information in most libraries. The writer must learn to use the systems to find what you need.

In addition to books, the writer may use *periodicals and journals* that are relevant to the topic. The *Reader's Guide to Periodical Literature* and *New York Times Index* are the two best sources for this information. *Indexes for special disciplines* such as psychology or medicine are available. Finally, various *abstracting services* are available to provide summaries of important recent articles and books relevant to a project.

After having discovered how to use these resources, the writer should develop a *working bibliography*, that is, *a list on index cards of all the sources that **might** be used in the paper*. The writer must be sure to include all the *bibliographic information* on one side of the cards (including *author, title, publisher, city of publication, year of publication*, and *any other identifying information necessary*). Put important notes on the other side of the cards, such as the author's thesis or main supporting evidence. The writer should do this in the beginning; these notes will be available when writing the formal bibliography at the end.

When at the end of the research effort during prewriting, the writer should write a *working outline* of the paper that shows what should be included in the sections of the paper (introduction, body, and conclusion). Use this outline as a rough idea of how and what should be included in the paper. Later, when revising the paper, data may be added as well as ideas that will affect the length and shape of the paper.

Original v. Derivative Research

Professors may ask for either *original* or *derivative research* or both, depending upon the topic. The opportunity to do *original research* rarely occurs to undergraduates, but this kind of research is characterized by finding out entirely new things in new areas of experiment or study. Most often, graduate students find themselves involved in this sort of research.

Derivative research is characterized by study and research from works already known and written by experts in a given field, from which the student researcher forms new opinions or from which information is used to support theses *derived from someone else's findings*.

Sometimes professors call upon students to write *a review of the literature* available in a given field. In this sort of research paper, the student is asked to find out what is generally known about a given topic and "review" the literature for its major findings or theses of the experts in the field. In sociology, a student may writer a paper about what is known about urban violence among teenagers in Philadelphia. Who are the authorities and what are the theories? Once a working bibliography is developed in addition to a rough outline, the rough draft can be begun.

Primary and Secondary Sources

Before launching into the draft the writer must make sure that both types of sources have been researched: *primary and secondary resources*. Some topics do not have primary resources, make sure that they are being dealt with if both exist. A *primary resource* is the original book, work of art, or artifact under study. For example, *Huckleberry Finn* is the primary resource for the study of the novel *Huckleberry Finn*. Anything written, spoken, or recorded about the primary source that is in the public domain is a *secondary source*. Some sources are better than others. While it may be interesting enough in its own right, Joe the plumber's view of the literary value of *Huckleberry Finn* is probably not as relevant as the view of an expert who has made his or her life study the life and work of Mark Twain. The value of secondary sources can be checked by asking the reference librarian and the professor who assigned the paper.

Outlining: The Fundamental Form for Research Papers

Research takes slightly different forms depending upon what field the paper is in; however, the basic form of introduction, body, and conclusion remains, and should be followed along with the current form used in the field of study. Get to know well the forms peculiar to the field.

Introduction, Background, Discussion and Analysis, Implications, Conclusions, and Recommendations

Although the basic pattern of organization is the same for research as for shorter essays, some differences are important to note.

The *introduction* to a research paper usually includes a statement of the paper's purpose, the topic to be explored, and the fundamental thesis or hypothesis of the writer.

The next section, or *background*, usually discusses the "history," or extant of published knowledge available about the topic, and summarizes the known theories and research. If researching the "causes of violence among urban teenagers in Philadelphia," the *background* section would summarize all the major known causes cited by authorities and independent studies in the field.

Next, the *discussion and analysis* section should offer views of what the known research indicates and how it affects the thesis (Does it support the thesis, contradict it, or do a little of both? Does the research found in favor of the thesis outweigh that opposed?). In this section, the writer should not offer any statements that are conclusive about the thesis, but only explain and analyze the findings that came out of the research.

In the next section, or *implications*, the writer should show what the information researched *implies* about the *thesis*, or say *what the trends are*; *what the dominant theories are*; and *what makes the most sense*. The writer must be sure to give credit to those scholars or researchers from whose work he has derived ideas, by quoting, paraphrasing, and always citing sources where necessary.

In the *conclusions and recommendations* section, the writer must list the findings and what he or she believes to be the truth about the topic and the power of the thesis. The conclusions should be (1) logically inescapable, given the research; (2) limited in scope appropriate to the level of research; and (3) not the restatement of someone else's ideas. A writer may include *recommendations* to add to the paper. Usually, if offering the solution to a problem, recommendations would be in order. Also, young researchers will often recommend areas of research that other researchers need to pursue further because they and/or others have been overlooked, slighted, or neglected areas or because the findings remain inconclusive. Generally, however, in a research paper about literature, the writer will limit his or her conclusions to the meaning or relevance of a work of literary art.

Format and Style for Research Papers

A List of Reference Style Books for Research Papers

American Psychological Association. *Publication Manual of the American Psychological Association*. Latest edition. Washington D.C.: American Psychological Association.

Associated Press. *The Associated Press Stylebook and Libel Manual.* Reading: Addison, 1987.

The Chicago Manual of Style. Latest edition. Chicago: U. of Chicago Press.

Gibaldi, Joseph, and Walter S. Achtert. *MLA Handbook for Writers of Research Papers.* Latest edition. New York: Modern Language Association.

REA's Handbook of English Grammar, Style and Writing. Latest edition. Piscataway, NJ: Research & Education Association.

Turabian, Kate L. *A Manual for Writers of Term Papers, Theses, and Dissertations.* Latest edition. Chicago: University of Chicago Press.

United States Government Printing Office. *Style Manual.* Rev. ed. Washington D.C.: GPO.

The "works cited" list is an alphabetical listing of every book, periodical, abstract, article, dissertation, interview, or any other information source that the writer incorporates into his or her paper through either paraphrasing or direct quotation. The writer should check the style manual that is appropriate for the paper's topic. If the researcher looked only at the title of a particular source—or just scanned it—without actually using any information from that source, he or she need not include it in the "works cited" list.

Documentation and Plagiarism

One of the serious problems in writing research papers is that students often have difficulty citing or *documenting correctly the research they have done.* If a researcher uses an idea and the very same words directly from some other writing or research, the researcher must make sure that he or she has correctly noted the sources for the reader. This type of documentation not only helps readers do further research if they want to work with the same information, but it also honors the work of those who previously spent so much time and effort to find out about the chosen topic.

Students and writers who do not note where they get information, or *take another person's ideas and represent them as their own,* are guilty of *plagiarism.* So egregious is this practice that it can result in expulsion. *The writer must not plagiarize.* It doesn't matter how much the writer borrows from another author as long as he or she acknowledges the borrowed ideas.

To document correctly, a writer must follow specific forms, depending upon the topic that is being written about (e.g., the American Psychological Association publishes a style book that addresses research-paper issues specific to the discipline of psychology). Each discipline uses a particular style manual; ask your professor which one to consult as the authoritative guide for your field. Professors prefer to see a variety of primary and secondary resources, demonstrating that the student rsearched a thorough range of possible sources.

Footnotes, Endnotes, and Parenthetical Documentation

In doing research documentation, the researcher may cite where he or she found the information for a particular idea in one of three basic ways: *footnotes*, *endnotes*, or *parenthetical documentation*. Writers generally number *footnotes* sequentially and list them at the bottom of each page in which the information or quotation is footnoted with a line separating the footnote from the text and with a superscript or other number to identify the item referred to within the text. Thus,

[1]Jones, R. H., *The Rise of Mammals After the Fall of Dinosaurs.* (New York: Biology Press), 1994, pp. 34–36.

Unlike the list of works cited, footnotes, endnotes, and parenthetical documentation usually include the particular pages on which the quoted or paraphrased information was found. *Endnotes* are basically the same as footnotes, except that, instead of printing each footnote that appears on a page at the bottom of the page, the researcher places endnotes after the text of the paper, numbering them sequentially on as many pages as needed. The writer usually places endnotes after any *appendices*, sections of information such as charts, graphs, or experimental data, but before the bibliography. The list of works cited is always the last section of any paper. Many students dread doing research; however, once they have a full grasp of the techniques, they will find that these techniques have many applications in most professional walks of life. Moreover, the student seldom forgets what he or she researches.

Parenthetical documentation is probably the most practical way to reference information in the body of the text. Using this method, the writer acknowledges the referenced work by inserting the author's name, and the page number where the reference was found, in parenthesis directly after the cited text. The full information of the work is then found on the works cited page.

If a writer quotes a piece of information directly from a research source, the source must be referenced. If a writer uses only a person's ideas in the form of a paraphrase—but not his or her exact words—the writer still must reference that paraphrase *just as if it were a quotation*. A student *may* arrive independently at an idea that some expert in the topic under study has already found, but that rarely happens. Such a random convergence of thought is usually a sign of weak research. The student who knows the available sources well enough will know that he or she shared an idea with an expert in the field. To be safe, reference *any* idea that is not original. It is better to reference too much rather than too little.

CHAPTER 3
ENGLISH LANGUAGE
SKILLS REVIEW

Chapter 3

ENGLISH LANGUAGE SKILLS REVIEW

The CLEP: Freshman College Composition does not require you to know grammatical terms such as *gerund, subject complement,* or *dependent clause,* although general familiarity with such terms may be helpful to you in determining whether a sentence or part of a sentence is correct or incorrect. You should watch for errors in grammar, spelling, punctuation, capitalization, sentence structure, and word choice. Remember: this is a test of language skills; therefore, your responses should be based on what you know to be correct for written work, not what you know to be appropriate for a casual conversation. For instance, in informal speech, you might say "Who are you going to choose?" But in formal academic writing, you would write "Whom are you going to choose?" Your choices, then, should be dictated by requirements for *written,* not *conversational* English.

WORD CHOICE SKILLS

Connotative and Denotative Meanings

The denotative meaning of a word is its *literal,* dictionary definition: what the word denotes or "means." The connotative meaning of a word is what the word connotes or "suggests"; it is a meaning apart from what the word literally means. A writer should choose a word based on the tone and context of the sentence; this ensures that a word bears the appropriate connotation while still conveying some exactness in denotation. For example, a gift might be described as "cheap," but the directness of this word has a negative connotation—something cheap is something of little or no value. The word "inexpensive" has a more positive connotation, though "cheap" is a synonym for "inexpensive." Questions of this type require you to make a decision regarding the appropriateness of words and phrases for the context of a sentence.

Wordiness and Conciseness

Effective writing is concise. Wordiness, on the other hand, decreases the clarity of expression by cluttering sentences with unnecessary words.

Wordiness questions test your ability to detect redundancies (unnecessary repetitions), circumlocution (failure to get to the point), and padding with loose synonyms. Wordiness questions require you to choose sentences that use as few words as possible to convey a message clearly, economically, and effectively.

Notice the difference in impact between the first and second sentences in the following pairs:

INCORRECT:	The medical exam that he gave me was entirely complete.
CORRECT:	The medical exam he gave me was complete.

INCORRECT:	Larry asked his friend John, who was a good, old friend, if he would join him and go along with him to see the foreign film made in Japan.
CORRECT:	Larry asked his good, old friend John if he would join him in seeing the Japanese film.

INCORRECT:	I was absolutely, totally happy with the present that my parents gave to me at 7 a.m. on the morning of my birthday.
CORRECT:	I was happy with the present my parents gave me on the morning of my birthday.

☞ Drill: Word Choice Skills

DIRECTIONS: Choose the correct option.

1. His <u>principal</u> reasons for resigning were his <u>principles</u> of right and wrong.

    (A) principal . . . principals   (C) principle . . . principles

    (B) principle . . . principals   (D) No change is necessary.

2. The book tells about Alzheimer's disease—how it <u>affects</u> the patient and what <u>effect</u> it has on the patient's family.

    (A) effects . . . affect   (C) effects . . . effects

    (B) affects . . . affect   (D) No change is necessary.

3. The <u>amount</u> of homeless children we can help depends on the <u>number</u> of available shelters.

    (A) number . . . number   (C) number . . . amount

    (B) amount . . . amount   (D) No change is necessary.

4. All students are <u>suppose to</u> pass the test before <u>achieving</u> upper-division status.

    (A) suppose to . . . acheiving

    (B) suppose to . . . being achieved

    (C) supposed to . . . achieving

    (D) No change is necessary.

5. The reason he <u>succeeded</u> is <u>because</u> he worked hard.

    (A) succeeded . . . that   (C) succede . . . because of

    (B) seceded . . . that   (D) No change is necessary.

DIRECTIONS: Select the sentence that clearly and effectively states the idea and has no structural errors.

6.   (A)   South of Richmond, the two roads converge together to form a single highway.

    (B)   South of Richmond, the two roads converge together to form an interstate highway.

    (C)   South of Richmond, the two roads converge to form an interstate highway.

    (D)   South of Richmond, the two roads converge to form a single interstate highway.

7.   (A)   The student depended on his parents for financial support.

    (B)   The student lacked the ways and means to pay for his room and board, so he depended on his parents for this kind of money and support.

    (C)   The student lacked the ways and means or the wherewithal to support himself, so his parents provided him with the financial support he needed.

    (D)   The student lacked the means to pay for his room and board, so he depended on his parents for financial support.

8.   (A)   Vincent van Gogh and Paul Gauguin were close personal friends and companions who enjoyed each other's company and frequently worked together on their artwork.

    (B)   Vincent van Gogh and Paul Gauguin were friends who frequently painted together.

    (C)   Vincent van Gogh was a close personal friend of Paul Gauguin's, and the two of them often worked together on their artwork because they enjoyed each other's company.

    (D)   Vincent van Gogh, a close personal friend of Paul Gauguin's, often worked with him on their artwork.

9.   (A)   A college education often involves putting away childish thoughts, which are characteristic of youngsters, and concentrating on the future, which lies ahead.

(B) A college education involves putting away childish thoughts, which are characteristic of youngsters, and concentrating on the future.

(C) A college education involves putting away childish thoughts and concentrating on the future.

(D) A college education involves putting away childish thoughts and concentrating on the future which lies ahead.

10. (A) I had the occasion to visit an Oriental pagoda while I was a tourist on vacation and visiting in Kyoto, Japan.

(B) I visited a Japanese pagoda in Kyoto.

(C) I had occasion to visit a pagoda when I was vacationing in Kyoto, Japan.

(D) On my vacation, I visited a Japanese pagoda in Kyoto.

SENTENCE STRUCTURE SKILLS

Parallelism

Parallel structure is used to express matching ideas. It refers to the grammatical balance of a series of any of the following:

Phrases:

The squirrel ran *along the fence, up the tree*, and *into his burrow* with a mouthful of acorns.

Adjectives:

The job market is flooded with *very talented, highly motivated*, and *well-educated* young people.

Nouns:

You will need a *notebook, pencil*, and *dictionary* for the test.

Clauses:

The children were told to decide which toy they would keep and which toy they would give away.

Verbs:

The farmer *plowed, planted*, and *harvested* his corn in record time.

Verbals:

> *Reading*, *writing*, and *calculating* are fundamental skills that all of us should possess.

Correlative conjunctions:

> *Either* you will do your homework *or* you will fail.

Repetition of structural signals:

(such as articles, auxiliaries, prepositions, and conjunctions)

> INCORRECT: I have quit my job, enrolled in school, and am looking for a reliable babysitter.

> CORRECT: I *have quit* my job, *have enrolled* in school, and *am looking* for a reliable babysitter.

Note: Repetition of prepositions is considered formal and is not necessary.

> You can travel *by car, by plane, or by train*; it's all up to you.

> OR

> You can travel *by car, plane, or train*; it's all up to you.

When a sentence contains items in a series, check for both punctuation and sentence balance. When you check for punctuation, make sure the commas are used correctly. When you check for parallelism, make sure that the conjunctions connect similar grammatical constructions, such as all adjectives or all clauses.

Misplaced and Dangling Modifiers

A misplaced modifier is one that is in the wrong place in the sentence. Misplaced modifiers come in all forms—words, phrases, and clauses. Sentences containing misplaced modifiers are often very comical: *Mom made me eat the spinach instead of my brother*. Misplaced modifiers, like the one in this sentence, are usually too far away from the word or words they modify. This sentence should read: *Mom made me, instead of my brother, eat the spinach*.

Modifiers like *only, nearly*, and *almost* should be placed next to the word they modify and not in front of some other word, especially a verb, that they are not intended to modify.

A modifier is misplaced if it appears to modify the wrong part of the sentence or if we cannot be certain what part of the sentence the writer intended it to modify. To correct a misplaced modifier, move the modifier next to the word it describes.

INCORRECT: She served hamburgers to the men on paper plates.

CORRECT: She served hamburgers on paper plates to the men.

Split infinitives also result in misplaced modifiers. Infinitives consist of the marker *to* plus the plain form of the verb. The two parts of the infinitive make up a grammatical unit that should not be split. Splitting an infinitive is placing an adverb between the *to* and the verb.

INCORRECT: The weather service expects temperatures to not rise.

CORRECT: The weather service expects temperatures not to rise.

Sometimes a split infinitive may be natural and preferable, though it may still bother some readers.

EX: Several U.S. industries expect *to* more than *triple* their use of robots within the next decade.

A squinting modifier is one that may refer to either a preceding or a following word, leaving the reader uncertain about what it is intended to modify. Correct a squinting modifier by moving it next to the word it is intended to modify.

INCORRECT: Snipers who fired on the soldiers often escaped capture.

CORRECT: Snipers who often fired on the soldiers escaped capture.

OR   Snipers who fired on the soldiers escaped capture often.

A dangling modifier is a modifier or verb in search of a subject: the modifying phrase (usually an *-ing* word group, an *-ed* or *-en* word group, or a *to* + *a verb* word group—participle phrase or infinitive phrase respectively) either appears to modify the wrong word or has nothing to modify. It is literally dangling at the beginning or the end of a sentence. The sentences often look and sound correct: *To be a student government officer, your grades must be above average.* (However, the verbal modifier has nothing to describe. Who is *to be a student government officer?* Your grades?) Questions of this type require you to determine whether a modifier has a headword or whether it is dangling at the beginning or the end of the sentence.

To correct a dangling modifier, reword the sentence by either: 1) changing the modifying phrase to a clause with a subject, or 2) changing the subject of the sentence to the word that should be modified. The following are examples of a dangling gerund, a dangling infinitive, and a dangling participle:

INCORRECT: Shortly after leaving home, the accident occurred.

Who is <u>leaving home</u>, the accident?

CORRECT: Shortly after we left home, the accident occurred.

INCORRECT: To get up on time, a great effort was needed.

<u>To get up</u> needs a subject.

CORRECT: To get up on time, I made a great effort.

Fragments

A fragment is an incomplete construction which may or may not have a subject and a verb. Specifically, a fragment is a group of words pretending to be a sentence. Not all fragments appear as separate sentences, however. Often, fragments are separated by semicolons.

INCORRECT: Traffic was stalled for ten miles on the freeway. Because repairs were being made on potholes.

CORRECT: Traffic was stalled for ten miles on the freeway because repairs were being made on potholes.

INCORRECT: It was a funny story; one that I had never heard before.

CORRECT: It was a funny story, one that I had never heard before.

Run-on/Fused Sentences

A run-on/fused sentence is not necessarily a long sentence or a sentence that the reader considers too long; in fact, a run-on may be two short sentences: *Dry ice does not melt it evaporates.* A run-on results when the writer fuses or runs together two separate sentences without any correct mark of punctuation separating them.

INCORRECT: Knowing how to use a dictionary is no problem each dictionary has a section in the front of the book telling how to use it.

CORRECT: Knowing how to use a dictionary is no problem. Each dictionary has a section in the front of the book telling how to use it.

Even if one or both of the fused sentences contains internal punctuation, the sentence is still a run-on.

> INCORRECT: Bob bought dress shoes, a suit, and a nice shirt he needed them for his sister's wedding.

> CORRECT: Bob bought dress shoes, a suit, and a nice shirt. He needed them for his sister's wedding.

Comma Splices

A comma splice is the unjustifiable use of only a comma to combine what really is two separate sentences.

> INCORRECT: One common error in writing is incorrect spelling, the other is the occasional use of faulty diction.

> CORRECT: One common error in writing is incorrect spelling; the other is the occasional use of faulty diction.

Both run-on sentences and comma splices may be corrected in one of the following ways:

> RUN-ON: Neal won the award he had the highest score.

> COMMA SPLICE: Neal won the award, he had the highest score.

Separate the sentences with a period:

> Neal won the award. He had the highest score.

Separate the sentences with a comma and a coordinating conjunction (*and, but, or, nor, for, yet, so*):

> Neal won the award for he had the highest score.

Separate the sentences with a semicolon:

> Neal won the award; he had the highest score.

Separate the sentences with a subordinating conjunction such as *although, because, since, if*:

> Neal won the award because he had the highest score.

Subordination, Coordination, and Predication

Suppose, for the sake of clarity, you wanted to combine the information in these two sentences to create one statement:

> I studied a foreign language. I found English quite easy.

How you decide to combine this information should be determined by the relationship you'd like to show between the two facts. *I studied a foreign language, and I found English quite easy* seems rather illogical. The **coordination** of the two ideas (connecting them with the coordinating conjunction *and* is ineffective. Using **subordination** instead (connecting the sentences with a subordinating conjunction) clearly shows the degree of relative importance between the expressed ideas:

> After I studied a foreign language, I found English quite easy.

When using a conjunction, be sure that the sentence parts you are joining are in agreement.

> INCORRECT: She loved him dearly but not his dog.

> CORRECT: She loved him dearly but she did not love his dog.

A common mistake that is made is to forget that each member of the pair must be followed by the same kind of construction.

> INCORRECT: They complimented them both for their bravery and they thanked them for their kindness.

> CORRECT: They both complimented them for their bravery and thanked them for their kindness.

While refers to time and should not be used as a substitute for *although, and,* or *but.*

> INCORRECT: While I'm usually interested in Fellini movies, I'd rather not go tonight.

> CORRECT: Although I'm usually interested in Fellini movies, I'd rather not go tonight.

Where refers to time and should not be used as a substitute for *that.*

> INCORRECT: We read in the paper where they are making great strides in DNA research.

> CORRECT: We read in the paper that they are making great strides in DNA research.

After words like reason and explanation, use that, not because.

> INCORRECT: His explanation for his tardiness was because his alarm did not go off.

> CORRECT: His explanation for his tardiness was that his alarm did not go off.

☞ Drill: Sentence Structure Skills

DIRECTIONS: Choose the sentence that expresses the thought most clearly and that has no error in structure.

1. (A) Many gases are invisible, odorless, and they have no taste.

   (B) Many gases are invisible, odorless, and have no taste.

   (C) Many gases are invisible, odorless, and tasteless.

   (D) Many gases are invisible and odorless and have no taste.

2. (A) Everyone agreed that she had neither the voice or the skill to be a speaker.

   (B) Everyone agreed that she had neither the voice nor the skill to be a speaker.

   (C) Everyone agreed that she had either the voice nor the skill to be a speaker.

   (D) Everyone agreed that she had not the voice nor the skill to be a speaker.

3. (A) The mayor will be remembered because he kept his campaign promises and because of his refusal to accept political favors.

   (B) The mayor will be remembered because he kept his campaign promises and because he refused to accept political favors.

   (C) The mayor will be remembered because of his refusal to accept political favors and because he kept his campaign promises.

   (D) The mayor will be remembered because of his refusal to accept political favors and that he kept his campaign promises.

4. (A) While taking a shower, the doorbell rang.

   (B) While I was taking a shower, the doorbell rang.

   (C) While taking a shower, someone rang the doorbell.

   (D) The doorbell rang, while taking a shower.

5. (A) He swung the bat, while the runner stole second base.

   (B) The runner stole second base while he swung the bat.

(C)   While he was swinging the bat, the runner stole second base.

(D)   The runner was stealing second base while he was swinging the bat.

DIRECTIONS: Choose the correct option.

6.   Nothing grows as well in Mississippi as <u>cotton. Cotton</u> being the state's principal crop.

   (A)   cotton, cotton   (C)   cotton cotton

   (B)   cotton; cotton   (D)   No change is necessary.

7.   It was a heartwrenching <u>movie; one</u> that I had never seen before.

   (A)   movie and   (C)   movie. One

   (B)   movie, one   (D)   No change is necessary.

8.   Traffic was stalled for three miles on the <u>bridge. Because</u> repairs were being made.

   (A)   bridge because   (C)   bridge, because

   (B)   bridge; because   (D)   No change is necessary.

9.   The ability to write complete sentences comes with <u>practice writing</u> run-on sentences seems to occur naturally.

   (A)   practice, writing   (C)   practice and

   (B)   practice. Writing   (D)   No change is necessary.

10. Even though she had taken French classes, she could not understand native French <u>speakers they</u> all spoke too fast.

   (A)   speakers, they   (C)   speaking

   (B)   speakers. They   (D)   No change is necessary.

VERBS

Verb Forms

This section covers the principal parts of some irregular verbs including troublesome verbs like *lie* and *lay*. The use of regular verbs like *look* and *receive* poses no real problem to most writers since the past and past participle forms end in *-ed*; it is the irregular forms which pose the most serious problems—for example, *seen, written,* and *begun.*

Verb Tenses
   Tense sequence indicates a logical time sequence.

Use present tense
   in statements of universal truth:

   > I learned that the sun *is* ninety-million miles from the earth.

   in statements about the contents of literature and other published works:

   > In this book, Sandy *becomes* a nun and *writes* a book on psychology.

Use past tense
   in statements concerning writing or publication of a book:

   > He *wrote* his first book in 1949, and it *was published* in 1952.

Use present perfect tense
   for an action that began in the past but continues into the future:

   > I *have lived* here all my life.

Use past perfect tense
   for an earlier action that is mentioned in a later action:

   > Cindy ate the apple that she *had picked.*

(First she picked it, then she ate it.)

Use future perfect tense
   for an action that will have been completed at a specific future time:

   > By May, I shall have graduated.

Use a present participle
   for action that occurs at the same time as the verb:

   > *Speeding* down the interstate, I saw a cop's flashing lights.

Use a perfect participle

for action that occurred before the main verb:

> *Having read* the directions, I started the test.

Use the subjunctive mood

to express a wish or state a condition contrary to fact:

> *If it were not raining,* we could have a picnic.

in *that* clauses after verbs like *request, recommend, suggest, ask, require*, and *insist*; and after such expressions as *it is important* and *it is necessary*:

> It is necessary that all papers *be* submitted on time.

Subject-Verb Agreement

Agreement is the grammatical correspondence between the subject and the verb of a sentence: *I do, we do, they do, he, she, it does.*

Every English verb has five forms, two of which are the bare form (plural) and the *-s* form (singular). Simply put, singular verb forms end in *-s;* plural forms do not.

Study these rules governing subject-verb agreement:

A verb must agree with its subject, not with any additive phrase in the sentence such as a prepositional or verbal phrase. Ignore such phrases.

> Your *copy* of the rules *is* on the desk.

> Ms. Craig's *record* of community service and outstanding teaching *qualifies* her for promotion.

In an inverted sentence beginning with a prepositional phrase, the verb still agrees with its subject.

> At the end of the summer *come* the best *sales.*

> Under the house *are* some old Mason *jars.*

Prepositional phrases beginning with compound prepositions such as *along with, together with, in addition to,* and *as well as* should be ignored, for they do not affect subject-verb agreement.

> *Gladys Knight,* as well as the Pips, *is* riding the midnight train to Georgia.

A verb must agree with its subject, not its subject complement.

Taxes are a problem.

A *problem is* taxes.

His main *source* of pleasure *is* food and women.

Food and women are his main source of pleasure.

When a sentence begins with an expletive such as *there, here,* or *it,* the verb agrees with the subject, not the expletive.

Surely, there *are* several *alumni* who would be interested in forming a group.

There *are* 50 *students* in my English class.

There *is* a horrifying *study* on child abuse in *Psychology Today.*

Indefinite pronouns such as *each, either, one, everyone, everybody,* and *everything* are singular.

Somebody in Detroit *loves* me.

Does either [one] of you have a pencil?

Neither of my brothers *has* a car.

Indefinite pronouns such as *several, few, both,* and *many* are plural.

Both of my sorority sisters *have* decided to live off campus.

Few seek the enlightenment of transcendental meditation.

Indefinite pronouns such as *all, some, most,* and *none* may be singular or plural depending on their referents.

Some of the food *is* cold.

Some of the vegetables *are* cold.

I can think of some retorts, but *none seem* appropriate.

None of the children *is* as sweet as Sally.

Fractions such as *one-half* and *one-third* may be singular or plural depending on the referent.

Half of the mail *has* been delivered.

Half of the letters *have* been read.

Subjects joined by *and* take a plural verb unless the subjects are thought to be one item or unit.

Jim and *Tammy were* televangelists.

Guns and Roses is my favorite group.

In cases when the subjects are joined by *or, nor, either . . . or,* or *neither . . . nor,* the verb must agree with the subject closer to it.

> Either the teacher or the *students are* responsible.

> Neither the students nor the *teacher is* responsible.

Relative pronouns, such as *who, which,* or *that,* which refer to plural antecedents require plural verbs. However, when the relative pronoun refers to a singular subject, the pronoun takes a singular verb.

> She is one of the girls *who cheer* on Friday nights.

> She is the only cheerleader *who has* a broken leg.

Subjects preceded by *every, each,* and *many a* are singular.

> *Every* man, woman, and child *was* given a life preserver.

> *Each* undergraduate *is* required to pass a proficiency exam.

> *Many a* tear *has* to fall before one matures.

A collective noun, such as *audience, faculty, jury,* etc., requires a singular verb when the group is regarded as a whole, and a plural verb when the members of the group are regarded as individuals.

> The *jury has* made its decision.

> The *faculty are* preparing their grade rosters.

Subjects preceded by *the number of* or *the percentage of* are singular, while subjects preceded by *a number of* or *a percentage of* are plural.

> *The number of* vacationers in Florida *increases* every year.

> *A number of* vacationers *are* young couples.

Titles of books, companies, name brands, and groups are singular or plural depending on their meaning.

> *Great Expectations is* my favorite novel.

> The *Rolling Stones are* performing in the Super Dome.

Certain nouns of Latin and Greek origin have unusual singular and plural forms.

Singular	Plural
criterion	criteria
alumnus	alumni
datum	data
medium	media

The *data are* available for inspection.

The only *criterion* for membership *is* a high GPA.

Some nouns such as *deer, shrimp,* and *sheep* have the same spellings for both their singular and plural forms. In these cases, the meaning of the sentence will determine whether they are singular or plural.

Deer are beautiful animals.

The spotted *deer is* licking the sugar cube.

Some nouns like *scissors, jeans,* and *wages* have plural forms but no singular counterparts. These nouns almost always take plural verbs.

The *scissors are* on the table.

My new *jeans fit* me like a glove.

Words used as examples, not as grammatical parts of the sentence, require singular verbs.

Can't is the contraction for "cannot."

Cats is the plural form of "cat."

Mathematical expressions of subtraction and division require singular verbs, while expressions of addition and multiplication take either singular or plural verbs.

Ten *divided* by two *equals* five.

Five *times* two *equals* ten.

OR   Five *times* two *equal* ten.

Nouns expressing time, distance, weight, and measurement are singular when they refer to a unit and plural when they refer to separate items.

Fifty yards is a short distance.

Ten years have passed since I finished college.

Expressions of quantity are usually plural.

Nine out of ten dentists *recommend* that their patients floss.

Some nouns ending in *-ics,* such as *economics* and *ethics,* take singular verbs when they refer to principles or a field of study; however, when they refer to individual practices, they usually take plural verbs.

Ethics is being taught in the spring.

His unusual business *ethics are* what got him into trouble.

Some nouns like *measles, news,* and *calculus* appear to be plural but are actually singular in number. These nouns require singular verbs.

> *Measles is* a very contagious disease.

> *Calculus requires* great skill in algebra.

A verbal noun (infinitive or gerund) serving as a subject is treated as singular, even if the object of the verbal phrase is plural.

> *Hiding* your mistakes *does* not make them go away.

> *To run* five miles *is* my goal.

A noun phrase or clause acting as the subject of a sentence requires a singular verb.

> What I need is to be loved.

> Whether there is any connection between them is unknown.

Clauses beginning with *what* may be singular or plural depending on the meaning, that is, whether *what* means "the thing" or "the things."

> What I want for Christmas is a new motorcycle.

> What matters are Clinton's ideas.

A plural subject followed by a singular appositive requires a plural verb; similarly, a singular subject followed by a plural appositive requires a singular verb.

> When the girls throw a party, *they* each bring a *gift.*

> The *board,* all ten members, *is* meeting today.

☞ Drill: Verbs

DIRECTIONS: Choose the correct option.

1. If you <u>had been concerned</u> about Marilyn, you <u>would have went</u> to greater lengths to ensure her safety.

   (A) had been concern . . . would have gone

   (B) was concerned . . . would have gone

   (C) had been concerned . . . would have gone

   (D) No change is necessary.

2. Susan <u>laid</u> in bed too long and missed her class.

   (A) lays   (C) lied

   (B) lay   (D) No change is necessary.

3. The Great Wall of China <u>is</u> fifteen hundred miles long; it <u>was built</u> in the third century B.C.

   (A) was . . . was built   (C) has been . . . was built

   (B) is . . . is built   (D) No change is necessary.

4. Joe stated that the class <u>began</u> at 10:30 a.m.

   (A) begins   (C) was beginning

   (B) had begun   (D) No change is necessary.

5. The ceiling of the Sistine Chapel <u>was</u> painted by Michelangelo; it <u>depicted</u> scenes from the Creation in the Old Testament.

   (A) was . . . depicts   (C) has been . . . depicting

   (B) is . . . depicts   (D) No change is necessary.

6. After Christmas <u>comes</u> the best sales.

   (A) has come   (C) is coming

   (B) come   (D) No change is necessary.

7. The bakery's specialty <u>are</u> wedding cakes.

   (A) is   (C) be

   (B) were   (D) No change is necessary.

8. Every man, woman, and child <u>were given</u> a life preserver.

   (A) have been given   (C) was given

   (B) had gave   (D) No change is necessary.

9. Hiding your mistakes <u>don't</u> make them go away.

   (A) doesn't   (C) have not

   (B) do not   (D) No change is necessary.

10. The Board of Regents <u>has recommended</u> a tuition increase.

   (A) have recommended   (C) had recommended

   (B) has recommend   (D) No change is necessary.

PRONOUNS

Pronoun Case

Pronoun case questions test your knowledge of the use of nominative and objective case pronouns:

Nominative Case	Objective Case
I	me
he	him
she	her
we	us
they	them
who	whom

This review section answers the most frequently asked grammar questions: when to use *I* and when to use *me*; when to use *who* and when to use *whom*. Some writers avoid *whom* altogether, and instead of distinguishing between *I* and *me*, many writers incorrectly use *myself*.

Use the nominative case (subject pronouns)

for the subject of a sentence:

> *We* students studied until early morning for the final.

> Alan and *I* "burned the midnight oil," too.

for pronouns in apposition to the subject:

> Only two students, Alex and *I*, were asked to report on the meeting.

for the predicate nominative/subject complement:

> The actors nominated for the award were *she* and *I*.

for the subject of an elliptical clause:

> Molly is more experienced than *he*.

for the subject of a subordinate clause:

> Robert is the driver *who* reported the accident.

for the complement of an infinitive with no expressed subject:

> I would not want to be *he*.

Use the objective case (object pronouns)

for the direct object of a sentence:

> Mary invited *us* to her party.

for the object of a preposition:

> The books that were torn belonged to *her*.

> Just between you and *me*, I'm bored.

for the indirect object of a sentence:

> Walter gave a dozen red roses to *her*.

for the appositive of a direct object:

> The committee elected two delegates, Barbara and *me*.

for the object of an infinitive:

> The young boy wanted to help *us* paint the fence.

for the object of a gerund:

> Enlisting *him* was surprisingly easy.

for the object of a past participle:

> Having called the other students and *us*, the secretary went home for the day.

for a pronoun that precedes an infinitive (the subject of an infinitive):

> The supervisor told *him* to work late.

for the complement of an infinitive with an expressed subject:

> The fans thought the best player to be *him*.

for the object of an elliptical clause:

> Bill tackled Joe harder than *me*.

for the object of a verb in apposition:

> Charles invited two extra people, Carmen and *me*, to the party.

When a conjunction connects two pronouns or a pronoun and a noun, remove the "and" and the other pronoun or noun to determine what the correct pronoun form should be:

> Mom gave ~~Tom and~~ myself a piece of cake.

> Mom gave ~~Tom and~~ I a piece of cake

> Mom gave ~~Tom and~~ me a piece of cake.

Removal of these words reveals what the correct pronoun should be:

> Mom gave *me* a piece of cake.

The only pronouns that are acceptable after *between* and other preposi-tions are: *me, her, him, them,* and *whom.* When deciding between *who* and *whom,* try substituting *he* for *who* and *him* for *whom;* then follow these easy transformation steps:

1. Isolate the *who* clause or the *whom* clause:

    whom we can trust

2. Invert the word order, if necessary. Place the words in the clause in the natural order of an English sentence, subject followed by the verb:

    we can trust whom

3. Read the final form with the *he* or *him* inserted:

    We can trust ~~whom~~ him.

When a pronoun follows a comparative conjunction like *than* or *as,* complete the elliptical construction to help you determine which pronoun is correct.

> EX: She has more credit hours than me [do].
>
> She has more credit hours than I [do].

Use the reflexive case

for the direct object of a sentence:

> Mary invited *us* us her party.

for the object of a preposition:

> The books that were torn belonged to *her.*
>
> Just between you and *me,* I'm bored.

for the indirect object of a sentence:

> Walter gave a dozen red roses to *her.*

for the appositive of a direct object:

> The committee elected two delegates, Barbara and *me.*

for the object of an infinitive:

> The young boy wanted to help *us* paint the fence.

for the object of a gerund:

> Enlisting *him* was surprisingly easy.

Pronoun-Antecedent Agreement

These kinds of questions test your knowledge of using an appropriate pronoun to agree with its antecedent in number (singular or plural form) and gender (masculine, feminine, or neuter). An antecedent is a noun or pronoun to which another noun or pronoun refers.

Here are the two basic rules for pronoun reference-antecedent agreement:

1. Every pronoun must have a conspicuous antecedent.

2. Every pronoun must agree with its antecedent in number, gender, and person.

When an antecedent is one of dual gender like *student, singer, artist, person, citizen*, etc., use *his* or *her*. Some careful writers change the antecedent to a plural noun to avoid using the sexist, singular masculine pronoun his:

> INCORRECT: Everyone hopes that he will win the lottery.

> CORRECT: Most people hope that they will win the lottery.

Ordinarily, the relative pronoun *who* is used to refer to people, *which* to refer to things and places, *where* to refer to places, and *that* to refer to places or things. The distinction between *that* and *which* is a grammatical distinction (see the section on Word Choice Skills).

Many writers prefer to use *that* to refer to collective nouns.

> EX: A family *that* traces its lineage is usually proud of its roots.

Many writers, especially students, are not sure when to use the reflexive case pronoun and when to use the possessive case pronoun. The rules governing the usage of the reflexive case and the possessive case are quite simple.

Use the possessive case

before a noun in a sentence:

> *Our* friend moved during the semester break.

> *My* dog has fleas, but *her* dog doesn't.

before a gerund in a sentence:

> *Her* running helps to relieve stress.

> *His* driving terrified her.

as a noun in a sentence:

Mine was the last test graded that day.

to indicate possession:

Karen never allows anyone else to drive *her* car.

Brad thought the book was *his,* but it was someone else's.

Use the reflexive case

as a direct object to rename the subject:

I kicked *myself.*

as an indirect object to rename the subject:

Henry bought *himself* a tie.

as an object of a prepositional phrase:

Tom and Lillie baked the pie for *themselves.*

as a predicate pronoun:

She hasn't been *herself* lately.

Do not use the reflexive in place of the nominative pronoun:

INCORRECT: Both Randy and *myself* plan to go.

CORRECT: Both Randy and *I* plan to go.

———————

INCORRECT: *Yourself* will take on the challenges of college.

CORRECT: *You* will take on the challenges of college.

———————

INCORRECT: Either James or *yourself* will paint the mural.

CORRECT: Either James or *you* will paint the mural.

Watch out for careless use of the pronoun form:

INCORRECT: George *hisself* told me it was true.

CORRECT: George *himself* told me it was true.

———————

INCORRECT: They washed the car *theirselves.*

CORRECT: They washed the car *themselves.*

Notice that reflexive pronouns are not set off by commas:

INCORRECT: Mary, *herself*, gave him the diploma.

CORRECT: Mary *herself* gave him the diploma.

INCORRECT: I will do it, *myself*.

CORRECT: I will do it *myself*.

Pronoun Reference

Pronoun reference questions require you to determine whether the antecedent is conspicuously written in the sentence or whether it is remote, implied, ambiguous, or vague, none of which results in clear writing. Make sure that every italicized pronoun has a conspicuous antecedent and that one pronoun substitutes only for another noun or pronoun, not for an idea or a sentence.

Pronoun reference problems occur

when a pronoun refers to either of two antecedents:

INCORRECT: Joanna told Tim that *she* was getting fat.

CORRECT: Joanna told Tim, "I'm getting fat."

when a pronoun refers to a remote antecedent:

INCORRECT: A strange car followed us closely, and *he* kept blinking his lights at us.

CORRECT: A strange car followed us closely, and its driver kept blinking his lights at us.

when *this, that,* and *which* refer to the general idea of the preceding clause or sentence rather than the preceding word:

INCORRECT: The students could not understand the pronoun reference handout, which annoyed them very much.

CORRECT: The students could not understand the pronoun reference handout, a fact which annoyed them very much.

OR   The students were annoyed because they could not understand the pronoun reference handout.

when a pronoun refers to an unexpressed but implied noun:

INCORRECT: My husband wants me to knit a blanket, but I'm not interested in it.

CORRECT: My husband wants me to knit a blanket, but I'm not interested in knitting.

when *it* is used as something other than an expletive to postpone a subject:

INCORRECT: It says in today's paper that the newest shipment of cars from Detroit, Michigan, seems to include outright imitations of European models.

CORRECT: Today's paper says that the newest shipment of cars from Detroit, Michigan, seems to include outright imitations of European models.

INCORRECT: The football game was canceled because it was bad weather.

CORRECT: The football game was canceled because the weather was bad.

when *they* or *it* is used to refer to something or someone indefinitely, and there is no definite antecedent:

INCORRECT: At the job placement office, they told me to stop wearing ripped jeans to my interviews.

CORRECT: At the job placement office, I was told to stop wearing ripped jeans to my interviews.

when the pronoun does not agree with its antecedent in number, gender, or person:

INCORRECT: Any graduate student, if they are interested, may attend the lecture.

CORRECT: Any graduate student, if he or she is interested, may attend the lecture.

OR All graduate students, if they are interested, may attend the lecture.

INCORRECT: Many Americans are concerned that the overuse of slang and colloquialisms is corrupting the language.

CORRECT: Many Americans are concerned that the overuse of slang and colloquialisms is corrupting their language.

INCORRECT: The Board of Regents will not make a decision about tuition increase until their March meeting.

CORRECT: The Board of Regents will not make a decision about tuition increase until its March meeting.

when a noun or pronoun has no expressed antecedent:

> INCORRECT: In the President's address to the union, he promised no more taxes.

> CORRECT: In his address to the union, the President promised no more taxes.

☞ Drill: Pronouns

DIRECTIONS: Choose the correct option.

1. My friend and <u>myself</u> bought tickets for *Cats*.

    (A) I

    (B) me

    (C) us

    (D) No change is necessary.

2. Alcohol and tobacco are harmful to <u>whomever</u> consumes them.

    (A) whom

    (B) who

    (C) whoever

    (D) No change is necessary.

3. Everyone is wondering <u>whom</u> her successor will be.

    (A) who

    (B) whose

    (C) who'll

    (D) No change is necessary.

4. Rosa Lee's parents discovered that it was <u>her who</u> wrecked the family car.

    (A) she who

    (B) she whom

    (C) her whom

    (D) No change is necessary.

5. A student <u>who</u> wishes to protest <u>his or her</u> grades must file a formal grievance in the Dean's office.

    (A) that ... their

    (B) which ... his

    (C) whom ... their

    (D) No change is necessary.

6. One of the best things about working for this company is that <u>they pay</u> big bonuses.

    (A) it pays

    (B) they always pay

    (C) they paid

    (D) No change is necessary.

7.   Every car owner should be sure that <u>their</u> automobile insurance is adequate.

    (A)   your   (C)   its

    (B)   his or her   (D)   No change is necessary.

8.   My mother wants me to become a teacher, but I'm not interested in <u>it</u>.

    (A)   this   (C)   that

    (B)   teaching   (D)   No change is necessary.

9.   Since I had not paid my electric bill, <u>they</u> sent me a delinquent notice.

    (A)   the power company   (C)   it

    (B)   he   (D)   No change is necessary.

10.   Margaret seldom wrote to her sister when <u>she</u> was away at college.

    (A)   who   (C)   her sister

    (B)   her   (D)   No change is necessary.

ADJECTIVES AND ADVERBS

Correct Usage

Adjectives are words that modify nouns or pronouns by defining, describing, limiting, or qualifying those nouns or pronouns.

Adverbs are words that modify verbs, adjectives, or other adverbs and that express such ideas as time, place, manner, cause, and degree. Use adjectives as subject complements with linking verbs; use adverbs with action verbs.

EX: The old man's speech was *eloquent*.	ADJECTIVE
Mr. Brown speaks *eloquently*.	ADVERB
Please be *careful*.	ADJECTIVE
Please drive *carefully*.	ADVERB

Good or well

Good is an adjective; its use as an adverb is colloquial and nonstandard.

INCORRECT: He plays *good*.

CORRECT: He looks *good* to be an octogenarian.

The quiche tastes very *good*.

Well may be either an adverb or an adjective. As an adjective, *well* means "in good health."

CORRECT: He plays *well*.　　　　ADVERB

My mother is not *well*.　　　　ADJECTIVE

Bad or badly
Bad is an adjective used after sense verbs such as *look, smell, taste, feel*, or *sound*, or after linking verbs (*is, am, are, was, were*).

INCORRECT: I feel *badly* about the delay.

CORRECT: I feel *bad* about the delay.

Badly is an adverb used after all other verbs.

INCORRECT: It doesn't hurt very *bad*

CORRECT: It doesn't hurt very *badly*.

Real or really
Real is an adjective; its use as an adverb is colloquial and nonstandard. It means "genuine."

INCORRECT: He writes *real* well.

CORRECT: This is *real* leather.

Really is an adverb meaning "very."

INCORRECT: This is *really* diamond.

CORRECT: Have a *really* nice day.

EX: This is *real* amethyst.　　　　ADJECTIVE

This is *really* difficult.　　　　ADVERB

This is a *real* crisis　　　　ADJECTIVE

This is *really* important.　　　　ADVERB

Sort of and kind of
Sort of and *kind of* are often misused in written English by writers who actually mean *rather* or *somewhat*.

INCORRECT: Jan was *kind of* saddened by the results of the test.

CORRECT: Jan was *somewhat* saddened by the results of the test.

Faulty Comparisons

Sentences containing a faulty comparison often sound correct because their problem is not one of grammar but of logic. Read these sentences closely to make sure that like things are being compared, that the comparisons are complete, and that the comparisons are logical.

When comparing two persons or things, use the comparative, not the superlative form, of an adjective or an adverb. Use the superlative form for comparison of more than two persons or things. Use *any, other,* or *else* when comparing one thing or person with a group of which it/he or she is a part.

Most one- and two-syllable words form their comparative and superlative degrees with *-er* and *-est* suffixes. Adjectives and adverbs of more than two syllables form their comparative and superlative degrees with the addition of *more* and *most*.

Positive	Comparative	Superlative
good	better	best
old	older	oldest
friendly	friendlier	friendliest
lonely	lonelier	loneliest
talented	more talented	most talented
beautiful	more beautiful	most beautiful

A double comparison occurs when the degree of the modifier is changed incorrectly by adding both *-er* and *more* or *-est* and *most* to the adjective or adverb.

INCORRECT: He is the *most nicest* brother.

CORRECT: He is the *nicest* brother.

INCORRECT: She is the *more meaner* of the sisters.

CORRECT: She is the *meaner* sister.

Illogical comparisons occur when there is an implied comparison between two things that are not actually being compared or that cannot be logically compared.

INCORRECT: The interest at a loan company is higher *than* a bank.

CORRECT: The interest at a loan company is higher *than* that *at* a bank.

OR The interest at a loan company is higher *than at* a bank.

Ambiguous comparisons occur when elliptical words (those omitted) create for the reader more than one interpretation of the sentence.

INCORRECT: I like Mary better than you. (than you *what?*)

CORRECT: I like Mary better than I like you.

OR I like Mary better than you do.

Incomplete comparisons occur when the basis of the comparison (the two categories being compared) is not explicitly stated.

INCORRECT: Skywriting is *more* spectacular.

CORRECT: Skywriting is *more* spectacular *than* billboard advertising.

Do not omit the words *other, any,* or *else* when comparing one thing or person with a group of which it/he or she is a part.

INCORRECT: Joan writes better *than any* student in her class.

CORRECT: Joan writes better *than any other* student in her class.

Do not omit the second *as* of *as . . . as* when making a point of equal or superior comparison.

INCORRECT: The University of West Florida is *as large* or larger than the University of North Florida.

CORRECT: The University of West Florida is *as large as* or larger than the University of Northern Florida.

Do not omit the first category of the comparison, even if the two categories are the same.

INCORRECT: This is one of the best, if not the best, college in the country.

CORRECT: This is one of the best colleges in the country, if not the best.

The problem with the incorrect sentence is that *one of the best* requires the plural word *colleges,* not *college.*

☞ Drill: Adjectives and Adverbs

DIRECTIONS: Choose the correct option.

1. Although the band performed <u>badly</u>, I feel <u>real bad</u> about missing the concert.

   (A) badly . . . real badly   (C) badly . . . very bad

   (B) bad . . . badly   (D) No change is necessary.

2. These reports are <u>relative simple</u> to prepare.

   (A) relatively simple   (C) relatively simply

   (B) relative simply   (D) No change is necessary.

3. He did <u>very well</u> on the test although his writing skills are not <u>good</u>.

   (A) real well . . . good   (C) good . . . great

   (B) very good . . . good   (D) No change is necessary.

4. Shake the medicine bottle <u>good</u> before you open it.

   (A) very good   (C) well

   (B) real good   (D) No change is necessary.

5. Though she speaks <u>fluently</u>, she writes <u>poorly</u> because she doesn't observe <u>closely</u> or think <u>clear</u>.

   (A) fluently, poorly, closely, clearly

   (B) fluent, poor, close, clear

   (C) fluently, poor, closely, clear

   (D) No change is necessary.

DIRECTIONS: Select the sentence that clearly and effectively states the idea and has no structural errors.

6. (A) Los Angeles is larger than any city in California.

   (B) Los Angeles is larger than all the cities in California.

   (C) Los Angeles is larger than any other city in California.

   (D) Los Angeles is larger than the cities in California.

7.　(A)　Art history is as interesting as, if not more interesting than, music appreciation.

　　(B)　Art history is as interesting, if not more interesting than, music appreciation.

　　(C)　Art history is as interesting as, if not more interesting, music appreciation.

　　(D)　Art history is as interesting as, if not more interesting as, music appreciation.

8.　(A)　The baseball team here is as good as any other university.

　　(B)　The baseball team here is as good as all the other universities.

　　(C)　The baseball team here is as good as any other university's.

　　(D)　The baseball team here is as good as the other universities.

9.　(A)　I like him better than you.

　　(B)　I like him better than I like you.

　　(C)　I like him better.

　　(D)　I like him more than you.

10.　(A)　You are the most stingiest person I know.

　　(B)　You are the most stingier person I know.

　　(C)　You are the stingiest person I know.

　　(C)　You are the more stingiest person I know.

PUNCTUATION

Commas

Commas should be placed according to standard rules of punctuation for purpose, clarity, and effect. The proper use of commas is explained in the following rules and examples.

In a series:

When more than one adjective describes a noun, use a comma to separate and emphasize each adjective. The comma takes the place of the word *and* in the series.

the long, dark passageway

another confusing, sleepless night

an elaborate, complex, brilliant plan

the old, grey, crumpled hat

Some adjective-noun combinations are thought of as one word. In these cases, the adjective in front of the adjective-noun combination needs no comma. If you inserted *and* between the adjective-noun combination, it would not make sense.

a stately oak tree

an exceptional wine glass

my worst report card

a china dinner plate

The comma is also used to separate words, phrases, and whole ideas (clauses); it still takes the place of *and* when used this way.

an apple, a pear, a fig, and a banana

a lovely lady, an elegant dress, and many admirers

She lowered the shade, closed the curtain, turned off the light, and went to bed.

The only question that exists about the use of commas in a series is whether or not one should be used before the final item. It is standard usage to do so, although many newspapers and magazines have stopped using the final comma. Occasionally, the omission of the comma can be confusing.

INCORRECT: He got on his horse, tracked a rabbit and a deer and rode on to Canton.

We planned the trip with Mary and Harold, Susan, Dick and Joan, Gregory and Jean and Charles.

With a long introductory phrase:

Usually if a phrase of more than five or six words or a dependent clause precedes the subject at the beginning of a sentence, a comma is used to set it off.

After last night's fiasco at the disco, she couldn't bear the thought of looking at him again.

Whenever I try to talk about politics, my wife leaves the room.

Provided you have said nothing, they will never guess who you are.

It is not necessary to use a comma with a short sentence.

> In January she will go to Switzerland.

> After I rest I'll feel better.

> During the day no one is home.

If an introductory phrase includes a verb form that is being used as another part of speech (a *verbal*), it must be followed by a comma.

INCORRECT: When eating Mary never looked up from her plate.

CORRECT: When eating, Mary never looked up from her plate.

INCORRECT: Because of her desire to follow her faith in James wavered.

CORRECT: Because of her desire to follow, her faith in James wavered.

INCORRECT: Having decided to leave Mary James wrote her a letter.

CORRECT: Having decided to leave Mary, James wrote her a letter.

To separate sentences with two main ideas:

To understand this use of the comma, you need to be able to recognize compound sentences. When a sentence contains more than two subjects and verbs (clauses), and the two clauses are joined by a conjunction (*and, but, or, nor, for, yet*), use a comma before the conjunction to show that another clause is coming.

> I thought I knew the poem by heart, but he showed me three lines I had forgotten.

> Are we really interested in helping the children, or are we more concerned with protecting our good names?

> He is supposed to leave tomorrow, but he is not ready to go.

> Jim knows you are disappointed, and he has known it for a long time.

If the two parts of the sentence are short and closely related, it is not necessary to use a comma.

> He threw the ball and the dog ran after it.

> Jane played the piano and Michael danced.

Be careful not to confuse a sentence that has a compound verb and a single subject with a compound sentence. If the subject is the same for both verbs, there is no need for a comma.

INCORRECT: Charles sent some flowers, and wrote a long letter explaining why he had not been able to attend.

CORRECT: Charles sent some flowers and wrote a long letter explaining why he had not been able to attend.

INCORRECT: Last Thursday we went to the concert with Julia, and afterwards dined at an old Italian restaurant.

CORRECT: Last Thursday we went to the concert with Julia and afterwards dined at an old Italian restaurant.

INCORRECT: For the third time, the teacher explained that the literacy level for high school students was much lower than it had been in previous years, and, this time, wrote the statistics on the board for everyone to see.

CORRECT: For the third time, the teacher explained that the literacy level for high school students was much lower than it had been in previous years and this time wrote the statistics on the board for everyone to see.

In general, words and phrases that stop the flow of the sentence or are unnecessary for the main idea are set off by commas.

Abbreviations after names:

Did you invite John Paul, Jr., and his sister?

Martha Harris, Ph.D., will be the speaker tonight.

Interjections (an exclamation without added grammatical connection):

Oh, I'm so glad to see you.

I tried so hard, alas, to do it.

Hey, let me out of here.

Direct address:

Roy, won't you open the door for the dog?

I can't understand, Mother, what you are trying to say.

> May I ask, Mr. President, why you called us together?
>
> Hey, lady, watch out for that car!

Tag questions:

> I'm really hungry, aren't you?
>
> Jerry looks like his father, doesn't he?

Geographical names and addresses:

> The concert will be held in Chicago, Illinois, on August 12.
>
> The letter was addressed to Mrs. Marion Heartwell, 1881 Pine Lane, Palo Alto, California 95824.

(Note: No comma is needed before the zip code, because it is already clearly set off from the state name.)

Transitional words and phrases:

> On the other hand, I hope he gets better.
>
> In addition, the phone rang constantly this afternoon.
>
> I'm, nevertheless, going to the beach on Sunday.
>
> You'll find, therefore, that no one is more loyal than I am.

Parenthetical words and phrases:

> You will become, I believe, a great statesman.
>
> We know, of course, that this is the only thing to do.
>
> In fact, I planted corn last summer.
>
> The Mannes affair was, to put it mildly, a surprise.

Unusual word order:

> The dress, new and crisp, hung in the closet.
>
> Intently, she stared out the window.

With nonrestrictive elements:

Parts of a sentence that modify other parts are sometimes essential to the meaning of the sentence and sometimes not. When a modifying word or group of words is not vital to the meaning of the sentence, it is set off by commas. Since it does not restrict the meaning of the words it modifies, it is called "nonrestrictive." Modifiers that are essential to the meaning of the sentence are called "restrictive" and are not set off by commas.

ESSENTIAL: The girl *who wrote the story* is my sister.

NONESSENTIAL: My sister, *the girl who wrote the story*, has always loved to write.

ESSENTIAL: John Milton's famous poem *Paradise Lost* tells a remarkable story.

NONESSENTIAL: Dante's greatest work, *The Divine Comedy*, marked the beginning of the Renaissance.

ESSENTIAL: The cup *that is on the piano* is the one I want.

NONESSENTIAL: The cup, *which my brother gave me last year*, is on the piano.

ESSENTIAL: The people *who arrived late* were not seated.

NONESSENTIAL: George, *who arrived late*, was not seated.

To set off direct quotations:

Most direct quotes or quoted materials are set off from the rest of the sentence by commas.

"Please read your part more loudly," the director insisted.

"I won't know what to do," said Michael, "if you leave me."

The teacher said sternly, "I will not dismiss this class until I have silence."

Who was it who said "Do not ask for whom the bell tolls; it tolls for thee"?

Note: Commas always go inside the closing quotation mark, even if the comma is not part of the material being quoted.

Be careful not to set off indirect quotes or quotes that are used as subjects or complements.

"To be or not to be" is the famous beginning of a soliloquy in Shakespeare's *Hamlet*. (subject)

She said she would never come back. (indirect quote)

Back then my favorite poem was "Evangeline." (complement)

To set off contrasting elements:

> Her intelligence, not her beauty, got her the job.

> Your plan will take you a little further from, rather than closer to, your destination.

> It was a reasonable, though not appealing, idea.

> He wanted glory, but found happiness instead.

In dates:

Both forms of the date are acceptable.

> She will arrive on April 6, 1998.

> He left on 5 December 1980.

> In January 1967, he handed in his resignation.

> On October 22, 1992, Frank and Julie were married.

Usually, when a subordinate clause is at the end of a sentence, no comma is necessary preceding the clause. However, when a subordinate clause introduces a sentence, a comma should be used after the clause. Some common subordinating conjunctions are:

after	so that
although	though
as	till
as if	unless
because	until
before	when
even though	whenever
if	while
inasmuch as	since

Semicolons

Questions testing semicolon usage require you to be able to distinguish between the semicolon and the comma, and the semicolon and the colon. This review section covers the basic uses of the semicolon: to separate independent clauses not joined by a coordinating conjunction, to separate independent clauses separated by a conjunctive adverb, and to separate items in a series with internal commas. It is important to be consistent; if you use a semicolon between *any* of the items in the series, you must use semicolons to separate *all* of the items in the series.

Usually, a comma follows the conjunctive adverb. Note also that a period can be used to separate two sentences joined by a conjunctive adverb. Some common conjunctive adverbs are:

accordingly	nevertheless
besides	next
consequently	nonetheless
finally	now
furthermore	on the other hand
however	otherwise
indeed	perhaps
in fact	still
moreover	therefore

Then is also used as a conjunctive adverb, but it is not usually followed by a comma.

Use the semicolon

to separate independent clauses which are not joined by a coordinating conjunction:

> I understand how to use commas; the semicolon I have not yet mastered.

to separate two independent clauses connected by a conjunctive adverb:

> He took great care with his work; *therefore*, he was very successful.

to combine two independent clauses connected by a coordinating conjunction if either or both of the clauses contain other internal punctuation:

> Success in college, some maintain, requires intelligence, industry, and perseverance; *but* others, fewer in number, assert that only personality is important.

to separate items in a series when each item has internal punctuation:

> I bought an old, dilapidated chair; an antique table which was in beautiful condition; and a new, ugly, blue and white rug.

> Call our customer service line for assistance: Arizona, 1-800-555-6020; New Mexico, 1-800-555-5050; California, 1-800-555-3140; or Nevada, 1-800-555-3214.

Do not use the semicolon

to separate a dependent and an independent clause:

> INCORRECT: You should not make such statements; even though they are correct.

> CORRECT: You should not make such statements even though they are correct.

to separate an appositive phrase or clause from a sentence:

> INCORRECT: His immediate aim in life is centered around two things; becoming an engineer and learning to fly an airplane.

> CORRECT: His immediate aim in life is centered around two things: becoming an engineer and learning to fly an airplane.

to precede an explanation or summary of the first clause:

Note: Although the sentence below is punctuated correctly, the use of the semicolon provides a miscue, suggesting that the second clause is merely an extension, not an explanation, of the first clause. The colon provides a better clue.

> WEAK: The first week of camping was wonderful; we lived in cabins instead of tents.

> BETTER: The first week of camping was wonderful: we lived in cabins instead of tents.

to substitute for a comma:

> INCORRECT: My roommate also likes sports; particularly football, basketball, and baseball.

> CORRECT: My roommate also likes sports, particularly football, basketball, and baseball.

to set off other types of phrases or clauses from a sentence:

> INCORRECT: Being of a cynical mind; I should ask for a recount of the ballots.

> CORRECT: Being of a cynical mind, I should ask for a recount of the ballots.

> INCORRECT: The next meeting of the club has been postponed two weeks; inasmuch as both the president and vice-president are out of town.

> CORRECT: The next meeting of the club has been postponed two weeks, inasmuch as both the president and vice-president are out of town.

Note: The semicolon is not a terminal mark of punctuation; therefore, it should not be followed by a capital letter unless the first word in the second clause ordinarily requires capitalization.

Colons

While it is true that a colon is used to precede a list, one must also make sure that a complete sentence precedes the colon. The colon signals the reader that a list, explanation, or restatement of the preceding will follow. It is like an arrow, indicating that something is to follow. The difference between the colon and the semicolon and between the colon and the period is that the colon is an introductory mark, not a terminal mark. Look at the following examples:

> The Constitution provides for a separation of powers among the three branches of government.
>
> **government.** The period signals a new sentence.
>
> **government;** The semicolon signals an interrelated sentence.
>
> **government,** The comma signals a coordinating conjunction followed by another independent clause.
>
> **government:** The colon signals a list.
>
> The Constitution provides for a separation of powers among the three branches of *government:* executive, legislative, and judicial.

Ensuring that a complete sentence precedes a colon means following these rules:

Use the colon to introduce a list (one item may constitute a list):

> I hate this one course: English.
>
> Three plays by William Shakespeare will be presented in repertory this summer at the University of Michigan: *Hamlet, Macbeth,* and *Othello.*

To introduce a list preceded by *as follows* or *the following*:

> The reasons he cited for his success are as follows: integrity, honesty, industry, and a pleasant disposition.

To separate two independent clauses, when the second clause is a restatement or explanation of the first:

> All of my high school teachers said one thing in particular: college is going to be difficult.

To introduce a word or word group which is a restatement, explanation, or summary of the first sentence:

> These two things he loved: an honest man and a beautiful woman.

To introduce a formal appositive:

> I am positive there is one appeal which you can't overlook: money.

To separate the introductory words from a quotation which follows, if the quotation is formal, long, or paragraphed separately:

> The actor then stated: "I would rather be able to adequately play the part of Hamlet than to perform a miraculous operation, deliver a great lecture, or build a magnificent skyscraper."

The colon should only be used after statements that are grammatically complete.

Do *not* use a colon after a verb:

> INCORRECT: My favorite holidays are: Christmas, New Year's Eve, and Halloween.
>
> CORRECT: My favorite holidays are Christmas, New Year's Eve, and Halloween.

Do *not* use a colon after a preposition:

> INCORRECT: I enjoy different ethnic foods such as: Greek, Chinese, and Italian.
>
> CORRECT: I enjoy different ethnic foods such as Greek, Chinese, and Italian.

Do *not* use a colon interchangeably with the dash:

> INCORRECT: Mathematics, German, English: These gave me the greatest difficulty of all my studies.
>
> CORRECT: Mathematics, German, English—these gave me the greatest difficulty of all my studies.

Information preceding the colon should be a complete sentence regardless of the explanatory information following the clause.

Do *not* use the colon before the words *for example, namely, that is,* or *for instance* even though these words may be introducing a list.

> INCORRECT: We agreed to it: namely, to give him a surprise party.
>
> CORRECT: There are a number of well-known American women writers: for example, Nikki Giovanni, Phillis Wheatley, Emily Dickinson, and Maya Angelou.

Colon usage questions test your knowledge of the colon preceding a list, restatement, or explanation. These questions also require you to be able to distinguish between the colon and the period, the colon and the comma, and the colon and the semicolon.

Apostrophes

Apostrophe questions require you to know when an apostrophe has been used appropriately to make a noun possessive, not plural. Remember the following rules when considering how to show possession.

Add *'s* to singular nouns and indefinite pronouns:

> Tiffany's flowers
>
> a dog's bark
>
> everybody's computer
>
> at the owner's expense
>
> today's paper

Add *'s* to singular nouns ending in *s*, unless this distorts the pronunciation:

> Delores's paper
>
> the boss's pen
>
> Dr. Yots' class
>
> for righteousness' sake
>
> Dr. Evans's office OR Dr. Evans' office

Add *an apostrophe* to plural nouns ending in *s* or *es*:

> two cents' worth
>
> ladies' night
>
> thirteen years' experience
>
> two weeks' pay

Add *'s* to plural nouns not ending in *s*:

> men's room
>
> children's toys

Add *'s* to the last word in compound words or groups:

> brother-in-law's car
>
> someone else's paper

Add *'s* to the last name when indicating joint ownership:

> Joe and Edna's home
>
> Julie and Kathy's party
>
> women and children's clinic

Add *'s* to both names if you intend to show ownership by each person:

> Joe's and Edna's trucks
>
> Julie's and Kathy's pies
>
> Ted's and Jane's marriage vows

Possessive pronouns change their forms *without* the addition of an apostrophe:

> her, his, hers
>
> your, yours
>
> their, theirs
>
> it, its

Use the possessive form of a noun preceding a gerund:

> His driving annoys me.
>
> My bowling a strike irritated him.
>
> Do you mind our stopping by?
>
> We appreciate your coming.

Add *'s* to words and initials to show that they are plural:

> no if's, and's, or but's
>
> the do's and don't's of dating
>
> three A's
>
> IRA's are available at the bank.

Add *s* to numbers, symbols, and letters to show that they are plural:

> TVs
>
> VCRs
>
> the 1800s
>
> the returning POWs

Quotation Marks and Italics

These kinds of questions test your knowledge of the proper use of quotation marks with other marks of punctuation, with titles, and with dialogue. These kinds of questions also test your knowledge of the correct use of italics and underlining with titles and words used as sample words (for example, *the word is is a common verb).*

The most common use of double quotation marks (") is to set off quoted words, phrases, and sentences.

> "If everybody minded their own business," said the Duchess in a hoarse growl, "the world would go round a great deal faster than it does."
>
> "Then you would say what you mean," the March Hare went on.
>
> "I do," Alice hastily replied: "at least—at least I mean what I say—that's the same thing, you know."
>
> —from Lewis Carroll's *Alice in Wonderland*

Single quotation marks are used to set off quoted material within a quote.

> "Shall I bring 'Rime of the Ancient Mariner' along with us?" she asked her brother.
>
> Mrs. Green said, "The doctor told me, 'Go immediately to bed when you get home!' "
>
> "If she said that to me," Katherine insisted, "I would tell her, 'I never intend to speak to you again! Goodbye, Susan!' "

When writing dialogue, begin a new paragraph each time the speaker changes.

> "Do you know what time it is?" asked Jane.
>
> "Can't you see I'm busy?" snapped Mary.
>
> "It's easy to see that you're in a bad mood today!" replied Jane.

Use quotation marks to enclose words used as words (sometimes italics are used for this purpose).

> "Judgment" has always been a difficult word for me to spell.
>
> Do you know what "abstruse" means?
>
> "Horse and buggy" and "bread and butter" can be used either as adjectives or as nouns.

If slang is used within more formal writing, the slang words or phrases should be set off with quotation marks.

Harrison's decision to leave the conference and to "stick his neck out" by flying to Jamaica was applauded by the rest of the conference attendees.

When words are meant to have an unusual or specific significance to the reader—in the service of irony or humor, for example—they are sometimes placed in quotation marks.

For years, women were not allowed to buy real estate in order to "protect" them from unscrupulous dealers.

The "conversation" resulted in one black eye and a broken nose.

To set off titles of TV shows, poems, stories, and book chapters, use quotation marks. (Book, motion picture, newspaper, and magazine titles are underlined when handwritten and italicized when printed.)

The article "Moving South in the Southern Rain," by Jergen Smith in the *Southern News*, attracted the attention of our editor.

The assignment is "Childhood Development," Chapter 18 of *Human Behavior.*

My favorite essay by Montaigne is "On Silence."

"Happy Days" led the TV ratings for years, didn't it?

You will find Keats' "Ode on a Grecian Urn" in Chapter 3, "The Romantic Era," in Lastly's *Selections from Great English Poets.*

Errors to avoid:

Be sure to remember that quotation marks always come in pairs. Do not make the mistake of using only one set.

INCORRECT: "You'll never convince me to move to the city, said Thurman. I consider it an insane asylum."

CORRECT: "You'll never convince me to move to the city," said Thurman. "I consider it an insane asylum."

INCORRECT: "Idleness and pride tax with a heavier hand than kings and parliaments," Benjamin Franklin is supposed to have said. If we can get rid of the former, we may easily bear the latter."

CORRECT: "Idleness and pride tax with a heavier hand than kings and parliaments," Benjamin Franklin is supposed to have said. "If we can get rid of the former, we may easily bear the latter."

When a quote consists of several sentences, do not put the quotation marks at the beginning and end of each sentence; put them at the beginning and end of the entire quotation.

INCORRECT: "It was during his student days in Bonn that Beethoven fastened upon Schiller's poem." "The heady sense of liberation in the verses must have appealed to him." "They appealed to every German." —John Burke

CORRECT: "It was during his student days in Bonn that Beethoven fastened upon Schiller's poem. The heady sense of liberation in the verses must have appealed to him. They appealed to every German." —John Burke

Instead of setting off a long quote with quotation marks, if it is longer than five or six lines you may want to indent and single space it. If you do indent, do not use quotation marks.

In his *First Inaugural Address,* Abraham Lincoln appeals to the war-torn American people:

We are not enemies, but friends. We must not be enemies. Though passion may have strained, it must not break, our bonds of affection. The mystic chords of memory, stretching from every battlefield and patriot grave to every living heart and hearthstone all over this broad land, will yet swell the chorus of the Union when again touched, as surely they will be, by the better angels of our nature.

Be careful not to use quotation marks with indirect quotations.

INCORRECT: Mary wondered "if she would get over it."

CORRECT: Mary wondered if she would get over it.

INCORRECT: The nurse asked "how long it had been since we had visited the doctor's office."

CORRECT: The nurse asked how long it had been since we had visited the doctor's office.

When you quote several paragraphs, it is not sufficient to place quotation marks at the beginning and end of the entire quote. Place quotation marks at the *beginning of each paragraph,* but only at the *end of the last paragraph.* Here is an abbreviated quotation for an example:

"Here begins an odyssey through the world of classical mythology, starting with the creation of the world . . .

"It is true that themes similar to the classical may be found in any corpus of mythology . . . Even technology is not immune to the influence of Greece and Rome . . .

"We need hardly mention the extent to which painters and sculptors . . . have used and adapted classical mythology to illustrate the past, to reveal the human body, to express romantic or antiromantic ideals, or to symbolize any particular point of view."

Remember that commas and periods are *always* placed inside the quotation marks even if they are not actually part of the quote.

INCORRECT: "Life always gets colder near the summit", Nietzsche is purported to have said, "—the cold increases, responsibility grows".

CORRECT: "Life always gets colder near the summit," Nietzsche is purported to have said, "—the cold increases, responsibility grows."

INCORRECT: "Get down here right away", John cried. "You'll miss the sunset if you don't."

CORRECT: "Get down here right away," John cried. "You'll miss the sunset if you don't."

INCORRECT: "If my dog could talk", Mary mused, "I'll bet he would say, 'Take me for a walk right this minute'".

CORRECT: "If my dog could talk," Mary mused, "I'll bet he would say, 'Take me for a walk right this minute'."

Other marks of punctuation, such as question marks, exclamation points, colons, and semicolons, go inside the quotation marks if they are part of the quoted material. If they are not part of the quotation, however, they go outside the quotation marks. Be careful to distinguish between the guidelines for the comma and period, which always go inside the quotation marks, and those for other marks of punctuation.

INCORRECT: "I'll always love you"! he exclaimed happily.

CORRECT: "I'll always love you!" he exclaimed happily.

INCORRECT: Did you hear her say, "He'll be there early?"

CORRECT: Did you hear her say, "He'll be there early"?

INCORRECT: She called down the stairs, "When are you going"?

CORRECT: She called down the stairs, "When are you going?"

INCORRECT: "Let me out"! he cried. "Don't you have any pity"?

CORRECT: "Let me out!" he cried. "Don't you have any pity?"

Remember to use only one mark of punctuation at the end of a sentence requiring a quotation mark.

INCORRECT: She thought out loud, "Will I ever finish this paper in time for that class?".

CORRECT: She thought out loud, "Will I ever finish this paper in time for that class?"

INCORRECT: "Not the same thing a bit!", said the Hatter. "Why, you might just as well say that 'I see what I eat' is the same thing as 'I eat what I see'!".

CORRECT: "Not the same thing a bit!" said the Hatter. "Why, you might just as well say that 'I see what I eat' is the same thing as 'I eat what I see'!"

☞ Drill: Punctuation

<u>DIRECTIONS:</u> Choose the correct option.

1. Indianola, <u>Mississippi, where B.B. King and my father grew up,</u> has a population of fewer than 50,000 people.

    (A) Mississippi where, B.B. King and my father grew up,

    (B) Mississippi where B.B. King and my father grew up,

    (C) Mississippi; where B.B. King and my father grew up,

    (D) No change is necessary.

2. John Steinbeck's best known novel, *The Grapes of Wrath,* is the story of the <u>Joads and Oklahoma family</u> who were driven from their Dust Bowl farm and forced to become migrant workers in California.

    (A) Joads, an Oklahoma family

    (B) Joads, an Oklahoma family,

    (C)   Joads; an Oklahoma family

    (D)   No change is necessary.

3.   All students who are interested in student teaching next <u>semester, must submit an application to the Teacher Education Office.</u>

    (A)   semester must submit an application to the Teacher Education Office.

    (B)   semester, must submit an application, to the Teacher Education Office.

    (C)   semester: must submit an application to the Teacher Education Office.

    (D)   No change is necessary.

4.   Whenever you travel by <u>car, or plane, you</u> must wear a seatbelt.

    (A)   car or plane you   (C)   car or plane, you

    (B)   car, or plane you   (D)   No change is necessary.

5.   Wearing a seatbelt is not just a good <u>idea, it's</u> the law.

    (A)   idea; it's   (C)   idea. It's

    (B)   idea it's   (D)   No change is necessary.

6.   Senators and representatives can be reelected <u>indefinitely; a</u> president can only serve two terms.

    (A)   indefinitely but a   (C)   indefinitely a

    (B)   indefinitely, a   (D)   No change is necessary.

7.   Students must pay a penalty for overdue library <u>books, however, there</u> is a grace period.

    (A)   books; however, there   (C)   books: however, there

    (B)   books however, there   (D)   No change is necessary.

8.   Among the states that seceded from the Union to join the Confederacy in 1860–1861 <u>were</u>: Mississippi, Florida, and Alabama.

    (A)   were   (C)   were.

    (B)   were;   (D)   No change is necessary.

9. The art exhibit displayed works by many famous <u>artists such as:</u> Dali, Picasso, and Michelangelo.

    (A) artists such as;

    (B) artists such as

    (C) artists. Such as

    (D) No change is necessary.

10. The National Shakespeare Company will perform <u>the following plays:</u> *Othello, Macbeth, Hamlet,* and *As You Like It.*

    (A) the following plays,

    (B) the following plays;

    (C) the following plays

    (D) No change is necessary.

CAPITALIZATION

When a word is capitalized, it calls attention to itself. This attention should be for a good reason. There are standard uses for capital letters. In general, capitalize (1) all proper nouns, (2) the first word of a sentence, and (3) the first word of a direct quotation.

You Should Also Capitalize

Names of ships, aircraft, spacecraft, and trains:

Apollo 13	*Mariner IV*
DC-10	S.S. *United States*
Sputnik 11	Boeing 707

Names of deities:

God	Jupiter
Allah	Holy Ghost
Buddha	Venus
Jehovah	Shiva

Geological periods:

Neolithic age	Cenozoic era
late Pleistocene times	Ice Age

Names of astronomical bodies:

Mercury	Big Dipper
the Milky Way	Halley's comet
Ursa Major	North Star

Personifications:

>   Reliable Nature brought her promised Spring.
>
>   Bring on Melancholy in his sad might.
>
>   She believed that Love was the answer to all her problems.

Historical periods:

the Middle Ages	World War I
Reign of Terror	Great Depression
Christian Era	Roaring Twenties
Age of Louis XIV	Renaissance

Organizations, associations, and institutions:

Girl Scouts	North Atlantic Treaty Organization
Kiwanis Club	League of Women Voters
New York Yankees	Unitarian Church
Smithsonian Institution	Common Market
Library of Congress	Franklin Glen High School
New York Philharmonic	Harvard University

Government and judicial groups:

United States Court of Appeals	Senate
Committee on Foreign Affairs	Parliament
New Jersey City Council	Peace Corps
Arkansas Supreme Court	Census Bureau
House of Representatives	Department of State

A general term that accompanies a specific name is capitalized only if it follows the specific name. If it stands alone or comes before the specific name, it is put in lowercase:

Washington State	the state of Washington
Senator Dixon	the senator from Illinois
Central Park	the park
Golden Gate Bridge	the bridge
President Clinton	the president of the United States
Pope John XXIII	the pope

Queen Elizabeth I	the queen of England
Tropic of Capricorn	the tropics
Monroe Doctrine	the doctrine of expansion
the Mississippi River	the river
Easter Day	the day
Treaty of Versailles	the treaty
Webster's Dictionary	the dictionary
Equatorial Current	the equator

Use a capital to start a sentence:

Our car would not start.

When will you leave? I need to know right away.

Never!

Let me in! Please!

When a sentence appears within a sentence, start it with a capital letter:

We had only one concern: When would we eat?

My sister said, "I'll find the Monopoly game."

He answered, "We can only stay a few minutes."

The most important words of titles are capitalized. Those words not capitalized are conjunctions (*and, or, but*) and short prepositions (*of, on, by, for*). The first and last word of a title must always be capitalized:

A Man for All Seasons	*Crime and Punishment*
Of Mice and Men	*Rise of the West*
Strange Life of Ivan Osokin	"Sonata in G Minor"
"Let Me In"	"Ode to Billy Joe"
"Rubaiyat of Omar Khayyam"	"All in the Family"

Capitalize newspaper and magazine titles:

U.S. News & World Report

National Geographic

the *New York Times*

the *Washington Post*

Capitalize radio and TV station call letters:

ABC	NBC
WNEW	WBOP
CNN	HBO

Do not capitalize compass directions or seasons:

west	north
east	south
spring	winter
autumn	summer

Capitalize regions:

the South	the Northeast
the West	Eastern Europe

BUT: the south of France

the east part of town

Capitalize specific military units:

the U.S. Army

the 7th Fleet

the German Navy

the 1st Infantry Division

Capitalize political groups and philosophies:

Democrat	Communist
Marxist	Nazism
Whig	Federalist
Existentialism	Transcendentalism

BUT do not capitalize systems of government or individual adherents to a philosophy:

democracy	communism
fascist	agnostic

☞ Drill: Capitalization

<u>DIRECTIONS:</u> Choose the correct option.

1. Mexico is the southernmost country in <u>North America</u>. It borders the United States on the north; it is bordered on the <u>south</u> by Belize and Guatemala.

    (A) north America . . . South

    (B) North America . . . South

    (C) North america . . . south

    (D) No change is necessary.

2. (A) Until 1989, Tom Landry was the only Coach the Dallas cowboys ever had.

    (B) Until 1989, Tom Landry was the only coach the Dallas Cowboys ever had.

    (C) Until 1989, Tom Landry was the only Coach the Dallas Cowboys ever had.

    (D) Until 1989, Tom Landry was the only Coach The Dallas Cowboys ever had.

3. The <u>Northern Hemisphere</u> is the half of the <u>earth</u> that lies north of the <u>Equator.</u>

    (A) Northern hemisphere . . . earth . . . equator

    (B) Northern hemisphere . . . Earth . . . Equator

    (C) Northern Hemisphere . . . earth . . . equator

    (D) No change is necessary.

4. (A) My favorite works by Ernest Hemingway are "The Snows of Kilamanjaro," *The Sun Also Rises,* and *For Whom the Bell Tolls.*

    (B) My favorite works by Ernest Hemingway are "The Snows Of Kilamanjaro," *The Sun Also Rises,* and *For Whom The Bell Tolls.*

    (C) My favorite works by Ernest Hemingway are "The Snows of Kilamanjaro," *The Sun also Rises,* and *For whom the Bell Tolls.*

    (D) My favorite works by Ernest Hemingway are "The Snows of Kilamanjaro," *The Sun also Rises,* and *For Whom the Bell Tolls.*

5.   Aphrodite (<u>Venus in Roman Mythology</u>) was the <u>Greek</u> goddess of love.

    (A) Venus in Roman mythology . . . greek

    (B) venus in roman mythology . . . Greek

    (C) Venus in Roman mythology . . . Greek

    (D) No change is necessary.

6.   The <u>Koran</u> is considered by <u>Muslims</u> to be the holy word.

    (A) koran . . . muslims   (C) Koran . . . muslims

    (B) koran . . . Muslims   (D) No change is necessary.

7.   (A) The freshman curriculum at the community college includes english, a foreign language, Algebra I, and history.

    (B) The freshman curriculum at the community college includes English, a foreign language, Algebra I, and history.

    (C) The Freshman curriculum at the Community College includes English, a foreign language, Algebra I, and History.

    (D) The freshman curriculum at the community college includes english, a foreign language, algebra I, and history.

8.   At the <u>spring</u> graduation ceremonies, the university awarded over 2,000 <u>bachelor's</u> degrees.

    (A) Spring . . . Bachelor's   (C) Spring . . . bachelor's

    (B) spring . . . Bachelor's   (D) No change is necessary.

9.   The fall of the <u>Berlin wall</u> was an important symbol of the collapse of <u>Communism</u>.

    (A) berlin Wall . . . communism

    (B) Berlin Wall . . . communism

(C) berlin wall . . . Communism

(D) No change is necessary.

10. A photograph of <u>mars</u> was printed in <u>the *New York Times*</u>.

(A) Mars . . . *The New York Times*

(B) mars . . . *The New York times*

(C) mars . . . *The New York Times*

(D) No change is necessary.

SPELLING

Spelling questions test your ability to recognize misspelled words. This section reviews spelling tips and rules to help you spot incorrect spellings. Problems such as the distinction between *to* and *too* and *lead* and *led* are covered under the Word Choice Skills section of this review.

- Remember, *i* before *e* except after *c*, or when sounded as "a" as in *neighbor* and *weigh*.

- There are only three words in the English language that end in -*ceed*:

    proceed, succeed, exceed

- There are several words that end in -*cede*:

    secede, recede, concede, precede

- There is only one word in the English language that ends in -*sede*:

    supersede

Many people learn to read English phonetically; that is, by sounding out the letters of the words. However, many English words are not pronounced the way they are spelled, and those who try to spell English words phonetically often make spelling *errors*. It is better to memorize the correct spelling of English words rather than relying on phonetics to spell correctly.

Frequently Misspelled Words

The following list of words are frequently misspelled words. Study the spelling of each word by having a friend or teacher drill you on the words. Then mark down the words that you misspelled and study those select ones again. (The words appear in their most popular spellings.)

a lot	affect	apply
ability	affectionate	appreciate
absence	again	appreciation
absent	against	approach
abundance	aggravate	appropriate
accept	aggressive	approval
acceptable	agree	approve
accident	aisle	approximate
accommodate	all right	argue
accompanied	almost	arguing
accomplish	already	argument
accumulation	although	arouse
accuse	altogether	arrange
accustomed	always	arrangement
ache	amateur	article
achieve	American	artificial
achievement	among	ascend
acknowledge	amount	assistance
acquaintance	analysis	assistant
acquainted	analyze	associate
acquire	angel	association
across	angle	attempt
address	annual	attendance
addressed	another	attention
adequate	answer	audience
advantage	antiseptic	August
advantageous	anxious	author
advertise	apologize	automobile
advertisement	apparatus	autumn
advice	apparent	auxiliary
advisable	appear	available
advise	appearance	avenue
advisor	appetite	awful
aerial	application	awkward

bachelor	career	concentration
balance	careful	conception
balloon	careless	condition
bargain	carriage	conference
basic	carrying	confident
beautiful	category	congratulate
because	ceiling	conquer
become	cemetery	conscience
before	cereal	conscientious
beginning	certain	conscious
being	changeable	consequence
believe	characteristic	consequently
benefit	charity	considerable
benefited	chief	consistency
between	choose	consistent
bicycle	chose	continual
board	cigarette	continuous
bored	circumstance	controlled
borrow	citizen	controversy
bottle	clothes	convenience
bottom	clothing	convenient
boundary	coarse	conversation
brake	coffee	corporal
breadth	collect	corroborate
breath	college	council
breathe	column	counsel
brilliant	comedy	counselor
building	comfortable	courage
bulletin	commitment	courageous
bureau	committed	course
burial	committee	courteous
buried	communicate	courtesy
bury	company	criticism
bushes	comparative	criticize
business	compel	crystal
cafeteria	competent	curiosity
calculator	competition	cylinder
calendar	compliment	daily
campaign	conceal	daughter
capital	conceit	daybreak
capitol	conceivable	death
captain	conceive	deceive

December
deception
decide
decision
decisive
deed
definite
delicious
dependent
deposit
derelict
descend
descent
describe
description
desert
desirable
despair
desperate
dessert
destruction
determine
develop
development
device
dictator
died
difference
different
dilemma
dinner
direction
disappear
disappoint
disappointment
disapproval
disapprove
disastrous
discipline
discover
discriminate
disease

dissatisfied
dissection
dissipate
distance
distinction
division
doctor
dollar
doubt
dozen
earnest
easy
ecstasy
ecstatic
education
effect
efficiency
efficient
eight
either
eligibility
eligible
eliminate
embarrass
embarrassment
emergency
emphasis
emphasize
enclosure
encouraging
endeavor
engineer
English
enormous
enough
entrance
envelope
environment
equipment
equipped
especially
essential

evening
evident
exaggerate
exaggeration
examine
exceed
excellent
except
exceptional
exercise
exhausted
exhaustion
exhilaration
existence
exorbitant
expense
experience
experiment
explanation
extreme
facility
factory
familiar
fascinate
fascinating
fatigue
February
financial
financier
flourish
forcibly
forehead
foreign
formal
former
fortunate
fourteen
fourth
frequent
friend
frightening
fundamental

further	incidental	labor
gallon	increase	laboratory
garden	independence	laid
gardener	independent	language
general	indispensable	later
genius	inevitable	latter
government	influence	laugh
governor	influential	leisure
grammar	initiate	length
grateful	innocence	lesson
great	inoculate	library
grievance	inquiry	license
grievous	insistent	light
grocery	instead	lightning
guarantee	instinct	likelihood
guess	integrity	likely
guidance	intellectual	literal
half	intelligence	literature
hammer	intercede	livelihood
handkerchief	interest	loaf
happiness	interfere	loneliness
healthy	interference	loose
heard	interpreted	lose
heavy	interrupt	losing
height	invitation	loyal
heroes	irrelevant	loyalty
heroine	irresistible	magazine
hideous	irritable	maintenance
himself	island	maneuver
hoarse	its	marriage
holiday	it's	married
hopeless	itself	marry
hospital	January	match
humorous	jealous	material
hurried	journal	mathematics
hurrying	judgment	measure
ignorance	kindergarten	medicine
imaginary	kitchen	million
imbecile	knew	miniature
imitation	knock	minimum
immediately	know	miracle
immigrant	knowledge	miscellaneous

mischief	opportune	persuasion
mischievous	opportunity	pertain
misspelled	optimist	picture
mistake	optimistic	piece
momentous	origin	plain
monkey	original	playwright
monotonous	oscillate	pleasant
moral	ought	please
morale	ounce	pleasure
mortgage	overcoat	pocket
mountain	paid	poison
mournful	pamphlet	policeman
muscle	panicky	political
mysterious	parallel	population
mystery	parallelism	portrayal
narrative	particular	positive
natural	partner	possess
necessary	pastime	possession
needle	patience	possessive
negligence	peace	possible
neighbor	peaceable	post office
neither	pear	potatoes
newspaper	peculiar	practical
newsstand	pencil	prairie
niece	people	precede
noticeable	perceive	preceding
o'clock	perception	precise
obedient	perfect	predictable
obstacle	perform	prefer
occasion	performance	preference
occasional	perhaps	preferential
occur	period	preferred
occurred	permanence	prejudice
occurrence	permanent	preparation
ocean	perpendicular	prepare
offer	perseverance	prescription
often	persevere	presence
omission	persistent	president
omit	personal	prevalent
once	personality	primitive
operate	personnel	principal
opinion	persuade	principle

privilege
probably
procedure
proceed
produce
professional
professor
profitable
prominent
promise
pronounce
pronunciation
propeller
prophet
prospect
psychology
pursue
pursuit
quality
quantity
quarreling
quart
quarter
quiet
quite
raise
realistic
realize
reason
rebellion
recede
receipt
receive
recipe
recognize
recommend
recuperate
referred
rehearsal
reign
relevant
relieve

remedy
renovate
repeat
repetition
representative
requirements
resemblance
resistance
resource
respectability
responsibility
restaurant
rhythm
rhythmical
ridiculous
right
role
roll
roommate
sandwich
Saturday
scarcely
scene
schedule
science
scientific
scissors
season
secretary
seize
seminar
sense
separate
service
several
severely
shepherd
sheriff
shining
shoulder
shriek
siege

sight
signal
significance
significant
similar
similarity
sincerely
site
soldier
solemn
sophomore
soul
source
souvenir
special
specified
specimen
speech
stationary
stationery
statue
stockings
stomach
straight
strength
strenuous
stretch
striking
studying
substantial
succeed
successful
sudden
superintendent
suppress
surely
surprise
suspense
sweat
sweet
syllable
symmetrical

sympathy
synonym
technical
telegram
telephone
temperament
temperature
tenant
tendency
tenement
therefore
thorough
through
title
together
tomorrow
tongue
toward
tragedy
transferred
treasury
tremendous
tries
truly
twelfth
twelve
tyranny
undoubtedly
United States
university
unnecessary
unusual
useful
usual
vacuum
valley
valuable
variety
vegetable
vein

vengeance
versatile
vicinity
vicious
view
village
villain
visitor
voice
volume
waist
weak
wear
weather
Wednesday
week
weigh
weird
whether
which
while
whole
wholly
whose
wretched

☞ **Drill: Spelling**

DIRECTIONS: Identify the misspelled word in each set.

1. (A) probly
   (B) accommodate
   (C) acquaintance
   (D) among

2. (A) auxiliary
   (B) atheletic
   (C) beginning
   (D) awkward

3. (A) environment
   (B) existence
   (C) Febuary
   (D) daybreak

4. (A) ocassion
   (B) occurrence
   (C) omitted
   (D) fundamental

5. (A) perspiration
   (B) referring
   (C) priviledge
   (D) kindergarten

DIRECTIONS: Choose the correct option.

6.   <u>Preceding</u> the <u>business</u> session, lunch will be served in a <u>separate</u> room.

    (A)   preceeding . . . business . . . seperate

    (B)   proceeding . . . bussiness . . . seperate

    (C)   proceeding . . . business . . . seperite

    (D)   No change is necessary.

7.   Monte <u>inadvertently</u> left <u>several</u> of his <u>libary</u> books in the cafeteria.

    (A)   inadverdently . . . serveral . . . libery

    (B)   inadvertently . . . several . . . library

    (C)   inadvertentely . . . several . . . librery

    (D)   No change is necessary.

8.   Sam wished he had more <u>liesure</u> time so he could <u>persue</u> his favorite hobbies.

    (A)   leisure . . . pursue   (B)   Liesure . . . pursue

    (C)   leisure . . . persue   (D)   No change is necessary.

9.   One of my <u>favrite charecters</u> in <u>litrature</u> is Bilbo from *The Hobbit*.

    (A)   favrite . . . characters . . . literature

    (B)   favorite . . . characters . . . literature

    (C)   favourite . . . characters . . . literature

    (D)   No change is necessary.

10.   Even <u>tho</u> Joe was badly hurt in the <u>accidant</u>, the company said they were not <u>lible</u> for damages.

    (A)   though . . . accidant . . . libel

    (B)   though . . . accident . . . liable

    (C)   though . . . acident . . . liable

    (D)   No change is necessary.

ENGLISH LANGUAGE SKILLS REVIEW

Drill: Word Choice Skills

1.	(D)	4.	(C)	7.	(A)	10.	(B)
2.	(D)	5.	(A)	8.	(B)		
3.	(A)	6.	(C)	9.	(C)		

Drill: Sentence Structure Skills

1.	(C)	4.	(B)	7.	(B)	10.	(B)
2.	(B)	5.	(A)	8.	(C)		
3.	(B)	6.	(A)	9.	(B)		

Drill: Verbs

1.	(C)	4.	(A)	7.	(A)	10.	(D)
2.	(D)	5.	(A)	8.	(C)		
3.	(D)	6.	(B)	9.	(A)		

Drill: Pronouns

1.	(A)	4.	(A)	7.	(B)	10.	(C)
2.	(C)	5.	(D)	8.	(B)		
3.	(A)	6.	(A)	9.	(A)		

Drill: Adjectives and Adverbs

1.	(C)	4.	(C)	7.	(A)	10.	(C)
2.	(A)	5.	(A)	8.	(C)		
3.	(D)	6.	(C)	9.	(B)		

Drill: Punctuation

1.	(D)	4.	(C)	7.	(A)	10.	(D)
2.	(A)	5.	(A)	8.	(A)		
3.	(A)	6.	(D)	9.	(B)		

Drill: Capitalization

1.	(D)	4.	(A)	7.	(B)	10.	(A)
2.	(B)	5.	(C)	8.	(D)		
3.	(C)	6.	(D)	9.	(B)		

Drill: Spelling

1.	(A)	4.	(A)	7.	(B)	10.	(B)
2.	(B)	5.	(C)	8.	(A)		
3.	(C)	6.	(D)	9.	(B)		

DETAILED EXPLANATIONS
OF ANSWERS

REVIEW

Drill: Word Choice Skills

1. **(D)** Choice (D) is correct. No change is necessary. *Principal* as a noun means "head of a school." *Principle* is a noun meaning "axiom" or "rule of conduct."

2. **(D)** Choice (D) is correct. No change is necessary. *Affect* is a verb meaning "to influence" or "to change." *Effect* as a noun meaning "result."

3. **(A)** Choice (A) is correct. Use *amount* with noncountable, mass nouns (*amount* of food, help, money); use *number* with countable, plural nouns (*number* of children, classes, bills).

4. **(C)** Choice (C) is correct. *Supposed to* and *used to* should be spelled with a final *d*. *Achieving* follows the standard spelling rule—*i* before *e*.

5. **(A)** Choice (A) is correct. Use *that*, not *because*, to introduce clauses after the word *reason*. Choice (A) is also the only choice that contains the correct spelling of "succeeded."

6. **(C)** Choice (C) is correct. *Converge together* is redundant, and *single* is not needed to convey the meaning of *a highway*.

7. **(A)** Choice (A) is correct. It is economical and concise. The other choices contain unnecessary repetition.

8. **(B)** Choice (B) is correct. Choices (A) and (C) pad the sentences with loose synonyms that are redundant. Choice (D), although a short sentence, does not convey the meaning as clearly as choice (B).

9. **(C)** Choice (C) is correct. The other choices all contain unnecessary repetition.

10. **(B)** Choice (B) is correct. Choices (A) and (C) contain circumlocution; they fail to get to the point. Choice (D) does not express the meaning of the sentence as concisely as choice (B).

Drill: Sentence Structure Skills

1. **(C)** Choice (C) is correct. Each response contains items in a series. In choices (A), (B), and (D) the word group after the conjunction is not an adjective like the first words in the series. Choice (C) contains three adjectives.

2. **(B)** Choice (B) is correct. Choices (A) and (C) combine conjunctions incorrectly. Choice (D) incorrectly uses the adverb *not*.

3. **(B)** Choice (B) is correct. Choices (A) and (C) appear to be parallel because the conjunction *and* connects two word groups that both begin with *because*, but the structure on both sides of the conjunction are very different. Choice (D) has the same structural problem as both (A) and (C) and it uses the conjunction *that* unnecessarily. *Because he kept his campaign promises* is a clause; *because of his refusal to accept political favors* is a prepositional phrase. Choice (B) connects two dependent clauses.

4. **(B)** Choice (B) is correct. Choices (A), (C), and (D) contain the elliptical clause *While . . . taking a shower*. It appears that the missing subject in the elliptical clause is the same as that in the independent clause—the *doorbell* in choice (A) and *someone* in choice (C), neither of which is a logical subject for the verbal *taking a shower*. Choice (B) removes the elliptical clause and provides the logical subject.

5. **(A)** Choice (A) is correct. Who swung the bat? Choices (B), (C), and (D) imply that it is the runner who swung the bat. Only choice (A) makes it clear that as *he* swung the bat, someone else (the *runner*) stole second base.

6. **(A)** Choice (A) is correct. The punctuation in the original sentence and in choice (B) creates a fragment. *Cotton being the state's principal crop* is not an independent thought because it lacks a complete verb—*being* is not a complete verb.

7. **(B)** Choice (B) is correct. The punctuation in the original sentence and in choice (A) creates a fragment. Both the semicolon and the

period should be used to separate two independent clauses. The word group *one that I have never seen before* does not express a complete thought and therefore is not an independent clause.

8.　**(C)**　Choice (C) is correct. The dependent clause *because repairs were being made* in choices (B) and (C) is punctuated as if it were a sentence. The result is a fragment.

9.　**(B)**　Choice (B) is correct. Choices (A) and (C) do not separate the complete thoughts in the independent clauses with the correct punctuation.

10.　**(B)**　Choice (B) is correct. Choices (A) and (C) do not separate the independent clauses with the correct punctuation.

Drill: Verbs

1.　**(C)**　Choice (C) is correct. The past participle form of each verb is required because of the auxiliaries (helping verbs) *had been* (concerned) and *would have* (gone).

2.　**(D)**　Choice (D) is correct. The forms of the irregular verb meaning *to rest* are *lie (rest), lies (rests), lay (rested),* and *has lain (has rested).* The forms of the verb meaning *to put* are *lay (put), lays (puts), laying (putting), laid (put),* and *have laid (have put).*

3.　**(D)**　Choice (D) is correct. The present tense is used for universal truths and the past tense is used for historical truths.

4.　**(A)**　Choice (A) is correct. The present tense is used for customary happenings. Choice (B), *had begun,* is not a standard verb form. Choice (C), *was beginning,* indicates that 10:30 a.m. is not the regular class time.

5.　**(A)**　Choice (A) is correct. The past tense is used for historical statements, and the present tense is used for statements about works of art.

6.　**(B)**　Choice (B) is correct. The subject of the sentence is the plural noun *sales,* not the singular noun *Christmas,* which is the object of the prepositional phrase.

7.　**(A)**　Choice (A) is correct. The subject *specialty* is singular.

8.   **(C)**   Choice (C) is correct. Subjects preceded by *every* are considered singular and therefore require a singular verb form.

9.   **(A)**   Choice (A) is correct. The subject of the sentence is the gerund *hiding*, not the object of the gerund phrase *mistakes*. *Hiding* is singular; therefore, the singular verb form *does* should be used.

10.   **(D)**   Choice (D) is correct. Though the form of the subject *Board of Regents* is plural, it is singular in meaning.

Drill: Pronouns

1.   **(A)**   Choice (A) is correct. Do not use the reflexive pronoun *myself* as a substitute for I.

2.   **(C)**   Choice (C) is correct. In the clause *whoever consumes them*, *whoever* is the subject. *Whomever* is the objective case pronoun and should be used only as the object of a sentence, never as the subject.

3.   **(A)**   Choice (A) is correct. Use the nominative case pronoun *who* as the subject complement after the verb *is*.

4.   **(A)**   Choice (A) is correct. In this sentence use the nominative case/subject pronouns *she who* as the subject complement after the *be* verb *was*.

5.   **(D)**   Choice (D) is correct. *Student* is an indefinite, genderless noun that requires a singular personal pronoun. While *his* is a singular personal pronoun, a genderless noun includes both the masculine and feminine forms and requires *his or her* as the singular personal pronoun.

6.   **(A)**   Choice (A) is correct. The antecedent *company* is singular, requiring the singular pronoun *it*, not the plural *they*.

7.   **(B)**   Choice (B) is correct. Choice (A) contains a person shift: *Your* is a second person pronoun, and *his* and *her* are third person pronouns. The original sentence uses the third person plural pronoun *their* to refer to the singular antecedent *every car owner*. Choice (B) correctly provides the masculine and feminine forms *his or her* required by the indefinite, genderless *every car owner*.

8. **(B)** Choice (B) is correct. The implied antecedent is *teaching*. Choices (A) and (C) each contain a pronoun with no antecedent. Neither *it* nor *this* are suitable substitutions for *teacher*.

9. **(A)** Choice (A) is correct. The pronoun *they* in the original sentence has no conspicuous antecedent. Since the doer of the action is obviously unknown (and therefore genderless), choice (B), *he*, is not the correct choice.

10. **(C)** Choice (C) is correct. The original sentence is ambiguous: the pronoun *she* has two possible antecedents; we don't know whether it is Margaret or her sister who is away at college.

Drill: Adjectives and Adverbs

1. **(C)** Choice (C) is correct. *Bad* is an adjective; *badly* is an adverb. *Real* is an adjective meaning *genuine* (*a real problem, real leather*). To qualify an adverb of degree to express how bad, how excited, how boring, etc., choose *very*.

2. **(A)** Choice (A) is correct. Use an adverb as a qualifier for an adjective. *How simple? Relatively simple*.

3. **(D)** Choice (D) is correct. *Good* is an adjective; *well* is both an adjective and an adverb. As an adjective, *well* refers to health; it means "not ill."

4. **(C)** Choice (C) is correct. All the other choices use *good* incorrectly as an adverb. *Shake* is an action verb that requires an adverb, not an adjective.

5. **(A)** Choice (A) is correct. The action verbs *speaks, writes, observe,* and *think* each require adverbs as modifiers.

6. **(C)** Choice (C) is correct. The comparisons in choices (A), (B), and (D) are illogical: these sentences suggest that Los Angeles is not in California because it *is larger than any city in California*.

7. **(A)** Choice (A) is correct. Do not omit the second *as* of the correlative pair *as . . . as* when making a point of equal or superior comparison, as in choice (B). Choice (C) omits *than* from "if not more interesting [than]." Choice (D) incorrectly uses *as* instead of *than*.

8.　**(C)**　Choice (C) is correct. Choice (A) illogically compares *baseball team* to a *university*, and choices (B) and (D) illogically compare *baseball team* to *other universities*. Choice (C) logically compares the baseball team here to the one at any other university, as implied by the possessive ending on university—*university's*.

9.　**(B)**　Choice (B) is correct. Choices (A), (C), and (D) are ambiguous; because these sentences are too elliptical, the reader does not know where to place the missing information.

10.　**(C)**　Choice (C) is correct. Choice (A) is redundant; there is no need to use *most* with *stingiest*. Choice (B) incorrectly combines the superlative word *most* with the comparative form *stingier*. Choice (D) incorrectly combines the comparative word *more* with the superlative form *stingiest*.

Drill: Punctuation

1.　**(D)**　Choice (D) is correct. Nonrestrictive clauses, like other nonrestrictive elements, should be set off from the rest of the sentence with commas.

2.　**(A)**　Choice (A) is correct. Use a comma to separate a nonrestrictive appositive from the word it modifies. "An Oklahoma family" is a nonrestrictive appositive.

3.　**(A)**　Choice (A) is correct. Do not use unnecessary commas to separate a subject and verb from their complement. Both choices (B) and (C) use superfluous punctuation.

4.　**(C)**　Choice (C) is correct. Do not separate two items in a compound with commas. The original sentence incorrectly separates "car or plane." Choice (A) omits the comma after the introductory clause.

5.　**(A)**　Choice (A) is correct. Use a semicolon to separate two independent clauses/sentences that are not joined by a coordinating conjunction, especially when the ideas in the sentences are interrelated.

6.　**(D)**　Choice (D) is correct. Use a semicolon to separate two sentences not joined by a coordinating conjunction.

7.　**(A)**　Choice (A) is correct. Use a semicolon to separate two sentences joined by a conjunctive adverb.

8.   **(A)**   Choice (A) is correct. Do not use a colon after a verb or a preposition. Remember that a complete sentence must precede a colon.

9.   **(B)**   Choice (B) is correct. Do not use a colon after a preposition, and do not use a colon to separate a preposition from its objects.

10.   **(D)**   Choice (D) is correct. Use a colon preceding a list that is introduced by words such as *the following* and *as follows*.

Drill: Capitalization

1.   **(D)**   Choice (D) is correct. *North America,* like other proper names, is capitalized. *North, south, east,* and *west* are only capitalized when they refer to geographic regions (*the Southwest, Eastern Europe);* as compass directions, they are not capitalized.

2.   **(B)**   Choice (B) is correct. Although persons' names are capitalized, a person's title is not (*coach,* not *Coach*). Capitalize the complete name of a team, school, river, etc. (Dallas Cowboys). *The,* whether it is part of the official title or not, is never capitalized when it appears in text.

3.   **(C)**   Choice (C) is correct. Capitalize all geographic units, and capitalize *earth* only when it is mentioned with other planets. *Equator* is not capitalized.

4.   **(A)**   Choice (A) is correct. Capitalize the first word in a title and all other words in a title except articles, prepositions with fewer than five letters, and conjunctions.

5.   **(C)**   Choice (C) is correct. Capitalize proper adjectives (proper nouns used as adjectives): *Greek* goddess, *Roman* mythology.

6.   **(D)**   Choice (D) is correct. Capitalize all religious groups, books, and names referring to religious deities.

7.   **(B)**   Choice (B) is correct. Do not capitalize courses unless they are languages (English) or course titles followed by a number (Algebra I).

8.   **(D)**   Choice (D) is correct. Do not capitalize seasons unless they accompany the name of an event such as *Spring Break.* Do not capitalize types of degrees (*bachelor's degrees*); capitalize only the name of the degree (*Bachelor of Arts degree*).

9.   **(B)**   Choice (B) is correct. As a landmark, *Berlin Wall* is capitalized; however, do not capitalize systems of government or individual adherents to a philosophy, such as *communism*.

10.   **(A)**   Choice (A) is correct. The names of planets, as well as the complete names of newspapers and other periodicals, are capitalized.

Drill: Spelling

1.   **(A)**   The correct spelling of choice (A) is "probably."

2.   **(B)**   The correct spelling is "athletic."

3.   **(C)**   Choice (C) should be spelled "February."

4.   **(A)**   The correct spelling of this word is "occasion."

5.   **(C)**   Choice (C) should be spelled "privilege."

6.   **(D)**   Choice (D) is the best response. *Business* has only three *-s's*. Separate has an *-e* at the beginning and the end, not in the middle.

7.   **(B)**   Choice (B) is the best response. *Library* has two *r's*.

8.   **(A)**   Choice (A) is the best response. *Leisure* is one of the few English words that does not follow the *i* before *e* except after *c* rule. *Pursue* has two *u's* and only one *e*.

9.   **(B)**   Choice (B) is the best response. "Favorite," "characters," and "literature" are commonly mispronounced, and when someone who mispronounces them tries to spell them phonetically, he or she often misspells them.

10.   **(B)**   Choice (B) is the best response. Advertisements often misspell words to catch the consumer's eye (*lite* for light, *tho* for though, etc.), and these misspellings are becoming more common in student writing. "Accident" and "liable" are examples of words that are not pronounced the way they are spelled.

PRACTICE
TEST 1

CLEP FRESHMAN COLLEGE COMPOSITION
Test 1

(Answer sheets appear in the back of this book.)

Section I

TIME: 45 Minutes
45 Minutes
55 Questions

DIRECTIONS: Each of the following sentences may contain an error in diction, usage, idiom, or grammar. Some sentences are correct. Some sentences contain one error. No sentence contains more than one error.

If there is an error, it will appear in one of the underlined portions labeled A, B, C, or D. If there is no error, choose the portion labeled E. If there is an error, select the letter of the portion that must be changed in order to correct the sentence.

EXAMPLE:

He drove <u>slowly</u> and <u>cautiously</u> in order to <u>hopefully</u> avoid having an
       A   **B**   **C**

<u>accident</u>. <u>No error</u>.
  D   **E**   Ⓐ Ⓑ ⬤ Ⓓ Ⓔ

---

1.   In 1877 Chief Joseph of the Nez Percé, <u>together with</u> 250 warriors
                                      A

    and 500 women and children, <u>were praised</u> by newspaper reporters
                              B

    for <u>bravery</u> during the 115-day fight <u>for</u> freedom. <u>No error</u>.
        C   **D**   **E**

2.   The ideals <u>upon which</u> American society <u>is based</u> <u>are</u> primarily
                          A   **B**   **C**
      those of Europe and not ones <u>derived from</u> the native Indian culture.
                                              D

      <u>No error.</u>
           E

3.   <u>Among</u> the activities <u>offered at</u> the local high school <u>through</u> the
          A   **B**   **C**
      community education program <u>are</u> singing in the couples' chorus,
                                        D
      ballroom dancing, and Chinese cooking. <u>No error.</u>
                                                   E

4.   If you are <u>disappointed by</u> an <u>inexpensive</u> bicycle, then an option
                      A   **B**
      you might consider is to work this summer and <u>save</u> your money for
                                                         C

      a <u>more expensive</u> model. <u>No error.</u>
           D   **E**

5.   Also being presented to the city council this morning <u>is</u> the mayor's
                                                                 A
      city budget for next year and plans <u>to renovate</u> the <u>existing</u> music
                                                B   **C**
      theater, so the session <u>will focus</u> on financial matters. <u>No error.</u>
                                   D   **E**

6.   "Scared Straight," a program designed <u>to inhibit</u> criminal <u>behavior in</u>
                                                  A   **B**
      juvenile offenders <u>who</u> seemed bound for prison as adults, had a
                             C
      significant <u>affect</u> on the youngsters. <u>No error.</u>
                      D   **E**

7.   The <u>average</u> American tourist feels <u>quite</u> at home in a Japanese
               A   **B**
      stadium filled <u>at capacity</u> with sports fans watching Japan's <u>most</u>
                          C   **D**
      popular sport, baseball. <u>No error.</u>
                                   E

8. My brother is <u>engaged</u> to a woman <u>who</u> my parents <u>have</u> not met
              A   **B**   **C**

    because she has not yet <u>emigrated from</u> her native country of Ecua-
                              D

    dor. <u>No error</u>.
        E

9. In the United States, <u>testing for</u> toxicity, determining the <u>proper</u>
                           A   **B**

    dose and timing between doses, and evaluating the vaccine for

    <u>effectiveness</u> <u>is</u> the method used in researching new drugs. <u>No error</u>.
       C   **D**   **E**

10. Rachel wants <u>to know if</u> <u>it is her</u> driving that expensive red sports
                 A   **B**

    car <u>at a rate of speed</u> <u>obviously exceeding</u> the posted speed limit.
           C   **D**

    <u>No error</u>.
    E

DIRECTIONS: In each of the following sentences, some portion of the sentence is underlined. Under each sentence are five choices. The first choice has the same wording as the original. The other four choices are reworded. Sometimes the first choice containing the original wording is the best; sometimes one of the other choices is the best. Choose the letter of the best choice. Your choice should produce a sentence which is not ambiguous or awkward and which is correct, clear, and precise.

This is a test of correct and effective English expression. Keep in mind the standards of English usage, punctuation, grammar, word choice, and construction.

EXAMPLE:

When you listen to opera, <u>a person may not appreciate it.</u>

(A) a person may not appreciate it.

(B) it may not be appreciated by a person.

(C) which may not be appreciated by one.

(D) you may not appreciate it.

(E) appreciating it may be a problem for you.   Ⓐ Ⓑ Ⓒ ⬤ Ⓔ

11. When the Mississippi River threatens to flood, sandbags are piled along its banks, <u>and they do this to keep its waters from overflowing</u>.

    (A) and they do this to keep its waters from overflowing.

    (B) to keep its waters from overflowing.

    (C) and then its waters won't overflow.

    (D) and, therefore, keeping its waters from overflowing.

    (E) and they keep its waters from overflowing.

12. <u>Having studied theology, music, along with medicine</u>, Albert Schweitzer became a medical missionary in Africa.

    (A) Having studied theology, music, along with medicine

    (B) Having studied theology, music, as well as medicine

    (C) Having studied theology and music, and, also, medicine

    (D) With a study of theology, music, and medicine

    (E) After he had studied theology, music, and medicine

13. According to a recent study by the Census Bureau, the more education anyone gets, <u>the more money you will make</u>.

    (A) the more money you will make.

    (B) the more money will be made.

    (C) the most money you will make.

    (D) the more money he will make.

    (E) the more money he will have made.

14. Bolivia, a South American country named for Simón Bolívar, who was a leader in freeing the Latin American colonies from Spain, <u>having a climate in which rainfall is seasonal</u>.

    (A) having a climate in which rainfall is seasonal.

    (B) the climate of which has seasonal rainfall.

    (C) has a climate in which rainfall is seasonal.

    (D) and it has a climate in which rainfall is seasonal.

    (E) the rainfall is seasonal in its climate.

15. Some pieces of the puzzle, in spite of Jane's search, <u>are still missing and probably will never be found</u>.

   (A) are still missing and probably will never be found.

   (B) is missing still but never found probably.

   (C) probably will be missing and never found.

   (D) are still probably missing and to never be found.

   (E) probably are missing and will not be found.

16. *Gone With the Wind* <u>is the kind of a movie</u> producers would like to release because it would bring them fame.

   (A) is the kind of a movie

   (B) is the sort of movie

   (C) is the kind of movie

   (D) is the type of a movie

   (E) is the category of movie

17. Eighteenth-century architecture, with its columns and balanced lines, <u>was characteristic of those of previous times in Greece and Rome</u>.

   (A) was characteristic of those of previous times in Greece and Rome

   (B) is similar to characteristics of Greece and Rome

   (C) is similar to Greek and Roman building styles

   (D) is characteristic with earlier Greek and Roman architecture

   (E) was similar to architecture of Greece and Rome

18. <u>In Harry Golden's "vertical Negro plan," he suggests</u> facetiously that a solution to the perceived problem of sit-ins in the 1950s would be to provide stand-up desks—with no seats—in the public schools.

   (A) In Harry Golden's "vertical Negro plan," he suggests

   (B) In his "vertical Negro plan" he suggests

   (C) Harry Golden's "vertical Negro plan" suggests

   (D) In the "vertical Negro plan" Harry Golden suggests

   (E) In his satiric "vertical Negro plan" Harry Golden suggests

19. A famous basketball player's reason for his uncanny ability to shoot hook shots accurately is that he has a <u>sense of where you are on the court</u>.

    (A) sense of where you are on the court.

    (B) sense of where he is on the court.

    (C) sense of where you were on the court.

    (D) sense of where he was on the court.

    (E) sense of where the court was in relation to his position on it.

20. Both Huckleberry Finn and Holden Caulfield wanted <u>to be a free person</u>, unburdened by social inconveniences.

    (A) to be a free person

    (B) each to be free persons

    (C) to be free persons each one

    (D) to be free persons

    (E) to be free people

DIRECTIONS: The following passages are considered early draft efforts of a student. Some sentences need to be rewritten to make the ideas clearer and more precise.

Read each passage carefully and answer the questions that follow. Some of the questions are about particular sentences or parts of sentences and ask you to make decisions about sentence structure, diction, and usage. Some of the questions refer to the entire essay or parts of the essay and ask you to make decisions about organization, development, appropriateness of language, audience, and logic. Choose the answer that most effectively makes the intended meaning clear and follows the requirements of standard written English. After you have chosen your answer, fill in the corresponding oval on your answer sheet.

EXAMPLE:

(1) On the one hand, I think television is bad, But it also does some good things for all of us. (2) For instance, my little sister thought she wanted to be a policemen until she saw police shows on television.

Which of the following is the best revision of the underlined portion of sentence 1 below?

On the one hand, I think television is bad. But it also does some good things for all of us.

(A)   is bad; But it also

(B)   is bad. but is also

(C)   is bad, and it also

(D)   is bad, but it also

(E)   is bad because it also

A B C ● E

QUESTIONS 21–26 are based on the following passage

(1) The melt-water stream draining out along the floor of a glacier cave gives evidence of its origin. (2) It goes without saying that the origin of another kind of cave can be gotten from the pounding of sea waves at the mouth of a sea cave. (3) Solution caves, however, have always been a source of wonder to man. (4) How do these extensive, complex, and in some places beautifully decorated passageways develop?

(5) Solution caves are formed in limestone and similar rocks by the action of the water. (6) Think of them as part of a huge subterranean plumbing system. (7) After a rain water seeps into cracks and pores of soil and rock and percolates beneath the land surface. (8) Eventually, some of the water reaches a zone of soil and rock where all the cracks are already filled with water. (9) The term <u>water table</u> refers to the upper surface of this saturated zone. (10) Calcite (calcium carbonate), the main mineral of limestone, is barely soluble in pure water. (11) Rainwater, however, absorbs some carbon dioxide as it passes through soil and decaying vegetation. (12) The water, combining chemically with the carbon dioxide, forms a weak carbonic acid solution which slowly dissolves calcite. (13) This acid slowly dissolves calcite, forms solution cavities, and excavates passageways. (14) This results in a solution cave.

(15) A second stage in cave development is when there is lowering of the water table. (16) During this stage, the solution cavities are stranded in the unsaturated zone where air can enter. (17) This leads to the deposition of calcite, which forms <u>dripstone</u> features, beautiful formations in strange shapes on the inside of caves.

21. Which of the following is the best revision of sentence 2 below?

It goes without saying that the origin of another kind of cave can be gotten from the pounding of sea waves at the mouth of a sea cave.

(A) It goes without saying that a sea cave can be formed by the pounding of waves at its mouth.

(B) The pounding waves at the mouth of a sea cave offer evidence of the origin of this cave.

(C) Evidence is offered of the origin of sea caves by the pounding of the waves.

(D) In saying that another kind of cave can be formed by the pounding of waves at the entrance of sea caves.

(E) It goes without saying that the pounding waves at the mouth of a sea cave offers evidence as to the origin of this kind of cave.

22. In the context of the sentences preceding and following sentence 6, which of the following is the best revision of sentence 6?

(A) These caves can be considered part of a huge subterranean plumbing system.

(B) You can think of these caves as part of a huge subterranean plumbing system.

(C) The formation of these caves can be thought of in terms of a huge subterranean plumbing system.

(D) If you think of it, these caves are similar to a huge subterranean plumbing system.

(E) When one visualizes the formation of these caves, one could compare them to part of a huge subterranean plumbing system.

23. Which of the following is the best way to combine sentences 13 and 14?

(A) This acid dissolving results in solution cavities, passageways, and caves.

(B) Solution caves are formed when this acid dissolves solution cavities and passageways.

(C) Slowly, this acid dissolves calcite, and the resulting effects are that cavities and passageways become caves.

    (D) Excavating cavities, passageways, and caves, the acid slowly dissolves calcite.

    (E) This acid slowly dissolves calcite, excavating cavities and passageways which eventually become solution caves.

24.   Which of the following is the best punctuation of the underlined portion of sentence 7?

<u>After a rain water seeps into</u> cracks and pores of soil and rock and percolates beneath the land surface.

    (A) After a rain, water seeps into

    (B) After, a rain water seeps into

    (C) After a rain: water seeps into

    (D) After a rain-water seeps into

    (E) Best as it is

25.   In relation to the passage as a whole, which of the following best describes the writer's intention in paragraph 2?

    (A) To provide an example

    (B) To propose a solution to a problem

    (C) To describe a location

    (D) To examine opposing evidence

    (E) To explain a process

26.   Which of the following is the best revision of the underlined portion of sentence 15 below?

A second stage in cave development <u>is when there is lowering of the water table</u>.

    (A) is because there is lowering of the water table

    (B) is due to the water table going lower

    (C) occurs after a lowering of the water table

    (D) happens to be when the water table is lowered

    (E) being when there is a lowering of the water table

QUESTIONS 27–32 are based on the following passage.

Dear Senator Simon,

(1) I am writing in support of your bill that, if passed, will be instrumental in getting legislation which will put a warning label on violent television programs. (2) Violence needs to be de-glamorized. (3) One must detest and deplore violence of excess and other such excesses in one's viewing choices.

(4) Unfortunately, violence sells. (5) One of the main reasons is because violent shows are easily translated and marketed to other countries. (6) Network executives have actually requested their script writers to include more violence in certain shows with a steady audience, as well as to create new violent shows for the late evening slot just before the news.

(7) The National Institute of Health did a study. (8) In this study children viewed violent scenes. (9) After this, children are more prone to violent acts. (10) Maybe parents will pay more attention to their children's viewing if this labeling system is enacted. (11) Maybe commercial sponsors will hesitate to sponsor programs that are labeled violent, so these programs will diminish in number and children will have fewer such programs to view.

(12) Yes, I think people need to be aware of violent events happening around the world and within our own country. (13) We need to know what is happening in the Balkans, Somalia, South Africa, as well in Los Angeles riots and the bombings in New York, are just to name two examples. (14) However, these are real events, not glamorizations.

(15) Please keep up your campaign to get rid of excessive violence!

Sincerely,
Sue Chan

27. Which of the following is the best revision of the underlined portion of sentence 1 below?

I am writing in support of your bill <u>that, if passed, will be instrumental in getting legislation which will put</u> a warning label on violent television programs.

(A) in order to pass legislation in order to put

(B) passing legislation which will require putting

(C) to pass a law that will legislate putting

(D) requiring passage of legislation requiring

(E) for a law requiring

28. In the context of the sentences preceding and following sentence 3, which of the following is the best revision of sentence 3?

(A) One should agree with me that excessive violence should be detested and deplored.

(B) I detest and deplore excessive violence.

(C) You can see that I think wanton violence should be detested and deplored.

(D) Detesting and deploring wanton violence and other such excesses is how I feel.

(E) Excessive violence should be detested and deplored.

29. In relation to the passage as a whole, which of the following best describes the writer's intention in paragraph 2?

(A) To present background information

(B) To contradict popular opinion

(C) To provide supporting evidence

(D) To outline a specific category

(E) To rouse the emotions of the reader

30. Which of the following is the best revision of the underlined portion of sentence 5 below?

One of the main reasons is because violent shows are easily translated and marketed to other countries.

(A) is being that violent shows

(B) being that violent shows are

(C) is that violent shows are

(D) is due to the fact that violent shows seem to be

(E) comes from violent shows containing violence being

31. Which of the following is the best way to combine sentences 7, 8, and 9?

(A) After doing a study, the children viewing violent scenes at the National Institute of Health were more prone to violent acts.

(B) Children viewing violent scenes at the National Institute of Health were more prone to violent acts.

(C) After viewing violent scenes, children at the National Institute of Health were more prone to doing violent acts themselves.

(D) The National Institute of Health did a study proving that after viewing violent scenes, children are more prone to violent acts.

(E) The National Institute of Health did a study proving that children viewing violent scenes are more prone to violent acts.

32. Which of the following would be the best revision of the underlined portion of sentence 13?

We need to know what is happening in the Balkans, Somalia, South Africa, <u>as well in Los Angeles riots and the bombings in New York, are just to name two examples</u>.

(A) as well as in Los Angeles riots, and bombings in New York just to name two examples.

(B) as well as, to name two examples, the Los Angeles riots and the bombings in New York.

(C) as well as riots in Los Angeles and the bombings in New York.

(D) as well as events such as the riots in Los Angeles and the bombings in New York.

(E) Best as it is.

QUESTIONS 33–38 are based on the following passage.

(1) Dripstone features are called <u>speleotherms,</u> and they can take several beautiful forms. (2) When these structures are highlighted by lanterns or electric lights, they transform a cave into a natural wonderland. (3) Some people feel that electric lights have no place in a cave. (4) The most familiar decorative dripstone features are <u>stalactites</u> and <u>stalagmites</u>. (5) Stalactites hang downward from the ceiling and are formed as drop after drop of water slowly trickles through cracks in the cave roof. (6) Each drop of water hangs from the ceiling. (7) The drop of water loses carbon dioxide. (8) It then deposits a film of calcite. (9) Stalagmites grow upward from the floor of the cave generally as a result of water dripping from overhead stalactites. (10) An impressive <u>column</u> forms when a stalactite and stalagmite grow until they join. (11) A <u>curtain</u> or <u>drapery</u> begins to

form in an inclined ceiling when the drops of water trickle along a slope. (12) Gradually, a thin sheet of calcite grows downward from the ceiling and hangs in graceful decorative folds like a drape.

(13) These impressive and beautiful features appear in caves in almost every state, making for easy access for tourists looking for a thrill. (14) In addition, the size and depth of many caves in the United States also impress even the most experienced tourist accustomed to many very unique sights. (15) Seven caves have more than 15 passage miles, the longest being the Flint-Mammoth Cave system in Kentucky with more than 169 miles. (16) The deepest cave in the United States is Neff Canyon in Utah. (17) Although many people seem to think that the deepest cave is Carlsbad Caverns, located in New Mexico. (18) However, Carlsbad Caverns boasts the largest room, the Big Room which covers 14 acres. (19) These are sights not to be missed by those who appreciate the handiwork of Mother Nature.

33. Which of the following is the best way to combine sentences 6, 7, and 8?

(A) Each drop of water deposits a film of calcite as it is hanging from the ceiling and losing carbon dioxide.

(B) When hanging, water drops lose carbon dioxide and create a film of calcite.

(C) In the process of losing carbon dioxide, the drops of water hang from the ceiling and deposit calcite.

(D) Hanging from the ceiling, losing carbon dioxide, and depositing calcite are the drops of water.

(E) Hanging from the ceiling, each drop of water loses carbon dioxide and deposits a film of calcite.

34. Which of the following sentences breaks the unity of paragraph 1 and should be omitted?

(A) Sentence 1   (D) Sentence 10

(B) Sentence 3   (E) Sentence 12

(C) Sentence 4

35. In relation to the passage as a whole, which of the following best describes the writer's intention in paragraph 2?

(A) To describe some examples

(B)   To provide a summary

(C)   To convince the reader to change an opinion

(D)   To persuade the reader to follow a course of action

(E)   To detail a chain of events

36.   Which of the following is the best revision of the underlined portion
      of sentence 14 below?

      In addition, the size and depth of many caves in the United States
      also impress even the most experienced tourist accustomed to many
      very unique sights.

      (A)   impressed the most experienced tourist also accustomed to
            very unique sights

      (B)   impress even the most experienced tourist also accustomed to
            very unique sights

      (C)   impress even the most experienced tourist accustomed to
            many unique sights

      (D)   also impress very experienced tourists accustomed to very
            unique sights

      (E)   also impress even the most experienced tourist accustomed to
            many unique sights

37.   In the context of the sentences preceding and following sentence 17,
      which of the following is the best revision of sentence 17?

      (A)   Although many people are thinking that the deepest cave is
            Carlsbad Caverns in New Mexico.

      (B)   Although, many people think the deepest cave is existing is
            Carlsbad Caverns in New Mexico.

      (C)   As a matter of fact, many people think the deepest cave exists
            in New Mexico in Carlsbad Caverns.

      (D)   However, many people think the deepest cave is Carlsbad
            Caverns in New Mexico.

      (E)   In addition, many people think the deepest cave is located in
            New Mexico in Carlsbad Caverns.

38.   Which of the following corrects the grammatical error in sentence 12?

(A)   Gradually, a thin sheet of calcite grow downward from the ceiling and hang in graceful decorative folds like a drape.

(B)   Gradually, a thin sheet of calcite grows downward from the ceiling and hangs in graceful decorative folds like a drape.

(C)   Gradually, a thin sheet of calcite grows downward from the ceiling and gracefully hang in decorative folds like a drape.

(D)   Gradually, a thin sheet of calcite grows downward from the ceilings and hang in graceful decorative folds like a drape.

(E)   Gradually, a thin sheet of calcite grows downward from the ceiling and hang from the ceiling like a drape.

QUESTIONS 39–44 are based on the following passage.

(1) Using Indians to track down and fight other Indians was not a new idea during the conflict between the Whites and the Indians during the mid-1800 Indian Wars during the conquest of the Apaches. (2) The English and the French from early colonial times had exploited traditional intertribal rivalries to their own advantage.

(3) What was a novel idea of the U.S. Army during its war against the Apaches was using an Indian against members of his own tribe. (4) Gen. George Crook believed that the best work would be done by an Indian who had only just been fighting him. (5) Crook had learned that such a scout would know alot because he would know the fighting habits, the hiding places, and the personalities of the Indians being pursued. (6) This method worked well for Crook and by the end of his career he had used about 500 Apache scouts.

(7) Crook demanded trust from all his troops and, in turn, he gave them his trust. (8) He paid his scouts well and on time, a very important factor. (9) Most importantly, Crook treated all the personnel under his command with dignity and respect. (10) These were good qualities. (11) These qualities no doubt earned Crook the admiration and loyalty of his Indian soldiers. (12) Though, the man himself won their respect. (13) Crook was like few West Point trained officers, for he understood his enemy well. (14) He learned to fight the Indians on their terms, to use the land and terrain to his advantage, and to abandon the textbook examples. (15) He got on a trail, and with his Apache scouts to guide him, he followed his quarry relentlessly.

(16) Crook's faith in his scouts never wavered. (17) Moreover, they gave him no grounds for worry. (18) In the annals of the Indian Wars, the story of Crook and his scouts is unique.

39. Which of the following is the best revision of the underlined portion of sentence 1 below?

Using Indians to track down and fight other Indians was not a new idea <u>during the conflict between Whites and the Indians during the mid-1800 Indian Wars during the conquest of the Apaches</u>.

(A) during the mid-1800 Indian Wars between Whites and Apaches.

(B) during the long years of conflict between Whites and Indians.

(C) during the mid-1800s when Indians and Whites came into conflict in the Indian Wars.

(D) when the Apaches and Whites were engaged in conflict.

(E) when, during the mid-1800 Indian Wars, Whites and Apaches engaged in fighting in the Indian Wars.

40. Which of the following is the best revision of the underlined portion of sentence 3 below?

<u>What was a novel idea of the U.S. Army during its war</u> against the Apaches was using an Indian against members of his own tribe.

(A) The U.S. Army's novel idea during this war

(B) What the U.S. Army had as a novel idea during its war

(C) The U.S. Army had the novel idea during this war

(D) During its war the U.S. Army's novelty

(E) A novelty of the U.S. Army's war during this time

41. Which of the following is the best revision of the underlined portion of sentence 5 below?

Crook had learned that such a scout <u>would know alot because he would know</u> the fighting habits, the hiding places, and the personalities of the Indians being pursued.

(A) would know alot about

(B) would know a lot about

(C) would know

(D) would have a great deal of useful knowledge concerning

(E) would have knowledge of

42. Which of the following is the best way to combine sentences 10, 11, and 12?

    (A) Admiring and loyal because of Crook's good qualities, the Indian soldiers gave him their respect.

    (B) Although earning the loyalty and admiration of the Indian soldiers, Crook won their respect.

    (C) Crook won the Indian soldier's respect, admiration, and loyalty because of his good qualities.

    (D) Although these good qualities no doubt earned Crook the admiration and loyalty of his Indian soldiers, the man himself won their respect.

    (E) Although the man himself earned respect, these good qualities earned Crook the Indian soldier's admiration and loyalty.

43. In relation to the passage as a whole, which of the following best describes the writer's intention in paragraph 4?

    (A) To narrate an important event

    (B) To describe the best features of the subject

    (C) To persuade readers to take a certain course of action

    (D) To provide a conclusion

    (E) To provide a summary of the passage

44. Which of the following would be the best way to revise sentence 15?

    (A) He got on a trail, with his Apache scouts to guide him, he followed his quarry relentlessly.

    (B) He got on a trail, and his Apache scouts guiding him, he followed his quarry relentlessly.

    (C) He would get on a trail, and with his Apache scouts to guide him, he followed his quarry relentlessly.

    (D) He got on a trail and he followed his quarry relentlessly, with his Apache scouts to guide him.

    (E) He would get on a trail, and with his Apache scouts to guide him, would follow his quarry relentlessly.

45. In a bibliography entry, the name of the publishing company appears just

    (A) before the city of publication.

    (B) after the city of publication.

    (C) before the publication title.

    (D) after the publication title.

    (E) after the author's name.

46. The most likely source for a brief overview of Mao Zedong's childhood would be

    (A) a magazine article.

    (B) an encyclopedia article.

    (C) a biography.

    (D) a world history book.

    (E) the biographical section of a dictionary.

47. In an encyclopedia article, a cross-reference

    (A) is a type of asterisk.

    (B) gives the titles of books on the same subject.

    (C) explains the difference between the subject discussed and another subject.

    (D) appears at the top of each page.

    (E) identifies a related article in the same encyclopedia.

48. When citing a single source in the text of a research paper, the page number is immediately followed by

    (A) a comma.   (D) a slash.

    (B) a period.   (E) a parenthesis.

    (C) a space.

49. Which of the following is the most likely source for the date a word was first used?

    (A) An encyclopedia

    (B) A dictionary

    (C) A book of quotations

    (D) A grammar and usage book

    (E) A literature textbook

50. In a student's research paper, which of the following does not need to be documented?

    (A) A bar chart from a textbook.

    (B) A paraphrase of an art critic's comment.

    (C) A direct quote from an ancient Greek philosopher.

    (D) A theory developed by the student who wrote the paper.

    (E) A comment recorded during an interview.

51. A book's index is most practical for

    (A) finding a little information on a specific subject.

    (B) locating every illustration in the book.

    (C) identifying subjects related to the book's main topic.

    (D) determining the reading level of the book.

    (E) finding the author's reference sources.

52. The least important information for finding a specific magazine article at the library is

    (A) the name of the magazine.

    (B) the issue number of the magazine.

    (C) the page numbers of the article.

    (D) whether the article is illustrated.

    (E) whether the article is continued in the next issue.

53. In text citations, an author's name usually appears

    (A) first name, then last name.

    (B) last name, then first name.

    (C) either last name only or last name plus first initial.

    (D) last name plus first initial in all cases.

    (E) last name only in all cases.

54. In a direct quote, a text citation should appear just after

    (A) the name of the person quoted.

    (B) the last word in the quote.

    (C) the period or ellipsis at the end of the quote.

    (D) the quotation mark ending the quote.

    (E) the last word in the paragraph.

55. When looking for a book in the library, it is least important to remember

    (A) the catalog call number.

    (B) the book title.

    (C) the author's name.

    (D) the date of publication.

    (E) whether the book is oversize.

Section II

TIME: 45 Minutes
45 Questions

DIRECTIONS: The following questions test your ability to recognize the content, form, and style of a passage as well as the writer's purpose. After reading each passage or poem, choose the best answer to each question and fill in the corresponding oval on the answer sheet.

QUESTIONS 56–62 are based on the following passage.

My daddy's face is a study. Winter moves into it and presides there. His eyes become a cliff of snow threatening to avalanche; his eyebrows bend like black limbs of leafless trees. His skin takes on the pale, cheerless yellow of winter
5   sun; for a jaw he has the edges of a snowbound field dotted with stubble; his high forehead is the frozen sweep of the Erie, hiding currents of gelid thoughts that eddy in darkness. Wolf killer turned hawk fighter, he worked night and day to keep one from the door and the other from under the
10 windowsills. A Vulcan guarding the flames, he gives us instructions about which doors to keep closed or opened for proper distribution of heat, lays kindling by, discusses qualities of coal, and teaches us how to rake, feed, and bank the fire. And he will not unrazor his lips until spring.
15   Winter tightened our heads with a band of cold and melted our eyes. We put pepper in the feet of our stockings, Vaseline on our faces, and stared through dark icebox mornings at four stewed prunes, slippery lumps of oatmeal, and cocoa with a roof of skin.
20   But mostly we waited for spring, when there could be gardens.
     By the time this winter had stiffened itself into a hateful knot that nothing could loosen, something did loosen it, or rather someone. A someone who splintered the knot into
25 silver threads that tangled us, netted us, made us long for the dull chafe of the previous boredom.

From The Bluest Eye, *by Toni Morrison*

56. It can be inferred from the opening paragraph that

    (A) the narrator's father was a cold and unloving man.

    (B) the house was besieged by wild animals in the winter.

    (C) the narrator's father was strange and alien to his children.

    (D) the narrator's father fought hunger and cold unceasingly.

    (E) the narrator's father was an accomplished hunter.

57. The sentence "My daddy's face is a study" (line 1) is best interpreted to mean that his face

    (A) reflects the formal learning he has acquired.

    (B) reflects the quiet of a study room.

    (C) is an expressive landscape.

    (D) is expressive of his extensive experiences in life.

    (E) is worthy of attention.

58. The phrase "will not unrazor his lips until spring" (line 14) evokes his

    (A) determination to win the battle for survival.

    (B) refusal to shave.

    (C) decision not to shave until spring comes.

    (D) preoccupation with his appearance.

    (E) stern, hostile attitude toward the family.

59. The image of a "hateful knot" (lines 22–23) is a reference to

    (A) the poverty of their home.

    (B) the unspent anger of their father.

    (C) the boredom of school.

    (D) the unyielding cold weather.

    (E) their cold, stiffened muscles.

60. In context, the phrase "dull chafe" (line 26) is best interpreted to mean

    (A) the rubbing of winter garments.

    (B) the discomfort of wearing the same old clothes.

    (C) the slow passage of time.

    (D) the absence of new people in their lives.

    (E) the unvaried rituals of winter life.

61. In line 25, the "silver threads that tangled us" most likely refer to

    (A) the icy tracings that winter left on their windows.

    (B) the net of poverty that envelopes them all.

    (C) the finery of Maureen's clothing.

    (D) the narrator and Frieda's plot to discredit Maureen.

    (E) itching threads of winter garments that chafe them.

62. The phrase "splintered the knot into silver threads" (lines 24–25) is

    (A) a simile.   (D) onomatopoeia.

    (B) dramatic irony.   (E) personification.

    (C) a mixed metaphor.

QUESTIONS 63–69 are based on the following poem

DO NOT GO GENTLE INTO THAT GOOD NIGHT

Do not go gentle into that good night,
Old age should burn and rave at close of day;
Rage, rage against the dying of the light.

Though wise men at their end know dark is right,
5   Because their words had forked no lightning they
Do not go gentle into that good night.

Good men, the last wave by, crying how bright
Their frail deeds might have danced in a green bay,
Do not go gentle into that good night.

10   Wild men who caught and sang the sun in flight,
      And learn, too late, they grieved it on its way,
      Do not go gentle into that good night.

      Grave men, near death, who see with blinding sight
      Blind eyes could blaze like meteors and be gay,
15   Rage, rage against the dying of the light.

      And you, my father, there on the sad height,
      Curse, bless, me now with your fierce tears, I pray.
      Do not go gentle into that good night.
      Rage, rage against the dying of the light.

      By Dylan Thomas

63. In the first stanza, the poet is addressing

     (A) the general audience.

     (B) wise men, good men, wild men, and grave men.

     (C) older people.

     (D) people of public notoriety.

     (E) "my father."

64. In the context of the first stanza, lines 2 and 3 express the belief that

     (A) old people should be less complaining.

     (B) old people should vent their anger regularly, and thus prolong
          their lives.

     (C) old people should fight against death in every way.

     (D) old people should fight against losing the will to live.

     (E) old people should be expected to be bitter and disappointed.

65. In the second stanza, the poet implies that

     (A) wise men cannot accept death, and so they must protest.

     (B) wise men always knew that their voices could not stop death,
          and so they accept it.

     (C) no wise person would willingly go gently into death.

(D) wise men accept the rightness of death, but they protest any-way.

(E) wise men feel frustrated that they could not expose death to the "light" of the truth they sense.

66. The "dying of the light" (lines 3, 15, 19) refers metaphorically to

(A) the passage of time.   (D) death.

(B) the aging of the body.   (E) the loss of the will to live.

(C) the aging of the spirit.

67. The use of the word "rage" throughout the poem has the greatest effect in

(A) increasing the emotional intensity of the statement.

(B) providing closure at the end of every stanza.

(C) providing "stock" figures with a vivid emotional reaction.

(D) providing the poet's audience with a clear statement of the poem's message.

(E) reinforcing the "curse" of the last stanza.

68. "Good men" (line 7), the poet implies, are best noted for

(A) their having done "frail deeds."

(B) the extent of their rage.

(C) their tendency to join wise men ("the last wave") in anger.

(D) the extent to which their deeds are recognized by others ("danced," etc.).

(E) the extent of their regret at not being recognized.

69. The fifth stanza is notable for its evident

(A) hyperbole.   (D) sexual innuendo.

(B) irony.   (E) paradox.

(C) synecdoche.

QUESTIONS 70–78 are based on the following passage.

The great fault of a modern school of poetry is that it is
an experiment to reduce poetry to a mere effusion of natural
sensibility; or what is worse, to divest it both of imaginary
splendor and human passion, to surround the meanest objects
5   with the morbid feelings and devouring egotism of the writers' own minds. Milton and Shakespeare did not so understand poetry. They gave a more liberal interpretation both to
nature and art. They did not do all they could to get rid of the
one and the other, to fill up the dreary void with the Moods
10   of their own Minds. They owe their power over the human
mind to their having had a deeper sense than others of human
life. But to the men I speak of there is nothing interesting,
nothing heroical, but themselves. To them the fall of gods or
of great men is the same. They do not enter into the feeling.
15   They cannot understand the terms. They are even debarred
from the last poor, paltry consolation of an unmanly triumph
over fallen greatness; for their minds reject, with a convul-
sive effort and intolerable loathing, the very idea that there
ever was, or was thought to be, anything superior to them-
20   selves. All that has ever excited the attention and admiration
of the world, they look upon with the most perfect indifference; and they are surprised to find that the world repays
their indifference with scorn. "With what measure they mete,
it has been meted to them again."
25   Shakespeare's imagination is of the same plastic kind as
his conception of character or passion. "It glances from
heaven to earth." Its movement is rapid and devious. It
unites the most opposite extremes: or, as Puck says, in
boasting of his own feats, "puts a girdle round about the
30   earth in forty minutes." He seems always hurrying from his
subject, even while describing it; but the stroke, like the
lightning's, is sure as it is sudden. He takes the widest
possible range, but from that very range he has his choice
of the greatest variety and aptitude of materials. He brings
35   together images the most alike, but placed at the greatest
distance from each other; that is, found in circumstances of
the greatest dissimilitude. From the remoteness of his combinations, and the celerity with which they are effected,
they coalesce the more indissolubly together.

From "On Shakespeare and Milton," by William Hazlitt

70. The primary distinction made in the first paragraph is one between

    (A) the poetry of the senses and the poetry of imagination.

    (B) the modern school of poetry and that of Shakespeare and Milton.

    (C) the poetry of Shakespeare and the poetry of Milton.

    (D) the poetry of egotism and the poetry of sensibility.

    (E) the modern school of poetry and the poetry of human mood.

71. Which of the following best describes the function of the first sentence in the first paragraph?

    (A) It sarcastically provides evidence of the critic's intention.

    (B) It establishes the critic as an authority.

    (C) It clearly states the topic which the rest of the passage elucidates.

    (D) It directly addresses a common misconception to prepare the ground for a discussion of the critic's main topic.

    (E) It advances an accepted viewpoint that therefore does not need extensive support in the rest of the paragraph.

72. The critic cited here seems particularly upset by what he terms the modernist's

    (A) "moods."   (D) "human passion."

    (B) "morbid feelings."   (E) "intolerable loathing."

    (C) "egotism."

73. In context, the sentence "They gave a more liberal interpretation both to nature and art" (lines 7–8) suggests which of the following?

    (A) Shakespeare and Milton did not espouse the political conservatism of the modernists.

    (B) Shakespeare and Milton were tolerant in matters concerning nature and art.

    (C) Shakespeare and Milton did not understand poetry in the same way as the modernists.

(D) The modernists had a greater right to their viewpoints than the Romantics.

(E) The modern age is one of egotism.

74. The passage suggests that Classical Tragedy would not be of interest to the "modern school" because they

(A) pay too much attention to their superiors and not enough to themselves.

(B) do not see any difference between "the fall of gods or of great men."

(C) they hate anything that holds the "admiration of the world."

(D) they cannot deal with the scorn the critical world has for them.

(E) they feel compelled to substitute their own "dreary world" for the real thing.

75. The author brings closure to his first paragraph by

(A) stating that the modernists are as surprised at their reception as he is at their views.

(B) implying that biblical injunctions are still in force, even though the modernists may be unbelievers.

(C) implying that the rest of the world is as indifferent to the modernists as they are to it.

(D) implying that the rest of the world scorns the modernists as much as he does.

(E) stating that there is nothing "heroical" in the modernist position.

76. Stylistically, the second paragraph is best characterized by the repeated use of

(A) descriptive adjectives.   (D) assonance.

(B) action verbs.   (E) metaphor.

(C) metaphor.

77. The structure of the second paragraph is such that

(A) most of the following sentences reinforce the contentions of the first sentence.

    (B)   the final sentence has been arrived at inductively.

    (C)   the central theme of the paragraph is stated in the middle of the paragraph.

    (D)   it relies heavily for contextual meaning on the statements of the first paragraph.

    (E)   each sentence is dependent on the previous one in establishing meaning.

78.   The critic demonstrates his admiration for Shakespeare in the second paragraph by

    (A)   using images from literary critics to reinforce his argument.

    (B)   praising Shakespeare repeatedly for doing simple tasks well.

    (C)   using occasional quotes from Shakespeare's poetry.

    (D)   speaking of Shakespeare's works in the same manner as he speaks of Milton's.

    (E)   describing Shakespeare's importance in grandiose terms such as "celerity."

DIRECTIONS: For each of the following questions, choose the best answer and fill in the corresponding oval on the answer sheet.

---

79.   The <u>mediocre</u> meal served in the cafeteria neither impressed nor satisfied us completely.

    Which of the following best captures the meaning of the underlined word above?

    (A) Light   (D) Second-rate

    (B) Tasteless   (E) Disappointing

    (C) Intolerable

80.   Based upon limited evidence, the police department <u>postulated</u> that the criminal entered the building at around 1:00 A.M.

    Which of the following best captures the meaning of the underlined word?

    (A) Attempted   (B) Verified

(C) Supposed   (D) Wondered

(E) Confirmed

81.   The lazy worker was fired from his company for failing to reach his daily sales quotas.

Which of the following substitutions for the underlined word presents a more neutral picture of the worker?

(A) inactive   (D) carefree

(B) slothful   (E) indolent

(C) easygoing

82.   We were promised by the loan officer that the decision would be reached by Monday.

Which of the following is a correct revision of the ambiguous sentence above?

(A) By Monday, the loan officer promised us, "A decision will be reached."

(B) "A decision will be reached," promised the loan officer by Monday.

(C) The loan officer promised us, "A decision will be reached by Monday."

(D) The loan officer promised us that "By Monday, a decision would be reached.

(E) "A decision by Monday will be reached," the loan officer promised us.

83.   Juanita decided to lead her class to the appropriate exit during the fire drill.

Which of the following substitutions for the underlined word presents a most emphatically negative picture of Juanita?

(A) advance   (D) dominate

(B) direct   (E) suddenly bring

(C) negatively influence

84. The torrential rains <u>impeded</u> our safe passage beyond the jagged mountain paths.

    Which of the following best captures the meaning of the underlined word?

    (A) Hindered

    (B) Unfortunately ruined

    (C) Relentlessly impelled

    (D) Luckily facilitated

    (E) Worsened

85. Diana decided to tell Jules that she would no longer accept his gifts.

    Which of the following is a correct revision of the ambiguous sentence above?

    (A) "Jules, I will no longer accept your gifts," Diana told him.

    (B) Diana told Jules, "I have decided to no longer accept your gifts."

    (C) Decided Diana, "I will no longer accept your gifts," she told Jules

    (D) Diana said to Jules that she had decided to no longer accept his gifts.

    (E) "I have decided," Diana told Jules, "to no longer accept your gifts."

86. The elderly man remained <u>stoic</u> during his wife's funeral.

    Which of the following best captures the meaning of the underlined word?

    (A) Apathetic

    (B) Expressionless

    (C) Impassive

    (D) Cheerful

    (E) Fervent

87. The neighboring tribes would <u>often pillage</u> the supplies of their enemies in times of need.

    Which of the following best captures the meaning of the underlined words?

    (A) Regularly trade

    (B) Usually negotiate

(C)   Outright demand   (D)   Frequently ravage

(E)   Repeatedly taint

88.   Unwilling to abandon the warmth and comfort of his bed, Jerry <u>lingered</u> under the blankets until noon.

Which of the following substitutions for the underlined word presents a most emphatically negative picture of Jerry?

(A)   delayed   (D)   procrastinated

(B)   secluded himself   (E)   slowly planned

(C)   carefully thought

89.   According to Carol, her style of dress reflects the current fashions from Paris.

Which of the following is a correct revision of the ambiguous sentence above?

(A)   "My style of dress," according to Carol reflects the "current fashions from Paris."

(B)   "The current Paris Fashions are reflected in this style," according to Carol.

(C)   "From Paris, my style of dress reflects the current fashions," said Carol.

(D)   Carol's current style reflects the current fashions from Paris.

(E)   Carol said, "My style of dress reflects the current Parisian fashions."

90.   Denise attempted to <u>legitimate</u> her poor attention span by criticizing the uselessness of the topics discussed.

Which of the following best captures the meaning of the underlined word?

(A)   Justify   (D)   Judge

(B)   Ignore   (E)   Analyze

(C)   Express

91. Believing that he could learn through <u>osmosis</u>, Dave often placed books under his pillow the night before an exam.

    Which of the following best captures the meaning of the underlined word?

    (A) Object relation   (D) Extended touching

    (B) Proximity   (E) Concentration

    (C) Absorption

92. Jake's <u>hearty</u> appetite and high metabolism allow him to ingest large quantities of food without gaining an ounce of weight.

    Which of the following substitutions for the underlined word presents a most emphatically negative picture of Jake?

    (A) enthusiastic   (D) gluttonous

    (B) abundant   (E) healthy

    (C) vigorous

93. Erika interrupted our discussion by telling us that she wanted to go home.

    Which of the following is a correct revision of the ambiguous sentence above?

    (A) Telling us she wanted to go home, Erika interrupted our conversation.

    (B) During our conversation, "I want to go home," Erika interrupted.

    (C) "To go home," Erika interrupted our conversation by telling us.

    (D) Erika interrupted our conversation by telling us, "I want to go home."

    (E) Telling us, Erika interrupted our conversation by saying, "I want to go home."

94. Our teacher told us that sometimes ideas seem <u>intangible</u> because they cannot be physically perceived.

    Which of the following best captures the meaning of the underlined word?

(A) Unrealized   (D) Abstract

(B) Unlikely to happen   (E) Visually impossible

(C) Invisible

QUESTIONS 95–97 refer to the following excerpts.

(A) The United States of America is a nation that was founded on such "self-evident" truths as racial tension, the inequality of women, and political partisanism; Misters Jefferson and Washington would be proud of their legacy.

(B) The replenishment of our rivers and streams is an issue of vital importance, yet they are continually exploited and depleted in the interest of progress and settlement. Will we realize our shortsightedness in time?

(C) The roots of colonization in the New World can be traced back to sixteenth-century Germany, when Martin Luther tacked his protest to the portals of the cathedral.

(D) In the iridescent flame of the candle, she could see the setting of the sun, with myriad of brilliant reds and bright yellows, as if rainbows and clouds had been set ablaze by a match of God.

(E) Emerging from the early decades of industrialization, the Roaring Twenties was a time in which the nation's focus returned to ideas of leisure and pleasure, marking it as a period of almost unimaginable euphoria.

95. In which excerpt is the tone nostalgic?

(A) (B) (C) (D) (E)

96. In which excerpt does the speaker's tone convey a sense of foreboding?

(A) (B) (C) (D) (E)

97. In which excerpt is the tone sarcastic?

(A) (B) (C) (D) (E)

QUESTIONS 98–100 refer to the following excerpt.

The bigtop was alive, a veritable cornucopia of sight and sound. At one end, the contortionist was twisting herself into shapes reminiscent of a pretzel, while next to her the strong man performed feats of strength that would make Atlas proud. The Ringmaster's voice boomed like thunder against the backdrop of the cheering crowd, and the roars of the lions could be heard clear across town. The highlight of the show was, of course, the clowns, whose antics amused young and old alike, and left more than one onlooker speechless and red in the face.

98. The performers are described using all of the following EXCEPT

    (A) metaphor.   (D) cliché.

    (B) allusion.   (E) simile.

    (C) hyperbole.

99. The description of the bigtop as "alive" is an example of

    (A) irony.   (D) hyperbole.

    (B) alliteration.   (E) metaphor.

    (C) personification.

100. In the first line of the excerpt, cornucopia can best be interpreted as meaning

    (A) abundance.   (D) enough.

    (B) scarcity.   (E) saturation.

    (C) rarity.

CLEP FRESHMAN COLLEGE COMPOSITION
TEST 1

Section I

1.	(B)	15.	(A)	29.	(A)	43.	(D)
2.	(E)	16.	(C)	30.	(C)	44.	(E)
3.	(E)	17.	(E)	31.	(D)	45.	(B)
4.	(A)	18.	(C)	32.	(D)	46.	(B)
5.	(A)	19.	(B)	33.	(E)	47.	(E)
6.	(D)	20.	(E)	34.	(B)	48.	(E)
7.	(C)	21.	(B)	35.	(D)	49.	(B)
8.	(B)	22.	(A)	36.	(C)	50.	(D)
9.	(E)	23.	(E)	37.	(D)	51.	(A)
10.	(B)	24.	(A)	38.	(B)	52.	(D)
11.	(B)	25.	(E)	39.	(A)	53.	(C)
12.	(E)	26.	(C)	40.	(A)	54.	(D)
13.	(D)	27.	(E)	41.	(C)	55.	(D)
14.	(C)	28.	(B)	42.	(D)		

Section II

56.	(D)	68.	(A)	79.	(D)	90.	(A)
57.	(C)	69.	(E)	80.	(C)	91.	(C)
58.	(A)	70.	(B)	81.	(A)	92.	(D)
59.	(D)	71.	(C)	82.	(C)	93.	(D)
60.	(E)	72.	(C)	83.	(D)	94.	(D)
61.	(C)	73.	(B)	84.	(A)	95.	(E)
62.	(C)	74.	(B)	85.	(B)	96.	(B)
63.	(E)	75.	(D)	86.	(A)	97.	(A)
64.	(C)	76.	(B)	87.	(D)	98.	(D)
65.	(D)	77.	(A)	88.	(D)	99.	(C)
66.	(D)	78.	(C)	89.	(E)	100.	(A)
67.	(A)						

DETAILED EXPLANATIONS OF ANSWERS

TEST 1

Section I

1. **(B)** "Were praised" is a plural verb; since the subject is Chief Joseph, a singular proper noun, the verb should be "was praised." The intervening phrase of choice (A), "together with 250 warriors and 500 women and children," does not change the singular subject. Choice (C), "bravery," is the correct noun form, and choice (D), "for," is idiomatically correct in that phrase.

2. **(E)** Choice (A), "upon which," is a correct prepositional phrase. Choice (B), "is based," agrees with its subject, "society." In choice (C) "are" agrees with its subject, "ideals." "Derived from" in choice (D) is correct idiomatic usage.

3. **(E)** Choice (A), "among," indicates choice involving more than two things. The prepositions in (B) and (C) are correct. "Are," (D), is a plural verb, agreeing in number with the compound subject "singing... dancing...cooking."

4. **(A)** One is "disappointed by" a person or action but "disappointed in" what is not satisfactory. "Inexpensive," (B), is the adjective form. Parallel with "to work," choice (C), "save," had the word "to" omitted. Choice (D) compares the two models, one "inexpensive" and one "more expensive."

5. **(A)** The verb should be plural, "are," in order to agree with the compound subject, "budget...plans." Choice (B) begins an infinitive phrase which includes a participle, "existing," (C). Choice (D) is idiomatically correct.

6.   **(D)**   The noun form, "effect," is the correct one to use. Choice (A), "to inhibit," is an infinitive; choice (B) is correctly worded; in choice (C), the nominative case "who" is the correct subject of "seemed."

7.   **(C)**   The idiom should be "filled to capacity." The adjective in choice (A), "average," is correct, as is the adverb in choice (B). Choice (D), "most," is appropriate for the superlative degree.

8.   **(B)**   The subordinate clause, "who my parents have not met," has as its subject "parents," which agrees with choice (C), "have . . . met." Therefore, the pronoun is a direct object of the verb and should be in the objective case, "whom." Both choice (A) and choice (D) are idiomatically correct.

9.   **(E)**   Choice (A), "testing," is parallel to "determining" and "evaluating." "Proper" in choice (B) and "effectiveness" in choice (C) are correct. In choice (D) "is" must be singular because all three steps mentioned comprise the one process.

10.   **(B)**   Choice (A) is correct. Choice (B) should read, "it is she"; nominative case pronoun is required following a linking verb. Choice (C) is proper English, and the correct form of the modifiers appears in choice (D).

11.   **(B)**   This sentence contains the ambiguous pronoun "they," for which there is no antecedent and fails to show the relationship of the ideas expressed. Choice (B) eliminates the clause with the ambiguous pronoun and correctly expresses the reason for the sandbag placement. Choice (C) suggests that the two clauses joined by "and" are equal and does not show the subordinate relationship of the second to the first. Choice (D) introduces a dangling phrase with a coordinating conjunction, "and," that suggests the joining of equals, and choice (E) retains both errors from the original sentence.

12.   **(E)**   This sentence presents two problems, namely use of a preposition instead of a coordinating conjunction to join the objects of the participle "having studied" and failure to show a time relationship. Choice (E) corrects both problems. Choice (B) simply replaces the preposition "along with" by "as well as"; choice (C) unnecessarily repeats the conjunction "and" rather than using the quite appropriate series construction. None of the choices (A), (B), (C), or (D) correctly shows the time relationship.

13. **(D)**   The original sentence contains a shift of pronoun from third person "anyone" to second person "you." Only choice (D) provides consistency in pronoun number without using an inappropriate tense, as in choice (E). Use of the passive voice in choice (B) loses parallelism in construction; and choice (C) retains the incorrect "you."

14. **(C)**   The words in this exercise result in a sentence fragment, not a complete sentence. Only choice (C) provides a predicate for the subject, "Bolivia." Choice (B) replaces the dangling phrase with a subordinate clause; choices (D) and (E) add main clauses but leave the subject, "Bolivia," without a predicate.

15. **(A)**   The correct answer has two concepts—pieces are missing and pieces will probably never be found. Choice (B) has a singular verb, "is." Choice (C) indicates the pieces "probably will be" missing, which is not the problem. Choice (D) and choice (E) both indicate the pieces are "probably" missing, which is illogical because the pieces either are or are not missing.

16. **(C)**   Choice (A), "the kind of a," and choice (D), "the type of a," are incorrect grammatical structures. Choice (E) introduces the new concept of "category." Choice (B), "sort of," is poor wording.

17. **(E)**   Choice (E) is clear and concise and shows the correct comparison of architecture. The antecedent of "those" in choice (A) is not clear. Choice (B) is comparing "characteristics," not just architecture. Choice (C) is awkward, and choice (D) incorrectly uses an idiom, "characteristic with."

18. **(C)**   The only concise (and clear in context) choice is (C). All the others, including the original, are wordy by comparison, except for choice (B). It does have one more word, even if it looks shorter than (C); and it fails to identify the antecedent of the pronouns.

19. **(B)**   The original awkwardly shifts pronoun voice from third person ("he") to second person ("you"). Choice (B) corrects the error and uses the appropriate present verb tense. Choice (C) repeats the initial error and changes the tense to the past. Choice (D) corrects the voice shift but uses past tense. Choice (E) uses tense and is hopelessly wordy.

20. **(E)**   The problem here is noun agreement. To be in agreement,

the underlined phrase must be plural, since the noun subject is compound. Choice (B) does use the plural but adds an unnecessary word, and the plural word is not the best choice. Choice (C) is similar in both ways. Choice (D) looks better, but the best word here is "people," thus choice (E). Incidentally, an even better rephrasing—not a choice—is "to be free."

21. **(B)**   Choice (B) is the most concise, least repetitive form of this sentence. Choices (A) and (E) contain the unnecessary phrase, "It goes without saying." Choice (C) leaves out the fact that waves are pounding at the mouth of a sea cave. Choice (D) is a fragment.

22. **(A)**   Choice (A) is the best revision because it is precise and uses a voice consistent with the rest of the passage. Choice (B) and (D) both slip into the less formal "you." Choice (E) is too formal, using "one." Choice (C) is somewhat acceptable but uses the passive voice construction, "can be thought of."

23. **(E)**   Choice (E) clearly shows the pattern of events, a sequence of cause-and-effect. Choice (A) contains the incorrect construction, "This acid dissolving"; it should be, "This acid's dissolving." Choice (B) neglects to extend clearly the process of cave formation to show that the passageways become caves. Choice (C) is somewhat acceptable, but it contains the awkward phrasing, "effects are that." Choice (D) reverses the cause with the effect, and so confuses the issues.

24. **(A)**   Choice (A) sets the prepositional phrase apart from the main subject and verb ("water seeps"). Choice (B) makes it seem as though we are talking about "a rain water." In (C) and (D) both a colon and a hyphen are inappropriate. In (E), the sentence as it stands is ambiguous, especially because we use the phrase "rain water" in other contexts, and unless the prepositional phrase is set-off by a comma, the sense is unclear.

25. **(E)**   The second paragraph explains the process (E) by which dripstone features are formed in a cave. This process takes place in a location—caves—but description, choice (C), is not the main intent of the paragraph. Choices (A), (B), and (D) would be more suitable to persuasion.

26. **(C)**   Choice (C) is the most precise wording and uses an action verb, "occurs." Choices (A), (D), and (E) use two forms of the verb "to be" in the same sentence, thus producing a weaker construction. Choice

(B) uses, "is due to," and so is a bit more awkward than choice (C).

27.   **(E)**   Choice (E) is the clearest and most concise rewording of the sentence portion. Choice (A) repeats the phrase, "in order to," and choice (D) contains repetition of "requiring." Choice (B) and choice (C) both contain unnecessary wordiness in the clauses beginning with "which will" and "that will."

28.   **(B)**   Choice (B) keeps the first person voice and states the main point using parallel structure and concise language. Choices (A), (C), and (D) are still excessively wordy; in addition, choice (A) changes the voice to "one." Choice (E), while somewhat more concise, uses passive voice; since this letter is a call to action, passive voice weakens the argument and intent of the letter.

29.   **(A)**   Paragraph 2 provides background information, choice (A), for the reason there is so much violence on television. Choice (B) is incorrect as the argument in paragraph 2 is not a contradiction to anything. Choice (C) would be correct if the paragraph contained support for the main argument. While the paragraph does give some specifics, choice (D), the evidence cannot be considered as categorizing anything. Choice (E) incorrectly implies that the paragraph is written in an emotionally charged manner.

30.   **(C)**   Although choice (C) employs two forms of the verb "to be," it is the best wording. Choices (A) and (B) both use the weak phrase "being that" and create fragments. Choice (D) is far too wordy and uses the weak wording "seem to be"; use of the word "seem" makes the writer appear uncertain and tentative, not precise. Choice (E) is still too wordy, using the phrase "shows containing violence" instead of the more concise phrase "violent shows."

31.   **(D)**   Choice (D) is the most concise combination, one which clearly shows time sequence and cause-and-effect. Choice (A), because it has a misplaced modifier, implies that the children conducted the study. Choices (B) and (E) imply that the children were prone to violence only while they were viewing the violent acts, a slight distortion of the correct finding. Choice (C) subtly suggests that only the children at the Institute were affected by this condition, with the implication that other children are not. This failure to indicate an extension of the findings subtly distorts the original meaning.

32. **(D)**   (D) would be the best revision; the phrase "are just to name two examples," besides being grammatically incorrect, is unnecessary, and the structure of (D) sets up the parallel best. (B) is the next best, but "to name two examples" is awkward and unnecessary. (A) and (C) are not specific about any particular riots (these would at least need the article "the" as in (B) and (D).

33. **(E)**   Choice (E) concisely combines ideas while effectively showing the sequence of events. Choice (A) puts the cause, "losing carbon dioxide," after the effect, "deposits a film of carbon dioxide." Choice (B) could be better worded by revising, "When hanging, water drops." Choice (C) erroneously presents hanging from the ceiling as part of the process of losing carbon dioxide. Choice (D) completely loses the cause-and-effect and lists events as an unrelated list.

34. **(B)**   Choice (B) breaks the unity of the paragraph by digressing slightly into an opinion about the presence of electric lights in a natural setting. As the main thrust of the passage is to discuss the beauty of caves in the United States, this idea is out of place. This sentence also mentions the opinions of "some people," a vague reference. The other choices contain no digressions.

35. **(D)**   The intent of the second paragraph builds to the last sentence, in which the persuasive (D) intent becomes evident. Although the paragraph provides some examples, choice (A), those examples bolster the persuasive intent. Choice (C) could be plausible if the writer had indicated an acknowledgment of the reader's aversion to caves. Choices (B) and (E) are more appropriate for the first paragraph.

36. **(C)**   Choice (C) is the most concise and accurate. Choices (A) and (B) use the incorrect grammatical structure, "very unique." A sight is unique, meaning "one of a kind"; therefore, "very unique" is incorrect. The sentence begins with the phrase, "in addition," so choices (D) and (E) are repetitive because they use the word "also."

37. **(D)**   Choice (D) makes a complete sentence that is correctly punctuated. Choice (A) is a fragment and contains the awkward "people are thinking." Choice (B) contains the poor phrase "is existing." Choices (C) and (E) could be moderately acceptable, but they have two prepositional phrases in a row beginning with "in" at the end of the sentence.

38.   **(B)**   Choice (B) is correct because both verbs must agree with the singular noun "sheet." Choice (A) brings "grow" into accord with "hang," but the plural verbs do not agree with the singular subject. Choice (C) uses "gracefully" as an adverb correctly, but does not correct the verb agreement problem. Choice (D) may appear correct: "hang" would be correct if it modified the plural "ceilings" but it modifies "sheet" which is singular. Similarly, (E) does not correct the subject-verb disagreement.

39.   **(A)**   Choice (A) is the best condensation of the wordy portion. Choice (B) and choice (D) omit the time period. Choice (C) is redundant, repeating the "conflict" idea twice. Choice (E) is almost as wordy and repetitive as the original.

40.   **(A)**   Choice (A) reduces wordiness through two means: deleting a subordinate clause by eliminating "What" and deleting a prepositional phrase by converting it to a possessive. Choice (B) keeps the subordinate clause. Choice (C) creates an incorrect sentence structure. Choice (D) trivializes the serious conflicts by using the word "novelty," which has light connotations. Choice (E) changes the focus of the action from the Army.

41.   **(C)**   Choice (C) is the best reduction of the wordy original. Choice (A) uses "alot" and choice (B) uses "a lot," both of which are not formal usage to mean "much." Choice (D) is almost wordier than the original. Choice (E) is a bit stiff for the tone of the article.

42.   **(D)**   Choice (D) presents the ideas correctly and concisely. Choices (A) and (C) use the awkward phrase "because of." Choice (B) sounds as if the first part of the sentence is unrelated to the last part. Choice (E) repeats the verb "earned" twice.

43.   **(D)**   Paragraph 4 is a conclusion (D), winding up the main idea, the good relationship between Crook and Indian soldiers. Choice (A) is not correct as there is no specific incident given. Choice (B) could be a second choice, but the best features of the subject are more fully discussed earlier in the paper. Choice (C) has no bearing on this essay. Choice (E) could be a choice if there were a recounting of the main points, but the major ideas of the last paragraph are the faith Crook and the Apaches had in one another and the uniqueness of their relationship.

44.   **(E)**   The past progressive tense is best, as it expresses Crook's

use of the scouts as a common occurrence, not as a single event, which may be implied by the past tense in the original. (A) eliminates "and" which further confuses the sentence and does not help the verb problem. (B) makes it sound even more like a singular occurrence. (C) changes only the first verb to the progressive. (D) is not incorrect, but does not clarify the sentence any, and lets the verb tense stand.

45. **(B)** According to the MLA Handbook and most other styles, the name of the publishing company appears just after the city of publication. It does not appear before the city of publication, so choice (A) is wrong. The publication title appears earlier than the publishing company name, making choice (C) incorrect. The city of publication appears between the publication title and the publishing company name, so choice (D) is wrong. The author's name is the first item, appearing long before the publishing company name, so (E) is incorrect.

46. **(B)** An encyclopedia article on the life of Mao Zedong would have a paragraph or two on his childhood—enough information for a brief overview without being overwhelming. A magazine article would most likely focus on a contemporary event, and even an in-depth profile article might not include childhood information, so (A) is incorrect. A biography would probably have a chapter or two on the subject's childhood, not merely a brief overview, so choice (C) is incorrect. Choice (D) is wrong as a world history book would have very little if any room for childhood information on any one person. The biographical section of a dictionary usually has only a line or two explaining the person's significance in the world, so choice (E) would be incorrect.

47. **(E)** A cross-reference, by definition, refers the reader to a related topic elsewhere in the book. It is not the name for any type of asterisk, so (A) is incorrect. Choice (B) is wrong as it describes a bibliography, not a cross-reference. A cross-reference doesn't explain anything, so (C) is incorrect. Choice (D) is also wrong as it describes a guide word, not a cross-reference.

48. **(E)** The page number is the last item in a citation and a citation appears in parentheses, so the page number would be followed by a closing parenthesis. There is no need for a comma after the page number, so (A) is incorrect. A period follows the page number in old-style footnotes but not in the current MLA citation style, making choice (B) wrong. Choice (C) is wrong as there should not be a space between the page

number and the parenthesis. A slash isn't used with the page number in citations, so (D) is incorrect.

49. **(B)** Many dictionaries list an approximate or exact year for the first use of a word as well as the word's definition. An encyclopedia has articles mainly on people, places, and events so it covers only a small percentage of words, making (A) an unlikely source. A book of quotations lists phrases, not words; it may have the original date for a phrase but definitely not for an individual word, making (C) incorrect. A grammar and usage book explains how to use words correctly, but doesn't give information on word origins, so choice (D) is incorrect. Literature text-books may give origin dates for selected words but the selection, if any, would be very small, so choice (E) does not describe a likely source.

50. **(D)** Any of the writer's original thoughts, including advanced theories, are the intellectual property of the writer and do not have to be documented. A bar chart is the graphical equivalent of a direct quote so it requires a reference, which means choice (A) is incorrect. A paraphrase must be documented as it is essentially another person's idea, so choice (B) is wrong. Choice (C) is wrong because no matter how ancient a quote is, it must still be referenced. An interview is considered a formal source, requiring documentation, just as a written source is, so choice (E) is incorrect.

51. **(A)** An index indicates pages where specific subjects can be found; each entry is usually no more than a few pages long. Illustrations would be listed in many separate places, according to their subjects, so choice (B) is wrong. Most indexes list hundreds of subjects and subtopics related to the book's main topic, so choice (C) would not be practical. An index gives little if any indication of a book's reading level, only a general idea of its content, making choice (D) incorrect. The author's reference sources are listed in the book's footnotes and/or bibliography, not in its index, so answer (E) is wrong.

52. **(D)** Illustrations in an article, or the lack of any, are not relevant to finding a magazine article. The name of a magazine is vitally important to locating it, so choice (A) is incorrect. The issue number of a magazine is also vital, as the correct number ensures that the correct issue will be found, so choice (B) is also incorrect. The page numbers are helpful in quickly locating the article; also, a magazine issue (and therefore an article) may be split between two microfiche cards, so (C) is not the best

choice. If an article is continued in another issue a reader may wish to read the next part of the article, so (E) is not a good choice.

53. **(C)** Only the author's last name should appear in a text citation unless more than one author has the same name, in which case the first initial is used. Choice (A) is incorrect as the full first name is not used. The last name, then first name style is used in bibliographies but not text citations, so choice (B) is wrong. The first initial isn't used if no other author has the same last name, making choice (D) incorrect. Choice (E) is wrong because first initials are necessary for identifying the author if more than one author has the same last name.

54. **(D)** According to MLA style the text citation is placed after the closing quotation mark. Choice (A) is incorrect as the name of the person quoted either precedes the quote, usually with text in between, or appears in the actual citation. The citation should appear outside the quotation marks surrounding the quote so placing it inside the quotes after the last word as choice (B) indicates would be wrong. Choice (C) is incorrect as the punctuation for a direct quote should be placed after the citation, not before it. A paragraph often continues after a direct quote, so placing the citation at the end of a paragraph as in choice (E) would be misleading.

55. **(D)** The date of publication of a book is never used in locating a book on a library shelf. (A) is an incorrect choice as the catalog call number is the most important item used to locate a book. The book title is useful if more than one book by the same author is on the same subject, and it is often the easiest information to see, so choice (B) is incorrect. The author's name is used for shelving books alphabetically if more than one book has the same call number (as is often the case), so choice (C) is incorrect. Choice (E) is incorrect as oversize books are often shelved in a separate section of the library.

Section II

56.   **(D)**   Answer (A) is wrong. Although he is described in wintery terms, he is never accused of harshness or indifference. His devotion to keeping them warm displays his love. Choices (B) and (E) are wrong because they stem from a misreading of the figurative expressions "wolf killer" and "hawk fighter," i.e., one who battles the wolf of hunger and the winds of winter. Choice (C) is wrong because it stems from a misreading of "Vulcan" to mean alien rather than the Roman god of fire and metalworking. Choice (D) is correct and is supported by lines 10–14.

57.   **(C)**   Choice (A) is wrong because it is based on a misreading of the word "study" to mean the acquisition of learning. Choice (B) is wrong because it interprets "study" to mean a room. Choice (C) is correct because "study" in this context means a description or portrait. Choice (D) is incorrect because the paragraph does not reveal anything about his experiences in life other than his actions to protect his family from the cold. Choice (E) is wrong because it arises from a misreading of the word "study" to mean "apply the mind," which it does not in this context.

58.   **(A)**   Choice (A) is correct because he will not relax or open up until the threat of winter disappears completely. Choices (B) and (C) are wrong because "unrazor" in this context does not have anything to do with shaving. Choice (D) is wrong because it implies that "unrazor" has a literal instead of a figurative meaning in this context, which it does not have. Choice (E) is wrong because it is unsupported by the paragraph. He does not scold, but instructs the family on how to keep the house warm.

59.   **(D)**   Choice (A) is wrong because the passage only implies their poverty and does not pass judgment on it. Choice (B) is wrong because nowhere in the passage is there any mention of the father's anger. Choice (C) is wrong because the passage makes no mention of being bored with school. They are bored with winter, not school. Choice (D) is the correct answer because the unyielding cold weather has tightened around them like a knot. Choice (E) is wrong because the passage states that the winter "stiffens," not their muscles.

60.   **(E)**   Choices (A) and (B) are wrong because they stem from a literal reading of the word "chafe" when it is meant metaphorically. Choice (C) is wrong. The days are slow because the activities are dull; not

vice versa. Choice (D) is wrong because although Maureen was new, more importantly, she was rich. Choice (E) is correct because the first two paragraphs include descriptions of winter life that rub them the same way day after day.

61. **(C)** Choice (A) is wrong because the "silver threads" do not represent the ice that clouds the windows. Choice (B) is wrong because they are caught up in a net of jealousy not poverty. Choice (C) is correct because Maureen's clothing upsets the girls most of all in that it makes them conscious of their own dull clothes. Choice (D) is incorrect because "silver threads" is too picturesque a phrase for something as mean as their plots against Maureen. Choice (E) is incorrect because there is no mention of garments that itch and chafe them.

62. **(C)** Choice (A) is wrong through the absence of "like" or "as." Choice (B) is wrong because dramatic irony involves a statement made by a character that ironically describes the character's fate later in the story. Choice (C) is correct because a knot is not splintered like a piece of wood but unraveled or slit with a knife. Choice (D) is wrong because the words do not contain or imitate the sound they make. Choice (E) is wrong because the knot is not imbued with human qualities.

63. **(E)** It may appear, on a quick and careless reading, that the poet is addressing wise men, good men, etc., but he is not. He is noting each of them in each of the stanzas as examples of others who do not go gently. He is addressing his father—as we find out in the last stanza. The confusion here may stem from Thomas' use of "And you ..." in the last stanza. Read the first and last stanza together without the middle stanzas and hear the difference.

64. **(C)** Thomas' message is perhaps unexpected. Acceptance of death is not the issue; rather, protest is encouraged. Maintaining the will to live is not enough; old people should rage against it in every possible way.

65. **(D)** Thomas honors seemingly contradictory notions: that death can be accepted and protested at the same time by "wise" minds. The reason why they do this ("because their words" ... etc.) is metaphorical and open to wider interpretation.

66. **(D)** While the image is used just before this and then later in the poem in conjunction with the passage of the sun across the sky, it is repeated

throughout as a metaphor for dying and death. It is interesting to note that, like "winter," "sunset" is usually taken to mean this, at least since Shakespeare's time ("In me thou sees the setting of the sun …"), yet Thomas uses the metaphor in a way that is both interesting and lyrically fresh.

67.   **(A)**   The repetition of "rage" serves many purposes, but its clearest purpose is to provide emotional intensity—and by an apt choice of a word which allows growing intensity with only slightly varied pronunciation of the heavy "r" which begins the word. Thomas' Welsh accent exaggerates this effect when recordings of his readings are reviewed.

68.   **(A)**   "Good men" are doers of deeds, although they cry "how bright / Their frail deeds might have danced." They too rage against death.

69.   **(E)**   In an artful dance of words, Thomas uses a contradictory phrase like "blinding sight," and the simile "Blind eyes could blaze like meteors." In addition, these dying men can be "gay" (meaning happy), and dying blind men can see (that) being blind is not as powerless a state as death. These are statements that seem to contradict common sense and yet are true—the definition of paradox.

70.   **(B)**   The first paragraph distinguishes between the "modernists" (here, the Romantics), who, Hazlitt says, are egotistical, and Milton and Shakespeare, who have a "deeper sense of human life."

71.   **(C)**   The entire paragraph deals with a discussion of the faults of the modernists in comparison to Shakespeare and Milton. The critic assumes an authoritative tone throughout. He provides no evidence in this first sentence, but rather an unconventional opinion.

72.   **(C)**   This line is from the middle of the first paragraph: "But to the men I speak of there is nothing interesting, nothing heroical, but themselves." This is the central point of an almost visceral dispute between Hazlitt and the "modern school," which he condemns as "egotism" at the end of his first sentence.

73.   **(B)**   According to the critic, Shakespeare and Milton were not determined "to get rid of" nature and art, introducing as much of their own personal views into their art as did the "modern school." Instead, they have a "deeper," and, by inference, "wider" understanding of human life—a greater tolerance in general.

74. **(B)** The key to tragedy, especially Classical Tragedy (the principles of which Shakespeare followed closely), is that a being of great or lofty station is brought down to a much lower level. A lesser personage—an "average" person—would not be a candidate for tragedy because he or she has less distance to fall. The modernists, says Hazlitt, are indifferent to the various distances different stations in life entail, and, therefore, they would not be interested in Classical Tragedy.

75. **(D)** The critic brings a sense of closure (bringing to an end) to the ideas in his first paragraph by referencing and magnifying the scorn he has for the modernists in his statement that "the world repays their indifference with scorn"—in effect, stating, "It is not just myself who feels this way, but everybody."

76. **(B)** The second paragraph, while it does employ some metaphor and simile (i.e., "like the lightning's") is characterized by the use of action verbs: glances, unites, hurrying, takes, brings, etc.

77. **(A)** Each of the sentences gives examples of the contention in the first sentence that "Shakespeare's imagination is of the same plastic kind …." Thus, the fact that his imagination "unites … puts a girdle …takes the widest possible range" etc., all stand in support of the "plastic" contention. Contrary to (E), this paragraph is also interesting structurally because each sentence following the first can stand independently as an example.

78. **(C)** Pope has said that poetry is "what oft was thought, but ne'er so well expressed." Hazlitt here shows his admiration for Shakespeare by using the Bard's own words instead of his own. There are no images here from other critics; he recognizes that Shakespeare has accomplished complex tasks. "Celerity" is not a word of importance (like "celebrity"), but rather a word that describes quickness.

79. **(D)** Second-rate is the best choice because it is synonymous with mediocre. (A), (B), (C), and (E) are incorrect because they are not synonymous with the word.

80. **(C)** "Supposed" is the correct answer. (A), (B), (D), and (E) are wrong because they are not synonymous with "postulated."

81. **(A)** (A) is the best choice. (B), (C), (D), and (E) do not have very neutral meanings.

82. **(C)** Answer choice (C) gives a clearer version of the sentence. (A) and (B) are incorrect because they provide a different meaning than the one intended. (D) and (E) are incorrect because they are unclear.

83. **(D)** "Dominate" has negative connotations, so it is the best choice. (A), (B), (C), and (E) are incorrect because they do not present the most emphatically negative picture.

84. **(A)** "Hindered" is synonymous with "impeded." (B), (C), (D), and (E) are incorrect because they are not close enough in meaning to "impeded."

85. **(B)** Choice (B) is the correct answer. (A), (C), (D), and (E) are not clear enough in meaning.

86. **(A)** Answer choice (A) is correct because it is synonymous with "stoic." (B), (C), (D), and (E) do not capture the meaning of the under-lined word.

87. **(D)** Choice (D) is the correct answer. (A), (B), (C), and (E) do not have the same meaning as "often pillage."

88. **(D)** "Procrastinated" is the most negative of the choices, so it is the correct answer. (A), (B), (C), and (E) do not present a negative picture.

89. **(E)** Answer choice (E) is correct. (A), (B), (C), and (D) do not clear up the ambiguity.

90. **(A)** Justify is synonymous with "legitimate," so (A) is correct. (B), (C), (D), and (E) are not synonymous with "legitimate."

91. **(C)** "Absorption" is synonymous with "osmosis," so (C) is correct. (A), (B), (D), and (E) do not have the same meaning as "osmosis."

92. **(D)** Answer choice (D) is correct. (A), (B), (C), and (E) do not have negative connotations.

93.   **(D)**   Choice (D) is the correct answer. (A), (B), (C), and (E) are unclear sentences.

94.   **(D)**   Answer choice (D) is correct. (A), (B), (C), and (E) are not synonymous with "intangible."

95.   **(E)**   (E) is the correct choice since the statement recalls the 1920s with fondness. (A), (B), (C), and (D) are not nostalgic in tone.

96.   **(B)**   Answer choice (B) conveys foreboding since it warns of the dangers of polluting rivers and streams. (A), (C), (D), and (E) do not convey a sense of warning, so they are incorrect.

97.   **(A)**   Answer choice (A) has a decidedly sarcastic tone. Using a term from the Declaration of Independence, "self-evident," it states the negatives upon which our country was built. (B), (C), (D), and (E) are not at all sarcastic.

98.   **(D)**   A cliché is a term or phrase that is over-used. None of the performers are described by clichés, so (D) is the correct answer. Metaphor, allusion, hyperbole, and simile are all used in the excerpt.

99.   **(C)**   Answer choice (C) is correct because the bigtop is described as having a property of a person. (A) is incorrect because there is no irony in the description, neither is there alliteration, so (B) is wrong. (D) and (E) are also incorrect because the description is neither a hyperbole nor a metaphor.

100.   **(A)**   Answer choice (A) is the correct meaning of cornucopia. (B), (C), (D), and (E) are not synonymous with the word.

PRACTICE
TEST 2

CLEP FRESHMAN COLLEGE COMPOSITION
Test 2

(Answer sheets appear in the back of this book.)

Section I

TIME: 45 Minutes
55 Questions

DIRECTIONS: Each of the following sentences may contain an error in diction, usage, idiom, or grammar. Some sentences are correct. Some sentences contain one error. No sentence contains more than one error.

If there is an error, it will appear in one of the underlined portions labeled A, B, C, or D. If there is no error, choose the portion labeled E. If there is an error, select the letter of the portion that must be changed in order to correct the sentence.

EXAMPLE:

He drove <u>slowly</u> and <u>cautiously</u> in order to <u>hopefully</u> avoid having an
            A   **B**   **C**
<u>accident</u>. <u>No error</u>.   Ⓐ Ⓑ ● Ⓓ Ⓔ
       D   **E**

---

1.   <u>An astute and powerful</u> woman, Frances Nadel <u>was</u> a beauty contest
                    A   **B**
       winner before she <u>became</u> president of the company <u>upon the death</u>
                            C   **D**
       of her husband. <u>No error</u>.
                              E

2. Representative Wilson <u>pointed out</u>, however, that the legislature
   A
   <u>had not finalized</u> the state budget and salary increases <u>had depended</u>
   B   **C**
   on decisions <u>to be made</u> in a special session. <u>No error</u>.
   D   **E**

3. Now the <u>city</u> librarian, doing more than checking out books, must
   A
   help <u>to plan</u> puppet shows and movies for children, garage sales for
   B
   <u>used</u> books, and <u>arranging for</u> guest lecturers and exhibits for adults.
   C   **D**
   <u>No error</u>.
   E

4. <u>Confronted with</u> a choice of either <u>cleaning up</u> his room or <u>cleaning</u>
   A   **B**   **C**
   <u>out</u> the garage, the teenager became very <u>aggravated</u> with his par-
   C   **D**
   ents. <u>No error</u>.
         E

5. My brother and <u>I</u> dressed as <u>quickly</u> as we could, but we missed the
                  A   **B**
   school bus, <u>which</u> made <u>us</u> late for class today. <u>No error</u>.
               C   **D**   **E**

6. Even a movement <u>so delicate</u> as a <u>fly's walking</u> triggers the Venus
                   A   **B**
   flytrap <u>to grow</u> extra cells on the outside of <u>its</u> hinge, immediately
           C   **D**
   closing the petals of the trap. <u>No error</u>.
                                   E

7. Unless an athlete is physically fit, there is no sense in <u>him</u> sacrific-
                                                            A
   ing <u>himself</u> for victory in <u>any one game</u> <u>and, therefore, facing</u> a
       B   **C**   **D**
   lifetime injury. <u>No error</u>.
                    E

8. <u>Insensible of</u> the pain from his burn, Father was <u>more concerned</u>
     A   **B**

with cooling off the overheated car and <u>assessing any</u> <u>damage to</u> the
                                     C   **D**

engine. <u>No error</u>.
      E

9. <u>Parasitic</u> plants, attaching <u>themselves</u> to other plants and <u>drawing</u>
     A   **B**   **C**

<u>nourishment</u> from them, thereby <u>sapping</u> the strength of the host
     C   **D**

plant, usually killing it. <u>No error</u>.
                         E

10. The Alaskan pipeline <u>stretches from</u> Prudhoe Bay <u>through</u> three
                           A   **B**

mountain ranges and <u>over</u> 800 rivers to Valdez, the northernmost
                       C

ice-free <u>port in</u> the United States. <u>No error</u>.
       D   **E**

DIRECTIONS: In each of the following sentences, some portion of the sentence is underlined. Under each sentence are five choices. The first choice has the same wording as the original. The other four choices are reworded. Sometimes the first choice containing the original wording is the best; sometimes one of the other choices is the best. Choose the letter of the best choice. Your choice should produce a sentence which is not ambiguous or awkward and which is correct, clear, and precise.

This is a test of correct and effective English expression. Keep in mind the standards of English usage, punctuation, grammar, word choice, and construction.

EXAMPLE:

When you listen to opera, <u>a person may not appreciate it.</u>

(A) a person may not appreciate it.

(B) it may not be appreciated by a person.

(C) which may not be appreciated by one.

(D) you may not appreciate it.

(E) appreciating it may be a problem for you. Ⓐ Ⓑ Ⓒ ● Ⓔ

11. The new secretary proved herself <u>to be not only capable and efficient but also a woman who was adept</u> at working under pressure and handling irate customers.

    (A) to be not only capable and efficient but also a woman who was adept

    (B) not only to be capable or efficient but also a woman who was adept

    (C) not only to be capable and efficient but also a woman who was adept

    (D) to be not only capable and efficient but also adept

    (E) to be not only capable and efficient but also an adept woman

12. <u>Hunting, if properly managed and carefully controlled</u>, can cull excess animals, thereby producing a healthier population of wild game.

    (A) Hunting, if properly managed and carefully controlled

    (B) Managing it wisely, carefully controlled hunting

    (C) Managed properly hunting that is carefully controlled

    (D) Properly and wisely controlled, careful hunting

    (E) If properly managed, hunting, carefully controlled

13. In spite of my reservations, <u>I agreed on the next day to help her put up new wallpaper</u>.

    (A) I agreed on the next day to help her put up new wallpaper.

    (B) I agreed on the next day to help put up her new wallpaper.

    (C) I agreed to help her put up new wallpaper on the next day.

    (D) I, on the next day, agreed to help her put up new wallpaper.

    (E) I agreed to, on the next day, help her put up new wallpaper.

14. Getting to know a person's parents <u>will often provide an insight to</u> his personality and behavior.

    (A) will often provide an insight to

    (B) will often provide an insight into

(C)   will often provide an insight for

(D)   will provide often an insight for

(E)   often will provide an insight with

15.   Upon leaving the nursery, Mr. Greene, together with his wife, <u>put</u> <u>the plants in the trunk of the car they had just bought</u>.

(A)   put the plants in the trunk of the car they had just bought.

(B)   put in the plants to the trunk of the car they had just bought.

(C)   put into the trunk of the car they had just bought the plants.

(D)   put the plants they had just bought in the trunk of the car.

(E)   put the plants into the trunk of the car.

16.   The way tensions are increasing in the Middle East, some experts <u>are afraid we may end up with a nuclear war</u>.

(A)   are afraid we may end up with a nuclear war.

(B)   being afraid we may end up with a nuclear war.

(C)   afraid that a nuclear war may end up over there.

(D)   are afraid a nuclear war may end there.

(E)   are afraid a nuclear war may occur.

17.   <u>Whether Leif Erickson was the first to discover America or not</u> is still a debatable issue, but there is general agreement that there probably were a number of "discoveries" through the years.

(A)   Whether Leif Erickson was the first to discover America or not

(B)   That Leif Erickson was the first to discover America

(C)   That Leif Erickson may have been the first to have discovered America

(D)   Whether Leif Erickson is the first to discover America or he is not

(E)   Whether or not Leif Erickson was or was not the first discoverer of America

18.   <u>People who charge too much are likely to develop</u> a bad credit rating.

(A)   People who charge too much are likely to develop

(B)   People's charging too much are likely to develop

(C)   When people charge too much, likely to develop

(D)   That people charge too much is likely to develop

(E)   Charging too much is likely to develop for people

19.   The Museum of Natural Science has a special exhibit of gems and minerals, <u>and the fifth graders went to see it on a field trip</u>.

(A)   and the fifth graders went to see it on a field trip.

(B)   and seeing it were the fifth graders on a field trip.

(C)   when the fifth graders took a field trip to see it.

(D)   which the fifth graders took a field trip to see.

(E)   where the fifth graders took their field trip to see it.

20.   <u>When the case is decided, he plans appealing</u> if the verdict is unfavorable.

(A)   When the case is decided, he plans appealing

(B)   When deciding the case, he plans appealing

(C)   After the case is decided, he is appealing

(D)   After deciding the case, he is planning to appeal

(E)   When the case is decided, he plans to appeal

DIRECTIONS: The following passages are considered early draft efforts of a student. Some sentences need to be rewritten to make the ideas clearer and more precise.

Read each passage carefully and answer the questions that follow. Some of the questions are about particular sentences or parts of sentences and ask you to make decisions about sentence structure, diction, and usage. Some of the questions refer to the entire essay or parts of the essay and ask you to make decisions about organization, development, appropriateness of language, audience, and logic. Choose the answer that most effectively makes the intended meaning clear and follows the requirements of standard written English. After you have chosen your answer, fill in the corresponding oval on your answer sheet.

EXAMPLE:

(1) On the one hand, I think television is bad, But it also does some good things for all of us. (2) For instance, my little sister thought she wanted to be a policemen until she saw police shows on television.

Which of the following is the best revision of the underlined portion of sentence 1 below?

On the one hand, I think television <u>is bad, But it also</u> does some good things for all of us.

(A)   is bad; But it also

(B)   is bad. but is also

(C)   is bad, and it also

(D)   is bad, but it also

(E)   is bad because it also   Ⓐ Ⓑ Ⓒ ● Ⓔ

QUESTIONS 21–26 are based on the following passage.

(1) In 1840 Dickens came up with the idea of using a raven as a character in his new novel, *Barnaby Rudge*. (2) Soon, the word got out among his friends and neighbors that the famous author was interested in ravens and wanted to know more about them. (3) When someone gave a raven as a pet, he was delighted. (4) The raven was named Grip by Dickens' children and became a successful member of the family. (5) Grip

began to get his way around the household, and if he wanted something, he took it, and Grip would bite the children's ankles when he felt displeased. (6) The raven in *Barnaby Rudge* is depicted as a trickster who slept "on horseback" in the stable and "has been known, by the mere superiority of his genius, to walk off unmolested with the dog's dinner." (7) So we get an idea of what life with Grip was like.

(8) Poe, however, was dissatisfied. (9) This was a comical presentation of the raven. (10) Poe felt that the large black bird should have a more prophetic use. (11) So, about a year after *Barnaby Rudge* was published, Poe began work on his poem, "The Raven." (12) Any schoolchild can quote the famous line, "Quoth the Raven, 'Nevermore,'" but almost no one knows about Grip. (13) What happened to Grip? (14) Well, when he died, the Dickens family had become so attached to him that they had him stuffed and displayed him in the parlor.

21. Which of the following is the best revision of the underlined portion of sentence 3 below?

When <u>someone gave a raven as a pet, he was delighted</u>.

(A) giving someone a raven as a pet, he was delighted.

(B) someone gave Dickens a raven for a pet, the author was delighted.

(C) someone delightedly gave a raven for a pet to Dickens.

(D) someone gave Dickens a raven as a pet, the result was that the author was delighted with the gift.

(E) receiving a raven as a pet, Dickens was delighted.

22. Which of the following is the best revision of the underlined portion of sentence 5 below?

Grip began to get his way around the household, and <u>if he wanted something, he took it, and Grip would bite the children's ankles when he felt displeased</u>.

(A) if he wanted something, he took it; if he felt displeased, he bit the children's ankles.

(B) if wanting something, he would take, and if unhappy, he would bite.

(C) when he wanted something, he would take it; being displeased, he would bite the children's ankles.

(D) when taking something that he wanted, he would bite the children's ankles.

(E) if displeased and if wanting something, Grip would bite the children's ankles and he would take it.

23. In the context of the sentences preceding and following sentence 7, which of the following is the best revision of sentence 7?

   (A) So, you can get an idea of what life with Grip was like.

   (B) Therefore, the challenges of living with Grip must have been numerous and varied.

   (C) So, an idea of the life with Grip can be gotten.

   (D) So, life with Grip must have been entertaining.

   (E) These are some examples I have given of what life with Grip was like.

24. Which of the following is the best way to combine sentences 8, 9, and 10?

   (A) Having dissatisfaction with the comical presentation of the big black bird, Poe felt it should be more prophetic.

   (B) As a result of dissatisfaction, Poe felt the big black bird should be presented more prophetically than comically.

   (C) However, Poe felt the comical presentation was not as good as the prophetic one.

   (D) Poe, however, dissatisfied with the comical presentation of the big black bird, felt a more prophetic use would be better.

   (E) Poe, however, was dissatisfied with this comical presentation and felt that the large black bird should have a more prophetic use.

25. In relation to the passage as a whole, which of the following best describes the writer's intention in the first paragraph?

   (A) To provide background information

   (B) To provide a concrete example of a humorous episode

   (C) To arouse sympathy in the reader

(D) To evaluate the effectiveness of the treatment of the subject

(E) To contrast with treatment of the subject in the second paragraph

26. Which of the following is the best revision of the underlined portion of sentence 4 below?

The raven was named Grip <u>by Dickens' children and became a successful member of the family</u>.

(A) by the children and it became a successful member of his family.

(B) by Dickens' children and was becoming a successful member of his family.

(C) by Dickens' children and became a successful member of the family.

(D) , Dickens' children named him that, and he became a successful member of the family.

(E) by Dickens' children and the raven also became a successful member of his family.

QUESTIONS 27–32 are based on the following passage.

(1) Medieval literature and art, throughout the predominance of religious themes, was greatly varied. (2) In literature, for example, the chivalric tradition embodied in such works as the Arthurian legends, as well as the Anglo-Saxon epic *Beowulf* and the French epic *Song of Roland,* showed the richness of themes. (3) Originating in France during the mid-1100s, the Gothic style spread to other parts of Europe. (4) However, it was in Gothic architecture that the Medieval religious fervor best exhibited itself. (5) Gothic cathedrals were the creation of a community, many artisans and craftsman working over many generations. (6) Most of the populace could not read or write, so donating funds or working on the building and its furnishings become a form of religious devotion as well as a means of impressing neighboring areas and attracting tourism. (7) The first Gothic structures were parts of an abbey and a cathedral. (8) Later during the twelfth and thirteenth centuries Gothic architecture reached its peak in the great cathedrals of Notre Dame in Paris, Westminster Abbey in England, and Cologne Cathedral in Germany.

(9) Gothic architecture strives to emphasize height and light. (10) Characteristic internal structures are the ribbed vault and pointed arches. (11) Thick stone walls give way to stained glass windows depicting religious scenes, and the masonry is embellished with delicate tracery. (12) Outside, slender beams called "flying buttresses" provide support for the height of the building. (13) Great spires complete the illusion of rising to the sky.

27. Which of the following would most appropriately replace "throughout" in sentence 1?

   (A) beyond   (D) unless

   (B) until   (E) under

   (C) despite

28. Which of the following should be plural rather than singular?

   (A) "art" in sentence 1

   (B) "architecture" in sentence 4

   (C) "craftsman" in sentence 5

   (D) "tracery" in sentence 11

   (E) "populace" in sentence 6

29. Which of the following would improve and clarify the structure of the first paragraph?

   (A) Eliminate sentence 5.

   (B) Place sentence 3 after sentence 7.

   (C) Reverse the order of sentences 2 and 4.

   (D) Place the first sentence at the end.

   (E) No change is necessary.

30. Which of the following words is used incorrectly in sentence 6?

   (A) populace   (D) devotion

   (B) donating   (E) tourism

   (C) become

31. How would the following underlined portion of sentence 8 be better clarified by punctuation?

Later during the twelfth and thirteenth centuries Gothic architecture reached its peak in the great cathedrals of Notre Dame in Paris, Westminster Abbey in England, and Cologne Cathedral in Germany.

(A) Later during the twelfth and thirteenth centuries, Gothic architecture reached its peak, in the great cathedrals

(B) Later, during the twelfth and thirteenth centuries: Gothic architecture reached its peak in the great cathedrals

(C) Later, during the twelfth, and thirteenth centuries, Gothic architecture reached its peak, in the great cathedrals

(D) Later, during the twelfth and thirteenth centuries, Gothic architecture reached its peak in the great cathedrals

(E) None of these.

32. Which of the following would best fit between sentences 10 and 11?

(A) Often, you can find gargoyles, grotesque demonic-looking creatures carved on the outside of the building.

(B) Particularly impressive to me are the carvings of realistic animals and plants on the pulpits.

(C) Tall, thin columns reach to the ceiling and help to support the roof.

(D) These buildings were designed to impress everyone who saw them with the glory of God.

(E) In the twelfth century, the Gothic style had reached its peak.

QUESTIONS 33–38 are based on the following passage.

(1) Actually, the term "Native Americans" is incorrect. (2) Indians migrated to this continent from other areas, just earlier then Europeans did. (3) The ancestors of the Anasazi—Indians of the four-state area of Colorado, New Mexico, Utah, and Arizona—probably crossed from Asia into Alaska. (4) About 25,000 years ago while the continental land bridge still existed. (5) This land bridge arched across the Bering Strait in the last Ice Age. (6) About A.D. 500 the ancestors of the Anasazi moved onto the

Mesa Verde a high plateau in the desert country of Colorado. (7) The Wetherills, five brothers who ranched the area, is generally given credit for the first exploration of the ruins in the 1870s and 1880s. (8) There were some 50,000 Anasazi thriving in the four-corners area by the 1200s. (9) At their zenith A.D. 700 to 1300, the Anasazi had established widespread communities and built thousands of sophisticated structures—cliff dwellings, pueblos, and kivas. (10) They even engaged in trade with Indians in surrounding regions by exporting pottery and other goods.

33.   Which of the following best corrects the grammatical error in sentence 7?

   (A)   The Wetherills, a group of five brothers who ranched in the area, is generally given credit for the first exploration of the ruins in the 1870s and 1880s.

   (B)   The Wetherills, five brothers who ranched in the area, are generally given credit for the first exploration of the ruins in the 1870s and 1880s.

   (C)   The Wetherills are generally given credit for the first exploration of the ruins in the 1870s and 1880s, five brothers who ranched in the area.

   (D)   The Wetherills, generally given credit for the first exploration of the area, is five brothers who ranched in the area.

   (E)   Best as it is.

34.   Which of the following sentences would best fit between sentences 9 and 10 of the passage?

   (A)   Artifacts recovered from the area suggest that the Anasazi were artistic, religious, agricultural, classless, and peaceful.

   (B)   By 12,000 to 10,000 B.C., some Indians had established their unique cultures in the southwest.

   (C)   The Navaho called their ancestors the Anasazi, the Ancient Ones.

   (D)   I think it is unfortunate that such a unique and innovative culture should have disappeared from the country.

   (E)   Before Columbus reached the New World, the Anasazi had virtually disappeared.

35. Which of the following is an incomplete sentence?

    (A) 4
    (B) 5
    (C) 6

    (D) 7
    (E) 10

36. Which of the following best corrects the underlined portion of sentence 9?

    <u>At their zenith A.D. 700 to 1300</u>, the Anasazi had established widespread communities and built thousands of sophisticated structures—cliff dwellings, pueblos, and kivas.

    (A) At their zenith which was from A.D. 700 to 1300

    (B) At their zenith B.C. 700 to 1300

    (C) At their zenith, from A.D. 700 to 1300,

    (D) At their zenith, being A.D. 700 to 1300,

    (E) At their zenith, of A.D. 700 to 1300,

37. Which of the following would be the best way to punctuate sentence 6?

    (A) About A.D. 500, the ancestors of the Anasazi moved onto the Mesa Verde a high plateau, in the desert country of Colorado.

    (B) About A.D. 500 the ancestors of the Anasazi moved, onto the Mesa Verde: a high plateau in the desert country of Colorado.

    (C) About A.D. 500 the ancestors of the Anasazi moved onto the Mesa Verde: a high plateau, in the desert country of Colorado.

    (D) About A.D. 500, the ancestors of the Anasazi moved onto the Mesa Verde, a high plateau in the desert country of Colorado.

    (E) Best as it is.

38. Which of the following sentences contains a spelling/grammatical error?

    (A) 1
    (B) 2
    (C) 3

    (D) 10
    (E) 5

QUESTIONS 39–44 are based on the following passage.

(1) A growing number of businesses are providing day care facilities for the children of their employees. (2) Some companies charge a standard fee, but most provide the day care free or at a nominal cost. (3) These care programs provide services that continue through the early teens of the children. (4) If they should help with day care at all is what many companies are trying to decide. (5) In the event parents need to work overtime, centers are even open on weekends, and some companies <u>showing</u> special initiative in building company loyalty of each employee by making arrangements for special field trips to zoos and museums. (6) Is this kind of care really necessary? (7) Should businesses really be in the business of day care.

(8) Experts in the field cite many advantages for this system. (9) Therefore, loyalty to the company is built, so morale climbs. (10) Studies show that when a company helps its employees blend parent and worker roles, absenteeism and tardiness drop. (11) In addition, workers feel the company has taken more of a personal interest in them. (12) Most companies also provide various health care programs for their employees. (13) Turnover becomes a much less significant factor for managers. (14) Human resource managers also estimate that every $1 spent on these programs returns $2 or more in increased productivity.

39. Which of the following best improves the underlined portion of sentence 3?

    These care programs provide services that <u>continue through the early teens of the children.</u>

    (A) continue, through the early teens, of the children.

    (B) continue through the children and their early teens.

    (C) continue through the children's early teens.

    (D) continue on through the early teens of the children.

    (E) Best as it is.

40. Which of the following would be a better way to structure sentence 4?

    (A) What many companies are trying to decide is if they should help with day care at all.

    (B) Unsure if they should help with day care at all, many companies are trying to decide.

(C) Many companies, unsure if they should help with day care at all, are trying to decide.

(D) Many companies are trying to decide if they should help with day care at all.

(E) Many companies are trying to help with day care at all.

41. Which of the following would be an acceptable substitution for the underlined word in sentence 5?

(A) show

(B) have been showing

(C) have shown

(D) (A) and (B).

(E) (A), (B), and (C).

42. Which of the following contains a punctuation error?

(A) Sentence 1

(B) Sentence 3

(C) Sentence 7

(D) Sentence 10

(E) None of these.

43. Which of the following sentences is irrelevant in the second paragraph and should be eliminated?

(A) 8

(B) 10

(C) 12

(D) 14

(E) None of these.

44. Which of the following best improves the sequence of ideas in the second paragraph?

(A) Reverse the order of sentences 8 and 9.

(B) Place sentence 13 before sentence 9.

(C) Delete sentence 11.

(D) Place sentence 9 after sentence 11

(E) Delete sentence 8.

DIRECTIONS: For each question, find the correct answer and fill in the appropriate oval on the answer sheet.

---

45. The fastest way to find the meaning of an unusual engineering term is to look in

    (A) an encyclopedia article on engineering.

    (B) an unabridged dictionary.

    (C) an engineering dictionary.

    (D) an engineering textbook.

    (E) a protessional engineering journal.

46. ```
    Boswell, James, 1740-1795
    The life of Samuel Johnson; abridged, with an
     introduction by Bergen Evans
    New York: Modern Library [1952]
    xv, [1], 559p, 19cm
    Other Entries: Johnson, Samuel, 1709-1784
     Biography
                     Evans, Bergen, 1904-
    ```

    The above book could be found in the library with the

    (A) history books, under Boswell.

    (B) history books, under Johnson.

    (C) biographies, under Boswell.

    (D) biographies, under Johnson.

    (E) literature, under Boswell.

47. ```
    Directing his own show. (Irvine Consulting
    Inc.) (Company Profile) by Dasha Jones il v23
    Black Enterprise Oct '92 p35(1)
    ```

    In the periodical index entry above, "v23" indicates

    (A) the page with the illustration.

    (B) the location of the microfiche card containing the article.

(C) the first page of the article.

(D) the computer code number for the magazine.

(E) the volume number of the magazine.

48. The most comprehensive source to check for the names of African poets is

(A) an anthology of world literature.

(B) a magazine article on contemporary African poets.

(C) an encyclopedia article on African literature.

(D) a world almanac containing names of poetry prize winners.

(E) a literary magazine published in Africa.

49. Which word is ignored in alphabetizing a library catalog system?

(A) An   (D) If

(B) Am   (E) Of

(C) I

50. Publications containing details of a town's political scandal in the 1920s will most likely be found in the

(A) encyclopedia.

(B) *The Reader's Guide to Periodical Literature*.

(C) town hall archives.

(D) Chamber of Commerce brochure display.

(E) state courthouse.

51. Which of the following is not an appropriate main resource for a college research paper?

(A) A television documentary

(B) The *Encyclopedia Americana*

(C) An interview with a local historian

(D) A book by a professor at that college

(E) The *Christian Science Monitor*

52. Which source is most likely to be biased in favor of herbal medicines?

    (A) A medical journal

    (B) A consumers' health guide

    (C) A natural-health guidebook

    (D) An allergy-remedy book

    (E) A city newspaper article

53. While researching a paper, what is the most efficient way to record research sources?

    (A) Listing the source of information on the back of each index card containing information on that source

    (B) Listing the source on the back of the first index card to contain information on that source

    (C) Listing the sources on a single piece of paper

    (D) Writing each source on a separate index card

    (E) Returning to the library at the end of research to match each card to its source

54. A paraphrase is

    (A) a quote with a couple of words changed.

    (B) a quote with some words or a couple of phrases changed.

    (C) a restatement describing the same idea as the quote but using different words and phrasing.

    (D) a statement that differs slightly from the opinion in the source.

    (E) a summary of a long passage.

55. A town's local newspaper is the most comprehensive primary source for a research paper when the topic

    (A) has local as well as national significance.

    (B) is a recent occurrence.

    (C) had its origin locally.

    (D) developed and concluded locally.

    (E) is well known to some local people.

Section II

TIME: 45 Minutes
          45 Questions

DIRECTIONS: The following questions test your ability to recognize the content, form, and style of a passage as well as the writer's purpose. After reading each passage or poem, choose the best answer to each question and fill in the corresponding oval on the answer sheet.

QUESTIONS 56–60 are based on the following passage.

It was there that, several years ago, I saw him for the first time; and the sight pulled me up sharp. Even then he was the most striking figure in Starkfield, though he was but the ruin of a man. It was not so much his great height
5   that marked him, for the "natives" were easily singled out by their lank longitude from the stockier foreign breed: it was the careless powerful look he had, in spite of a lameness checking each step like the jerk of a chain. There was something bleak and unapproachable in his face, and he
10 was so stiffened and grizzled that I took him for an old man and was surprised to hear that he was not more than fifty-two. I had this from Harmon Gow, who had driven the stage from Bettsbridge to Starkfield in pre-trolley days and knew the chronicle of all the families on his line.

15 Harmon drew a slab of tobacco from his pocket, cut off a wedge and pressed it into the leather pouch of his cheek. "Guess he's been in Starkfield too many winters. Most of the smart ones get away."

Though Harmon Gow developed the tale as far as his
20 mental and moral reach permitted there were perceptible gaps between his facts, and I had the sense that the deeper meaning of the story was in the gaps. But one phrase stuck in my memory and served as the nucleus about which I grouped my subsequent inferences: "Guess he's been in
25 Starkfield too many winters."

Before my own time there was up I had learned to know what that meant. Yet I had come in the degenerate day of trolley, bicycle and rural delivery, when communi-

cation was easy between the scattered mountain villages,
30 and the bigger towns in the valleys, such as Bettsbridge and
Shadd's Falls, had libraries, theatres and Y. M. C. A. halls
to which the youth of the hills could descend for recreation.
But when winter shut down on Starkfield, and the village
lay under a sheet of snow perpetually renewed from the
35 pale skies, I began to see what life there—or rather its
negation—must have been in Ethan Frome's young man-
hood.

From Ethan Frome, *by Edith Wharton*

56. The phrase "checking each step like the jerk of a chain" (line 8) is
best interpreted to mean that Ethan

   (A) had served time on a chain gang.

   (B) moved about with uncertainty and timidity.

   (C) dragged along the dead weight of his injured leg.

   (D) was obviously one of the "stockier" breed.

   (E) bore the characteristics of a corrupt and criminal past.

57. The phrase "singled out by their lank longitude" (lines 5–6) evokes
the

   (A) tall stature of the town "natives."

   (B) sailing history of the townfolk.

   (C) prejudice "natives" had for their own kind.

   (D) animosity shown toward the "natives" by the foreigners in town.

   (E) "natives'" superiority over the foreign breed.

58. In context, which of the following supports Harmon Gow's observation "Guess he's been in Starkfield too many winters" (line 17)?

   (A) Ethan's being the town's most striking figure

   (B) Ethan's great height

   (C) Ethan's careless, powerful look

   (D) Ethan's bleak and unapproachable face

   (E) Ethan's awareness of Gow's opinion of him

59. In context, the phrase "degenerate day" (lines 27–28) is best interpreted to mean

(A) a time when winters were more severe.

(B) a time of inferior trolley and mail service.

(C) an earlier time of restricted communication between villages.

(D) the time when winter clamped down on the village.

(E) a time of modern worldly influence on the village.

60. The tone of the first paragraph is best described as

(A) cynical glee.   (D) feigned sympathy.

(B) sympathetic curiosity.   (E) worshipful awe.

(C) mild sarcasm.

QUESTIONS 61–67 are based on the following poem.

> Unnumbered suppliants crowd Preferment's gate,
> Athirst for wealth, and burning to be great;
> Delusive Fortune hears the incessant call,
> They mount, they shine, evaporate, and fall.
> 5 On every stage the foes of peace attend,
> Hate dogs their flight, and Insult mocks their end.
> Love ends with hope, the sinking statesman's door
> Pours in the morning worshiper no more;
> For growing names the weekly scribbler lies,
> 10 To growing wealth the dedicator flies;
> From every room descends the painted face,
> That hung the bright palladium of the place;
> And smoked in kitchens, or in auctions sold,
> To better features yields the frame of gold;
> 15 For now no more we trace in every line
> Heroic worth, benevolence divine:
> The form distorted justifies the fall,
> And Detestation rids the indignant wall.
> But will not Britain hear the last appeal,
> 20 Sign her foes' doom, or guard her favorites' zeal?
> Through Freedom's sons no more remonstrance rings,
> Degrading nobles and controlling kings;

Our supple tribes repress their patriot throats,
And ask no questions but the price of votes,
25   With weekly libels and septennial ale.
Their wish is full to riot and to rail.

From "The Vanity of Human Wishes," by Samuel Johnson

61.   In line 1–4, the desire for fame is seen chiefly as

   (A)   everyone's birthright.

   (B)   the right of a select few.

   (C)   motivated by an urge to improve society.

   (D)   a disappearing phenomenon.

   (E)   a universal aspiration.

62.   In line 5, the phrase "the foes of peace" refers to

   (A)   the enemies of the realm.

   (B)   "Delusive Fortune."

   (C)   poverty, envy, and disease.

   (D)   plots to overthrow the government.

   (E)   worries that plague celebrities.

63.   According to the speaker, "The morning worshiper" (line 8), "the weekly scribbler" (line 9), and "the dedicator" (line 10) lack all of the following EXCEPT

   (A)   compassion.   (D)   insensitivity.

   (B)   piety.   (E)   honor.

   (C)   loyalty.

64.   The main point about those described in lines 5–18 is that

   (A)   they are abandoned when fortune frowns on them.

   (B)   they become deeply religious because of their success.

   (C)   they are remembered long after they are gone.

   (D)   they form friendships that last a lifetime.

   (E)   they are sorely missed when gone.

65. In lines 19–26, the speaker regards the integrity of his countrymen as

    (A) politically unblemished.

    (B) sound for their opposition to abuses by the nobility.

    (C) evident in their condemnation of their country's foes.

    (D) best expressed in their raillery for justice.

    (E) non-existent or up for sale.

66. According to the speaker, the common people are

    (A) innocent of wrongdoing.

    (B) simply bystanders to history.

    (C) victims of their own greed.

    (D) guardians of freedom.

    (E) the moral backbone of the country.

67. This excerpt is written in which of the following?

    (A) Ballad meter   (D) Terza rima

    (B) Iambic dimeter   (E) Heroic couplets

    (C) Blank verse

QUESTIONS 68–78 are based on the following passage.

       She had suffered badly during the period of poverty.
    Nothing, however, could shake the curious, sullen, animal
    pride that dominated each member of the family. Now, for
    Mabel, the end had come. Still she would not cast about
5   her. She would follow her own way just the same. She
    would always hold the keys of her own situation. Mind-
    less and persistent, she endured from day to day. Why
    should she think? Why should she answer anybody? It
    was enough that this was the end, and there was no way
10 out. She need not pass any more darkly along the main
    street of the small town, avoiding every eye. She need not
    demean herself any more, going into the shops and buying
    the cheapest food. This was at an end. She thought of

15 nobody, not even of herself. Mindless and persistent, she seemed in a sort of ecstasy to be coming nearer to her fulfillment, her own glorification, approaching her dead mother, who was glorified.

In the afternoon, she took a little bag, with shears and sponge and a small scrubbing-brush, and went out. It was a
20 gray, wintry day, with saddened dark green fields and an atmosphere blackened by the smoke of foundries not far off. She went quickly, darkly along the causeway, heeding nobody, through the town to the churchyard.

There she always felt secure, as if no one could see her,
25 although as a matter of fact she was exposed to the stare of everyone who passed along under the churchyard wall. Nevertheless, once under the shadow of the great looming church, among the graves, she felt immune to the world, reserved within the thick churchyard wall as in another
30 country.

Carefully, she clipped the grass from the grave, and arranged the pinky-white, small chrysanthemums in the tin cross. When this was done, she took an empty jar from a neighboring grave, brought water, and carefully, most scru-
35 pulously sponged the marble headstone and coping-stone.

It gave her sincere satisfaction to do this. She felt in immediate contact with the world of her mother. She took minute pains, went through the park in a state bordering on pure happiness, as if in performing this task she came into a
40 subtle, intimate connection with her mother. For the life she followed here in the world was far less real than the world of death she inherited from her mother.

"The Horse Dealer's Daughter," by D.H. Lawrence

68. Which of the following best summarizes the subject of the first paragraph of the passage?

(A) The debilitating effect of poverty on a family

(B) The liberating effects of impoverishment

(C) The ability of hope to overcome the debilitating effects of poverty

(D) The ecstasy that results when death is imminent

(E) The insanity caused by total despair

69. The tone of the author towards Mabel is

    (A) sympathetic.   (D) patronizing.

    (B) sarcastic.   (E) uninterested.

    (C) horrified.

70. The author implies that Mabel's questioning

    (A) is an act of information gathering.

    (B) is an expression of self-doubt.

    (C) is a defiant expression of self-assurance.

    (D) is simply an attempt by the author to indicate what she is thinking.

    (E) is an attempt by the author to gain the reader's sympathy for her situation.

71. The attainment of glory is associated in Mabel's mind with

    (A) the attainment of riches.

    (B) the loss of riches.

    (C) the pursuit of spiritual immortality.

    (D) the arrival of death.

    (E) the triumph of the individual mind.

72. Mabel's liberation from misery is based mostly on the fact that she

    (A) no longer has to contend with poverty.

    (B) is full of a sullen pride, like the rest of her family.

    (C) no longer thinks of herself.

    (D) has grown closer to her dead mother.

    (E) no longer has to demean herself when she goes to town.

73. The second paragraph of this selection is remarkable stylistically in that it

    (A) portrays a woman more involved with death than with life.

    (B) sustains a pattern of death imagery almost throughout.

(C)   concentrates on seemingly unimportant minor details.

(D)   uses natural description to portray Mabel's despair.

(E)   is written in a style unlike the surrounding paragraphs.

74.   The author's placement of the description of Mabel's bag in the same paragraph with the description of the landscape

(A)   underscores the stylistic challenges the author typically presents to the reader.

(B)   indicates that Mabel is as intent on eliminating the grime of her life as she is in "scrubbing" the soot off her mother's grave.

(C)   foreshadows her impending suicide.

(D)   is meant to indicate the disorder of her mind; no well-adjusted person would go out in this weather.

(E)   reinforces the picture of Mabel as a character who gives no outward indication of her "dark" intentions.

75.   The third paragraph of this passage ("There she always...") (line 24) presents the reader with the basic contradiction that

(A)   Mabel believes the graveyard will not hide her; she is more obvious to the prying public when she goes there.

(B)   Mabel feels immune from the world even though she is more exposed to it.

(C)   Mabel can feel most alive surrounded by a world of death.

(D)   Mabel can only find independence by communing with the spirit of her dead mother.

(E)   Mabel can only feel secure within the insecure and threatening world of death.

76.   The details supplied in the description of the graveyard clearing indicate that

(A)   Mabel has not cleaned the grave in a long time.

(B)   Mabel is unique in cleaning her mother's grave.

(C)   cleaning her mother's grave is a fulfilling, even happy task.

(D)   it is unusual for Mabel to clean the grave alone.

(E)   headstone cleaning is a seasonal occurrence.

77.   Mabel enjoys cleaning her mother's grave because

(A)   she believes she is defying the world of death by entering its confines.

(B)   she is able to escape her real world of troubles by contemplating the afterlife.

(C)   she feels she is returning all the favors her mother did for her when she was alive

(D)   she enjoys the park-like atmosphere of the graveyard.

(E)   she comes in contact with the more real world of death.

78.   The churchyard wall represents for Mabel

(A)   the boundary between the living and the dead.

(B)   a border between her native land and that of foreigners.

(C)   a mere physical obstacle of little consequence.

(D)   a forbidding symbol of death.

(E)   a religious boundary, representing hallowed ground.

DIRECTIONS: For each of the following questions choose the best answer and fill in the correspondmg oval on the answer sheet.

---

79.   Anna's friendly smile <u>emanates with</u> kindness and hospitality.

Which of the following substitutions best captures the meaning of the underlined words?

(A)   diffuses   (D)   seeks

(B)   provides a source of   (E)   provides evidence of

(C)   constantly reveals

80. When asked by the therapist, the boy expressed a particular <u>resentment of</u> his father.

    Which of the following substitutions creates a more negative connotation for the underlined words?

    (A) unhappiness with

    (B) dissatisfaction with

    (C) fear of

    (D) grudge against

    (E) embarrassment of

81. Paul's <u>esoteric</u> vocabulary is largely due to his singular and extensive interest in classical philosophy.

    Which of the following best captures the meaning of the underlined word?

    (A) Varied

    (B) Expansive

    (C) Amazing

    (D) Limited

    (E) Common

82. Geena found that her new class in Economics was not challenging enough for her.

    Which of the following is a correct revision of the ambiguous sentence above?

    (A) For her, Geena found her new class in economics to be "Not challenging enough."

    (B) Geena found, "My new class in Economics is not challenging enough," for her.

    (C) "My new Economics class is not challenging enough for me," said Geena.

    (D) "The new Economics class," is not challenging enough "for me," said Geena.

    (E) Geena said that "The new class in Economics is not challenging enough for me."

83. Emily Dickinson's seemingly <u>limpid</u> style of poetry often leads new readers to mistakenly believe that her work is easily interpreted.

    Which of the following best captures the meaning of the underlined word?

    (A) Needlessly wordy

    (B) Artfully charismatic

    (C) Concise and simple

    (D) Ordinary

    (E) Penetrating

84. Unlike other less dedicated professors in his department, Dr. Owens was serious about <u>pedagogy</u>; and therefore an excellent instructor.

    Which of the following substitutions best captures the meaning of the underlined word?

    (A) the profession of teaching

    (B) spelling and grammar

    (C) science

    (D) verbal communication

    (E) pupil interaction

85. According to a widely circulating rumor, Leroy was <u>reputed</u> to be the fastest runner in his high school class.

    Which of the following best captures the meaning of the underlined word?

    (A) Unknown to many

    (B) Discussed

    (C) Considered by many

    (D) Discovered

    (E) Found by a few

86. When asked, the victim described the dog as being small and spotted.

    Which of the following is a correct revision of the ambiguous sentence above?

    (A) "The dog," the victim described was "small and spotted" when asked.

    (B) When asked, "Small and spotted was the dog," the victim described the animal.

    (C) The victim said that "The animal was small" not to mention "spotted," when asked.

(D) "Being small and spotted," the victim described the dog.

(E) When asked, the victim answered, "The dog was small and spotted."

87. Despite mother's threats, the <u>obstinate</u> old cat would not be moved from her favorite spot next to the stove.

Which of the following substitutions best captures the meaning of the underlined word?

(A) stubborn   (D) unruly

(B) foolhardy   (E) loathsome

(C) senile

88. When he had fulfilled all of the difficult tasks, the young prince <u>superseded</u> his father's position as the king.

Which of the following best captures the meaning of the underlined word?

(A) Stole through trickery   (D) Replaced

(B) Bargained for   (E) Earned through bravery

(C) Challenged

89. Their father <u>admonished</u> them for their rude behavior and sent the twins to their room as punishment.

Which of the following substitutions creates a more positive connotation for the underlined word?

(A) needlessly punished   (D) spanked

(B) praised   (E) gently scolded

(C) harshly reproved

90. Andrew stood his ground and <u>adamantly</u> refused to take part in the activities at the carnival.

Which of the following best captures the meaning of the underlined word?

(A) Nonchalantly   (D) Relentlessly

(B) Reasonably   (E) Actively

(C) Gently

91   According to his mother, when he was a child, Michael often misbe-
      haved.

      Which of the following is a correct revision of the ambiguous sen-
      tence above?

      (A) Mother said, "Michael often misbehaved," according to her,
           when he was a child.

      (B) "Misbehaved is what Michael did when he was a child," said
           Michael's mother.

      (C) Michael's mother said, "Michael often misbehaved when he
           was a child."

      (D) "My son misbehaved when he was a child," said Michael's
           mother.

      (E) Often, according to Michael's mother, "He misbehaved."

92.   Our neighbor's fence <u>encompassed</u> their expansive backyard as well
      as their inground pool.

      Which of the following best captures the meaning of the underlined
      word?

      (A) Enclosed   (D) Ended

      (B) Divided   (E) Protected

      (C) Exposed

93.   James showed us the magic trick with great <u>confidence</u> in his ability
      to amaze us.

      Which of the following substitutions for the underlined word pre-
      sents most emphatically a negative picture of James?

      (A) desire   (D) strength

      (B) pomposity   (E) pride

      (C) greed

94.   In the movie, Fiona told her to return to the island as a storm
      approached.

      Which of the following is a correct revision of the ambiguous sen-
      tence above?

(A) "The storm is approaching, but you should return to the is-land," said Fiona in the movie.

(B) "I'm telling you to return" said Fiona to her, "as the storm is approaching" in the movie.

(C) In the movie, Fiona told her, "Despite the approaching storm you must return to the island."

(D) To return to the island in the movie despite the approaching storm Fiona told her.

(E) "As a storm approaches, return to the island," Fiona told her in the movie.

QUESTIONS 95–97 refer to the following excerpts.

(A) Villages are decimated, its young men and women slain by impersonal ideology, their land raped and laid bear, and their children left alone to be fed on the harsh fare of memory, all is in the name of peace.

(B) The narrow, cobbled street wound up through the city, passing the various shops of merchants and craftsmen, numerous eat-ing houses and watering holes, before ending abruptly at the horizon, overlooking the bay.

(C) Out of this culture of fear and distrust grew an almost obses-sive self-examination and self-critique, which resulted in a constant state of unease, often bordering on paranoia.

(D) Out of the mist of the clouds could be seen the pristine river, flowing through the enchanted valley as if borne on the wings of a light heart and the first rays of light of a new day, touch-ing the hearts of all who witnessed its sacred flow.

(E) American Indians are historically maligned peoples, suffer-ing ignominy and slander in the history of the country, a history whose few centuries pale in comparison to the Indian's millennia.

95. In which excerpt does the speaker's tone convey a sense of bitter irony?

(A) (B) (C) (D) (E)

96. In which excerpt is the tone reverential?

(A) (B) (C) (D) (E)

97. In which excerpt is the speaker's tone one of resentment?

(A) (B) (C) (D) (E)

QUESTIONS 98–100 refer to the following excerpt.

The jurors were amazed at how much of a foil the two lawyers were to each other. The prosecutor had concluded his closing statements by summarizing the hard evidence of the case, leaving what he clearly thought was evidence beyond any doubt. The defense attorney, in turn, had delivered her closing statements without even a reference to the evidence, instead focusing on the notion of motive. During deliberations, one juror remarked about the closing statement of the defense, "That was clever." "Clever!" replied a second juror, "that was brilliant!"

98. To create emphasis, the second juror uses

(A) metaphor.

(B) exclamatory tone.

(C) hyperbole.

(D) structure contrasting to that of the first juror.

(E) speculation.

99. The defense attorney ignored the evidence in an effort to avoid

(A) sexist language.   (D) cliché.

(B) jargon.   (E) speculation.

(C) redundancy.

100. In the first line of the excerpt, foil can be best interpreted as meaning

(A) juxtaposition.   (D) complimentary.

(B) different.   (E) contrasting.

(C) similar.

CLEP FRESHMAN COLLEGE COMPOSITION
TEST 2

Section I

1.	(B)	15.	(D)	29.	(B)	43.	(C)
2.	(C)	16.	(E)	30.	(C)	44.	(D)
3.	(D)	17.	(B)	31.	(D)	45.	(C)
4.	(D)	18.	(A)	32.	(C)	46.	(D)
5.	(C)	19.	(D)	33.	(B)	47.	(E)
6.	(A)	20.	(E)	34.	(A)	48.	(C)
7.	(A)	21.	(B)	35.	(A)	49.	(A)
8.	(A)	22.	(A)	36.	(C)	50.	(C)
9.	(D)	23.	(D)	37.	(D)	51.	(B)
10.	(E)	24.	(E)	38.	(B)	52.	(C)
11.	(D)	25.	(A)	39.	(C)	53.	(A)
12.	(A)	26.	(C)	40.	(D)	54.	(C)
13.	(C)	27.	(C)	41.	(E)	55.	(D)
14.	(B)	28.	(C)	42.	(C)		

Section II

56.	(C)	68.	(D)	79.	(B)	90.	(D)
57.	(A)	69.	(A)	80.	(D)	91.	(C)
58.	(D)	70.	(C)	81.	(B)	92.	(A)
59.	(E)	71.	(D)	82.	(C)	93.	(B)
60.	(B)	72.	(C)	83.	(C)	94.	(C)
61.	(E)	73.	(B)	84.	(A)	95.	(A)
62.	(E)	74.	(B)	85.	(C)	96.	(D)
63.	(D)	75.	(B)	86.	(E)	97.	(E)
64.	(A)	76.	(C)	87.	(A)	98.	(B)
65.	(E)	77.	(E)	88.	(D)	99.	(C)
66.	(C)	78.	(B)	89.	(E)	100.	(E)
67.	(E)						

DETAILED EXPLANATIONS OF ANSWERS

TEST 2

Section I

1.   **(B)**   Two past actions are mentioned. The earlier of two past actions should be indicated by past perfect tense, so the answer is "had been." Choice (C) is correct. Choice (A) contains two adjectives as part of an appositive phrase modifying the subject, and choice (D), "upon the death," is idiomatically correct.

2.   **(C)**   Choice (C) should be "depend," not "had depended" because that use of past perfect would indicate prior past action. There is a series of events in this sentence: first, the legislature "had not finalized" the budget (B); then, Representative Wilson "pointed out" this failure (A). Choice (C) needs to be present tense as this situation still exists, and (D) is future action.

3.   **(D)**   In order to complete the parallelism, choice (D) should be "arrangements." Choice (A) is a noun used as an adjective. "To plan" (B) is an infinitive phrase followed by noun objects: "puppet shows and movies" and "garage sales." Choice (C), "used," is a participate modifying books.

4.   **(D)**   Choice (D) should read, "became very irritated." "To aggravate" means "to make worse"; "to irritate" means "to excite to impatience or anger." A situation is "aggravated" and becomes worse, but one does not become "aggravated" with people. Choices (A), (B), and (C) are correctly used idioms.

5.   **(C)**   The reference in choice (C) is vague because it sounds as if the bus made the two students late. Choice (A) is a correct subject pronoun; choice (B) is the correct adverb form to modify "dressed"; choice

(D) is a correct object pronoun.

6.   **(A)**   The expression should be phrased, "as delicate as." Choice (B) uses a possessive before a gerund; choice (C) is correctly used; and choice (D) is a possessive pronoun of neuter gender which is appropriate to use in referring to a plant.

7.   **(A)**   "Sacrificing" is a gerund, and a possessive form is always used before a gerund. The phrase should read, "no sense in his sacrificing." Choice (B) is the reflexive form of the pronoun, and the pronoun in choice (C) is correct also. The punctuation in choice (D) is correct as "therefore" is an interrupter.

8.   **(A)**   The correct idiom is "insensible to" pain. Choice (B), "more concerned," is the correct comparative degree; choices (C) and (D) are correct.

9.   **(D)**   This is a fragment which can be corrected by changing "sapping" to "sap." Choice (A), "parasitic," is an adjective form; the pronoun "themselves," choice (B), refers to "plants." Choice (C), "drawing nourishment," is parallel to "attaching."

10.   **(E)**   Every preposition in this sentence is used correctly.

11.   **(D)**   The conjunction "not only . . . but also" must be properly placed to indicate which qualities are being discussed and to maintain proper parallelism. Choice (D) contains three adjectives to follow the verb "to be": "capable and efficient" and "adept." Choices (A), (B), (C), and (E) are not parallel. In addition, choices (B) and (C) have "to be" after the conjunction, and this construction would require another verb after the second conjunction, "but also."

12.   **(A)**   This sentence contains two concepts, proper management and careful control. In choice (A) these two concepts are concisely worded and appear in parallel form. Choice (B) has no noun for "Managing" to modify. Choice (C) would be acceptable with the addition of commas to set off the introductory phrase. Choice (D) mangles the concepts, and the wording in choice (E) is poor.

13.   **(C)**   Choice (A) is a "squinting" modifier: it is unclear if "on the next day" tells when "I agreed" or when "to put up." Choice (B) does not

clarify this problem. Choice (D) unnecessarily splits the subject and the verb, and choice (E) unnecessarily splits an infinitive.

14. **(B)**   The correct idiom is to have an insight into a situation or person. While "to" in choice (A) is close in meaning, it is not exact; "for" and "with" of choices (C), (D), and (E) are unacceptable. The location of "often" in choice (D) is poor, and the location of "often" in choice (E) makes no significant change in the meaning.

15. **(D)**   It is obvious that the Greenes have just purchased plants: "Upon leaving the nursery." The location of the modifying phrase, "they had just brought," should be carefully placed in the sentence so it clearly modifies "plants" and not "car." Choice (D) has the modifying phrase immediately following "plants," and the meaning is clear. The wording of choices (A), (B), and (C) makes the reader think the car has just been purchased. Choice (E) omits the concept "they had just bought."

16. **(E)**   Choice (E) retains the central idea while eliminating the wording problems of the other choices. There is no antecedent for "we" in choices (A) and (B). Also, the phrase "end up" is redundant; "up" should be eliminated. Therefore, choice (C) is incorrect. Choice (D) introduces a new concept of "war may end over there," an idea clearly not intended by the original.

17. **(B)**   Choice (B) clearly and precisely states the issue of debate. Choice (C) is eliminated because it is too wordy and not the precise issue under debate. The correlative conjunctions, "whether . . . or," should be followed by parallel structures. Choice (A) follows "Whether" with a subject-verb combination not seen after "not." Choice (D) is parallel but in the wrong tense. Choice (E) has "Whether or not" run together and uses poor wording in the rest of the sentence.

18. **(A)**   Choice (A) has both correct agreement and clear reference. Choice (B) has a subject-verb agreement problem, "charging . . . are." Choice (C) produces a fragment. It is unclear in choice (D) who will have the bad credit rating, and the wording of choice (E) has the obvious subject, "people," in a prepositional phrase.

19. **(D)**   Choice (D) correctly presents the fifth grade field trip in a subordinate clause modifying "exhibit." Choices (A) and (B) have the coordinating conjunction "and," but the first part of the sentence is not

equal in meaning or importance to the second part of the sentence. Choice (C) introduces "when" with no antecedent. Choice (E) uses "where" as the subordinating conjunction, but it is too far from its antecedent and is not the important idea of the sentence.

20. **(E)** In choice (E) the present infinitive is correctly used to express an action following another action: "plans to appeal." Choices (A) and (B) use the wrong form, "appealing." Choice (C) uses the wrong tense, "is appealing." Choice (D) sounds as if the same person is deciding the case and appealing the case.

21. **(B)** Choice (B) clears up the pronoun usage problem, eliminating the ambiguous reference of "he"; it is clear that Dickens is delighted. Choice (A) does not clearly identify the antecedent of "he." Choice (C) incorrectly identified the "delighted" person as the giver, not Dickens. Choices (D) and (E) both create fragments.

22. **(A)** Choice (A) combines all the elements correctly and uses parallel structure, creating a balanced sentence. Choice (B) is not exactly parallel, and the many commas create confusion. Choice (C) does not have parallel verbs: "wanted" and "being." Choices (D) and (E) incorrectly combine the two ideas, making it seem as if the children are blocking Grip's action.

23. **(D)** Choice (D) keeps the formal tone of the essay and avoids passive voice. Choice (A) and choice (E) both break the formal tone and use another voice: "you" and "I." Choice (B) is perhaps too formal and not straightforward. Choice (C) uses the passive voice.

24. **(E)** Choice (E) smoothly combines both major ideas as a cause-and-effect sequence. Choice (A) is the next best choice, but it is not as smoothly worded in the first half; also, this choice eliminates the idea of "use" in the second half. Choice (B) does not clarify the source of Poe's dissatisfaction. Choice (C) does not clearly present the idea that the prophetic use was Poe's, not Dickens'. Choice (D) has too many interruptions.

25. **(A)** Choice (A) is incorrect; the paragraph gives information on the origin of the bird. Although the paragraph gives one or two humorous incidents, choice (B) cannot be the main intention. Choice (C) is unlikely; the bird's biting is presented as more humorous than tragic. Choice (D)

would be a more effective label for paragraph two. Choice (E) is partly correct, but the second paragraph returns to the Dickens' household.

26.   **(C)**   Choice (C) clears up the confusion caused by the possessive pronoun "his," which in this sentence would incorrectly refer to "Dickens' children." "Their" would also be fine, but "the" is probably best, as it is clear from the context which family we are referring to. Choice (A) adds "it," which is unnecessary and redundant. Choice (B) replaces the past with the past progressive tense, which does not agree with the verb tense throughout the passage. Choice (D) replaces a neat prepositional phrase with an awkward clause. Choice (E) is repetitive; it is clear that "the raven" is still the subject of the sentence.

27.   **(C)**   "Despite" best fits the relation between the religious and secular themes. Choice (A), "beyond," would be the next best choice, though it sounds a bit overzealous. Choice (B), "until," would be inappropriate since the rest of the passage does not suggest that the secular themes preceded the religious, but rather that they coexisted. "Unless" (D) and "under" (E) are nonsensical in this context.

28.   **(C)**   "Craftsman" should be plural to agree with the other noun "artisans." We assume that there was not only one "craftsman" "working over many generations," so the singular would be nonsensical.

29.   **(B)**   Sentence 3, as it stands, introduces a wholly new subject without transition. Sentence 4 best carries this transition and should follow sentence 2. Sentence 3 introduces the spread of Gothic style throughout Europe, and this point is directly supported in sentence 8.

30.   **(C)**   "Become" should be in the past tense ("became") to accord with the rest of the passage.

31.   **(D)**   Choice (D) sets the clause off with commas, and best clarifies the sentence. Choice (A) uses commas to disrupt the main idea of the sentence. Choice (B) sets the clause off well, but the colon is inappropriate and should be a comma. Choice (C) employs too many commas; the second and fourth should be eliminated, as they disrupt the flow of the sentence.

32.   **(C)**   Choice (C) continues to describe the internal physical characteristics of Gothic cathedrals and best fits between sentences 10 and 11.

Choice (A) switches to the external aspect of the building. Choice (B) introduces the author's opinion, which is not necessary at this part of the passage. Choice (D) is a relevant thought, but would best be placed elsewhere: it describes the purpose of the architecture, where sentences 10 and 11 are describing the physical qualities of the interior of the buildings. Choice (E) is an unrelated, and possibly factually incorrect, statement.

33.   **(B)**   "The Wetherills" is plural, and the verb must agree. Choice (B) correctly changes "is" to "are"; the rest of the sentence is fine. (A) adds the singular "a group" which may make the verb "is" seem right, though it still modifies "The Wetherills" and must agree accordingly. (C) corrects the verb problem, but misplaces the clause "five brothers who ranched in the area" at the end of the sentence where it is unclear. (D) fails to correct the verb disagreement and places the clause at the end of the sentence, which alters the sense.

34.   **(A)**   Choice (A) best continues the topic of sentence 9, which concerns the cultural achievements of the Anasazi, and provides a nice transition toward the final sentence. (B) concerns an entirely different historical epoch and is clearly irrelevant. (C) may fit somewhere in this essay, but not between sentences 9 and 10, where this new fact would seem obtrusive. (D) introduces the personal voice of the author which is contrary to the expository tone in the passage thus far, and which would not fit between the factual content of sentences 9 and 10. (E) would be a good topic sentence for a new paragraph, but would not be good here.

35.   **(A)**   Sentence 4 is a dependent prepositional clause and would be best added onto sentence 3.

36.   **(C)**   The years of the Anasazi's zenith are best set off by commas and turned into a prepositional phrase, and of the two choices which do this, (C) uses "from," which is more appropriate than (D) "being." Without the punctuation, choice (A) is awkward; if the phrase were set off by commas, it would be acceptable, though (C) is more concise. (B) is just wrong; from the context of the passage, it is clear that the Anasazi thrived in the years A.D and not B.C.

37.   **(D)**   Choice (D) best utilizes commas which clarify the sense of the sentence. Choice (A) places the second comma incorrectly. (B) and (C) both utilize a colon, and each has an unnecessary comma. Choice (E) is correct as written.

38. **(B)** Sentence 2 uses "then," a temporal reference, instead of "than," which should be used for the comparison in this sentence.

39. **(C)** "Children's early teens" is much neater and clearer than "the early teens of the children." (A) introduces unnecessary punctuation. (B) is nonsensical ("continue through the children"). (D) adds "on" which does nothing but further convolute the original sentence.

40. **(D)** (D) makes a clear and simple sentence out of the clumsy original. The structures of (A), (B), and (C) duplicate the confusions of the original.

41. **(E)** "Showing" in the original sentence is clearly wrong, and any of these three forms would be acceptable.

42. **(C)** Sentence 7 is a rhetorical question, like sentence 6, and needs a question mark.

43. **(C)** Sentence 12 introduces a new issue in the middle of the paragraph and would best be eliminated.

44. **(D)** The idea in sentence 9 about company morale and employee loyalty would be best placed in support of the ideas in sentence 11, that the workers feel that the company has taken interest in them. "Therefore" sets up a logical relation which is not present between sentences 8 and 9.

45. **(C)** An engineering dictionary, limited exclusively to definitions of engineering words, would allow the reader to find the definition of a particular word in the shortest period of time. An encyclopedia article on engineering may not include that particular term and if it does, the term may be buried in any paragraph in the article, so choice (A) is not the best answer. (The article may or may not have a glossary of terms.) Unabridged dictionaries are extremely large and would take longer to search than an engineering dictionary, so (B) is not a good answer. Choice (D) is incorrect as an engineering textbook is more likely to have a glossary than an encyclopedia article but would not be as comprehensive as an engineering dictionary. A professional engineering journal would not include definitions as its audience would be familiar with most engineering terms, so choice (E) is wrong.

46. **(D)** The book listed is a biography, and biographies are shelved

alphabetically by the name of the book's subject. A biography would not be filed with history books, either under the author's name, as in choice (A), or the subject's name, as in choice (B), so both these choices are incorrect. Choice (C) is wrong as the author's name is not used for shelving a biography. Choice (E) is incorrect as even famous biographies such as the one listed are not shelved in the literature section.

47.   **(E)**   In periodical listings, "v" followed by a number stands for "volume" and indicates the volume number of the magazine listed. Choice (A) is wrong as a periodical index entry indicates whether an article is illustrated but not where the illustration appears. The letter "v" does not indicate a microfiche number or code, so choice (B) is incorrect. The number of the first page of the article appears after the letter "p" not "v," making choice (C) wrong. Choice (D) is also incorrect as "v23" is not part of the computer code for the magazine's location.

48.   **(C)**   An encyclopedia article on any type of literature usually has a listing of writers who fit that category, in either a bibliography, timeline, or the text. Choice (A) is incorrect as an anthology of world literature would include only a few poets from each continent, so the total number of names in its table of contents would be small. A magazine article on contemporary African poets would not include the names of poets from earlier periods, so choice (B) is wrong. Choice (D) would also be incorrect as a world almanac would list only the winners of the major poetry prizes, so only a few of the greatest poets would be listed there. As a literary magazine publishes only contemporary works, and therefore lists only contemporary poets, choice (E) is also wrong.

49.   **(A)**   Indefinite articles such as "a" and "an" are the only words that are ignored when alphabetizing a library catalog system. Choice (B) is incorrect as all verbs, no matter how small, are included in alphabetizing. Pronouns such as "I" are also used in alphabetizing, so choice (C) is incorrect. "If" is not an indefinite article, so choice (D) is incorrect. Although "of" is not usually capitalized, it is still used in alphabetization so choice (E) is also wrong.

50.   **(C)**   The town archives would contain minutes from town council meetings and possibly proceedings from any hearings or trials resulting from the scandal, and would be the most likely source for the details of a local political scandal. An encyclopedia article on a town would have only the basics such as the rounding date and major industries, so choice (A) is

incorrect. *The Reader's Guide* would refer a researcher to magazines and journals. Only a few publications would date back to the 1920s and few if any of them would cover a town scandal, so choice (B) is incorrect. Choice (D) is wrong because the Chamber of Commerce would only have brochures covering local businesses, accommodations, and buildings and sites of interest; the brochures would have little if any information on town scandals. The state courthouse would have information on a town scandal only if the scandal resulted in a trial or other government deliberations at the state level, making (E) an unlikely answer.

51.   **(B)**   Encyclopedias, even sophisticated ones, are not considered appropriate resources for a college research paper, partly because they represent someone else's research. Choice (A) is incorrect because a television program, if the program is developed by a reliable source and well-researched, is a valid source for a college paper. An interview with a local historian or other expert is also a valid resource, so choice (C) is incorrect. Any reliable book, even if it is written by a professor at the research paper writer's college, is an appropriate source, so choice (D) is wrong. Choice (E) is also incorrect as the *Christian Science Monitor* is a well-respected newspaper and therefore an excellent source for a college research paper.

52.   **(C)**   A natural-health guidebook would actively promote herbal medicines as more natural and therefore more healthy than conventional medicines. A medical journal would be biased against herbal medicines, if it had any bias, as most medical professionals are trained in and trust only conventional medicines, so choice (A) is incorrect. A consumers' health guide would be concerned with what the writers believed was in the best interests of the consumer, so it could be biased in favor of natural remedies or conventional medicines, or balanced between both; therefore, (B) is not the most likely answer. An allergy remedy book, similarly, may favor only conventional medicines, only herbal medicines, or both—the main point would be to use what works for curing or easing allergies. Therefore, choice (D) is also an unlikely answer. A city newspaper article could have any bias or none, depending on the bias of the staff and the focus of the article, so choice (E) is incorrect.

53.   **(A)**   If the source is listed on the back of each note card, the researcher can always quickly find the source of any information that was noted. If the source is listed only on the first card containing information from that source, then any other cards based on that source will not have the source connected with them, so choice (B) is inappropriate. If the

sources are all listed separately whether on a single sheet of paper as in choice (C) or each on a separate index card as in choice (D), there is no way to connect the information with the source, so choices (C) and (D) are wrong. Choice (E) is also incorrect as it is nearly impossible to remember at the end of research which information came from which book.

54.   **(C)**   A paraphrase is a restatement of a direct quote that uses few of the exact words and phrases of the original. A quote with only a couple of words changed is practically still a direct quote, so choice (A) is wrong. Choice (B) is also incorrect as a quote with only part of the statement changed is still not a paraphrase. A statement that differs in meaning is a new idea and not exactly a paraphrase, so choice (D) is incorrect. Choice (E) describes a summary, something else entirely, so it is incorrect.

55.   **(D)**   If the issue the topic is based on developed and concluded locally, then most of the events occurred locally and local newspaper articles would have a rich collection of details. Also, such a topic probably would not be well-covered outside the local area, so the local paper is almost certain to be the most comprehensive source on that topic. Many events have local as well as national significance, but the primary significance is usually national. Therefore, a national publication would be more comprehensive than a local source and choice (A) would be incorrect. A topic based on a recent occurrence would require recent publications such as newspapers but a local newspaper would not necessarily be the most comprehensive source, so choice (B) is wrong. An event that began locally may have good coverage in the local paper, but if the scope of the event expanded, other publications may have more comprehensive coverage, making choice (C) incorrect. If a topic is well-known to some local people, it is probably well-known to others outside the area (unless the topic has only local significance), so choice (E) is not the best answer.

Section II

56. **(C)**   Choice (A) is incorrect because it comes from a failure to recognize and understand the simile "like the jerk of a chain," which may suggest a chain gang, but which is not meant to be taken literally. Choice (B) is incorrect because it is inconsistent with previous observation by the narrator about "the careless, powerful look" Ethan had. Choice (C) is correct because his physical handicap creates a noticeable contrast with his "careless, powerful look." Choice (D) is incorrect because Ethan is clearly identified as one of the taller "natives." Choice (E) is incorrect because it, too, stems from a misreading of the line just as choice (A) does.

57. **(A)**   Choice (A) is a correct interpretation of the figurative expression "lank longitude." Only this interpretation makes sense in the context where the "natives" are compared to the shorter and heavier "foreign breed" who have recently settled there. Choice (B) is incorrect because it interprets "longitude" in a sailing context, which it does not have here. Choice (C) is incorrect because nothing in the passage supports the idea of the "natives" being prejudiced towards their own kind. Choices (D) and (E) are incorrect because they are unsupported in the passage.

58. **(D)**   Choice (A) is incorrect because Ethan's appearance is more a matter of genetics, i.e., his size and height, than it is due to his residence in the town. Choice (B) is incorrect because it is contradicted by line 4. Choice (C) is incorrect because Ethan retains these aspects of his appearance in spite of his personal history. Choice (D) is correct because the look on his face is a direct result of his personal history. Choice (E) is incorrect because the passage does not support it.

59. **(E)**   Choice (A) is incorrect because it is not supported by anything in the passage. The word "degenerate" carries moral overtones unsuitable for describing weather in this passage. Choice (B) is incorrect because these artifacts of the outside culture are not degenerate in and of themselves as much as the cultural changes they encourage and convey. Choice (C) is incorrect because it is contrary to the meaning of lines 28–29. Choice (D) is incorrect because it erroneously connects the new age and the recurring season of winter. Choice (E) is correct because the trolley, the bicycle, and rural mail delivery opened the village to outside corrupting influences that had not been experienced previously.

60. **(B)**   Choice (A) is incorrect because the narrator expresses no amusement toward Ethan and there is no distrust expressed towards Ethan's motives. Choice (B) is correct because the sight of Ethan pulls the narrator up sharply and arouses his curiosity. Choice (C) is incorrect because the narrator expresses no sarcasm towards Ethan. He does not view Ethan as someone deserving criticism. Choice (D) is incorrect because Ethan's appearance intrigues the narrator but he has yet to learn anything about the man to evoke sympathy. Choice (E) is incorrect because the narrator is struck by this unusual man but there is nothing in his description to suggest a worshipful attitude.

61. **(E)**   Most individuals desire fame but it is not labeled a birthright (A) in the poem. The "unnumbered suppliants" in line 1 contradict the idea that it is a right of a select few (B). Like Wolsey, individuals are motivated toward fame and fortune for strictly personal reasons, the least of which is a desire to improve society (C). The words "unnumbered" and "incessant" do not support the idea that this is a disappearing phenomenon (D). However, the words "unnumbered" and "the incessant call" both suggest that it is a universal aspiration (E).

62. **(E)**   Only a misreading of the word "foes" can make them the enemies of the realm (A), or poverty, envy, and disease (C). These are the foes of domestic peace which is not the meaning of "peace" in this passage. "Delusive Fortune" (B) is not the antecedent of "foes." Neither do the "foes" reside within the government and plot its overthrow (D). The correct answer is (E) in that the meaning of "peace" in this line is the tranquility of life that is shattered by the many worries that come to plague a celebrity.

63. **(D)**   By abandoning the former celebrity when hard times struck, the "worshiper," "scribbler," and "dedicator" show a lack of compassion (A), loyalty (C) and honor (E). Choice (B) is wrong because it stems from a misreading of the word "worshiper," which in the context of the poem means those who come to offer flattery in return for favors. Choice (D) is correct because the behavior of these individuals demonstrates "insensitivity."

64. **(A)**   The correct answer is (A) because of the selfish interests of those who attend them, i.e., the "worshiper," "scribbler," and "dedicator." Their success does not make them (B), as that is not the meaning of "worshiper" in this context. Choices (C), (D), and (E) are wrong because the actions described in each contradicts the meaning of the lines, which essentially catalogue how the "worshiper" and others abandon them.

65. **(E)** The speaker charges his countrymen with selling their votes, hence (A) is wrong. They used to be watchful of abuses by the nobility, but are no longer (B). There is no condemnation of their country's foes (C), and neither do they "rail" for justice (D). Rather they "riot and rail" for pure devilment. Choice (E) is correct because the portrait is that of men who lack integrity and sell their votes for a drink of ale.

66. **(C)** The common people are not innocent of blame (A), because they no longer safeguard liberty (line 21). Neither are they onlookers (B), in that their votes are for sale (line 24), which makes them victims of their own greed (C). Their role as guardians of liberty (D) is denied by line 21. Choices (D) and (E) are wrong because they contradict the accusations made in lines 21–26.

67. **(E)** Ballad meter alternates three and four stresses in the lines, the lines of this poem have five (A). The line uses iambic feet, but dimeter means only two stresses per line (B). These lines rhyme and blank verse does not (C). Terza rima (D) is a three-line stanza which is not evident in this sample. Choice (E) is correct because every two lines of a couplet rhyme.

68. **(D)** Mabel is in a state of "ecstasy," not because she is impoverished, or because she is in despair, but because she has decided to "end it all" and kill herself. There are strong hints throughout this passage, yet a casual reader might think she is speaking of the "end," meaning, perhaps, eviction from her property. By the time she thinks about being near her mother in the graveyard, however, the meaning should be clear.

69. **(A)** The author describes Mabel's actions in careful detail, stressing her pleasurable bond to death and her new found self-control. The author does not sound disparaging or repulsed; rather Mabel is presented in a sympathetic light, inviting emotional response from the reader.

70. **(C)** Mabel's self-questioning expresses her new-found defiance, and her growing independence from the onus of responding to the prejudices of the wider world. When Lawrence asks: "Why should she answer anybody?" we can hear the tragically directed Mabel saying: "I don't have to answer you or anybody," as she walks down the "dark main street of the small town."

71. **(D)** Mabel looks forward to her death, says Lawrence, as a personal fulfillment and "glorification," and as a way of getting closer to her mother — not just in a physical sense as she cleans up at the graveyard, but in a spiritual way as well.

72. **(C)** It is surprising, or so Lawrence implies, that a person who is about to commit suicide thinks "of nobody, not even of herself." Yet, it might be precisely this feeling that provides the sensation of liberation and which actually allows her to contemplate suicide.

73. **(B)** Lawrence presents us with a machine-gun procession of depressing images: "gray, wintry … saddened, dark green … blackened by the smoke." Along with this are the depressing images of foundries and graveyards.

74. **(B)** Mabel has already decided on the path she will take to eliminate her troubles. The brief description of Mabel and her bag seems almost medical. Perhaps she is gone to perform an operation — and in this sense it might be an omen. But Lawrence places this description next to the smoky and depressing landscape: Mabel will clean the headstone, Mabel will wipe her own slate clean.

75. **(B)** Lawrence points out that Mabel is more obvious to the public in the graveyard than she imagines herself to be: yet she feels immune.

76. **(C)** Cleaning her mother's grave gave her "sincere satisfaction." Lawrence implies that this task is performed often.

77. **(E)** Lawrence states in the last line: "For the life she followed here in the world was far less real than the world of death she inherited from her mother." Thus, a trip to the graveyard and a contemplation of death is not an escape from the "real" world, but a return to the more real world her mother left to her.

78. **(B)** Lawrence states: "She felt reserved within the thick churchyard wall as in another country." It is a difficult concept for the reader to understand fully until he or she confronts the concept again in the last paragraph quoted in this passage.

79. **(B)** Answer choice (B) is synonymous with "emanates with." (A), (C), (D), and (E) do not capture the meaning of the underlined words.

80. **(D)** Answer choice (D) is correct because it has negative connotations. (A), (B), (C), and (E) do not have negative meanings.

81. **(B)** Answer choice (B) is correct because it is synonymous with "esoteric." (A), (C), (D), and (E) are wrong because they do not capture the meaning of the underlined word.

82. **(C)** Answer choice (C) is the correct revision. (A), (B), (D), and (E) are not clear in meaning.

83. **(C)** Answer choice (C) best captures the meaning of the underlined word. (A), (B), (D), and (E) are not synonymous with "limpid."

84. **(A)** Answer choice (A) defines the underlined word. Choices (B), (C), (D), and (E) do not.

85. **(C)** Answer choice (C) defines "reputed," while choices (A), (B), (D), and (E) do not.

86. **(E)** Answer choice (E) is the correct revision, while choices (A), (B), (C), and (D) are unclear.

87. **(A)** Answer choice (A) is synonymous with "obstinate" and is therefore correct. (B), (C), (D), and (E) do not have the same meaning as the underlined word.

88. **(D)** Answer choice (D) is the best choice because it is synonymous with "superseded." Choices (A), (B), (C), and (E) are not.

89. **(E)** Answer choice (E) is correct because it is a more positive way of saying "admonished." (A), (C), and (D) are more negative and (B) is the opposite of "admonished," so these choices are incorrect.

90. **(D)** Answer choice (D) is the best choice because it is closest in meaning to the underlined word. (A), (B), (C), and (E) are not close in meaning to "adamantly."

91. **(C)** Answer choice (C) is a correct revision of the sentence. Choices (A), (B), (D) and (E) are unclear in their meaning.

92. **(A)**   Answer choice (A) is closest in meaning to "encompassed." Choices (B), (C), (D), and (E) are incorrect because they do not have the same meaning as the underlined word.

93. **(B)**   Answer choice (B) is correct because it carries negative connotations. Choices (A), (C), (D), and (E) are incorrect because they do not have the same meaning, nor are they as negative as (B).

94. **(C)**   Answer choice (C) is a correct revision, while choices (A), (B), (D), and (E) are unclear sentences.

95. **(A)**   Answer choice (A) is correct since its tone is ironic. Choices (B), (C), (D), and (E) are not ironic in tone and therefore are incorrect.

96. **(D)**   Answer choice (D) is the only excerpt that is reverential. The river is described using words such as "pristine" and "sacred," which convey reverence. Choices (A), (B), (C), and (E) do not convey reverence.

97. **(E)**   Answer choice (E) is correct because its tone is resentful. Choices (A), (B), (C), and (D) do not convey resentment.

98. **(B)**   Answer choice (B) is correct because, according to the punctuation, the juror makes an exclamation. The juror does not use metaphor, hyperbole, or speculation, so (A), (C) and (E) are wrong. Nor does he contrast his statement to that of the first juror, so (D) is incorrect too.

99. **(C)**   Redundancy is the correct answer since the prosecutor had summarized the evidence in his statement, the defense attorney would only be repeating it unnecessarily. Nothing indicates any of the other choices, so (A), (B), (D) and (E) are wrong.

100. **(E)**   Answer choice (E) is closest in meaning to "foil," as it is used in this case. Choices (A), (B), (C), and (D) are not synonymous with the word.

PRACTICE
TEST 3

CLEP FRESHMAN COLLEGE COMPOSITION
Test 3

(Answer sheets appear in the back of this book.)

Section I

TIME: 45 Minutes
       55 Questions

DIRECTIONS: Each of the following sentences may contain an error in diction, usage, idiom, or grammar. Some sentences are correct. Some sentences contain one error. No sentence contains more than one error.

If there is an error, it will appear in one of the underlined portions labeled A, B, C, or D. If there is no error, choose the portion labeled E. If there is an error, select the letter of the portion that must be changed in order to correct the sentence.

EXAMPLE:

He drove <u>slowly</u> and <u>cautiously</u> in order to <u>hopefully</u> avoid having an

            A   **B**   **C**

<u>accident</u>. <u>No error</u>.

   D   **E**   Ⓐ Ⓑ ⬤ Ⓓ Ⓔ

---

1.   Each campus appointed <u>their</u> own committee to apply the <u>findings of</u>

                            A   **B**

       the city-wide survey concerning ways <u>in which</u> the school district <u>can</u>

                                              C   **D**

       save money. <u>No error</u>.

                      E

---

2. When I asked Gary and John what would be good for dinner, the
        A   B
    boys said they could care less about eating liver for the main dish
                      C   D
    with spinach for a vegetable. No error.
                              E

3. If a person is a criminal, he should be punished for it; unfortunately,
        A   B   C
    many criminals are never caught. No error.
                    D   E

4. An intriguing habit many hawks have is bringing a fresh green
                                          A
    branch daily to line the nest during the season in which they are
            B   C   D
    mating and rearing their young. No error.
                           E

5. Hawks and owls can be seen more frequent in populated areas than
                                 A
    most people suppose, and it is possible to hear screech owls at night
        B   C   D
    when the adult birds feed their chicks. No error.
                                 E

6. Totaling more than expected, the groom's wedding expenses
                    A
    included hiring a limousine for the trip to the airport after the wed-
        B
    ding, buying gifts for his groomsmen, and a tuxedo for the cer-
            C   D
    emony. No error.
          E

7. Our viewing these photographs of Dad standing in front of the throne
        A
    at Macchu Pichu brings back pleasant memories for we children,
                    B   C
    reminding us of the need for more family get-togethers. No error.
               D   E

8. Finally confessing to the <u>theft of</u> money collected for a class movie,
                             A

    Jules said <u>he only</u> stole money once in his life and <u>his</u> conscience
             B   **C**

    would not allow <u>him</u> to enjoy spending it. <u>No error</u>.
                 D   **E**

9. <u>After seeing</u> the technique demonstrated on television, Janie baked
       A

    homemade bread for the first time yesterday, <u>and her</u> brother
                                                    B

    thought it tasted <u>good</u>, an opinion everyone <u>agreed with</u>. <u>No error</u>.
                       C   **D**   **E**

10. Although not <u>so</u> prevalent as they once were, <u>hood</u> ornaments still
                   A   **B**

    exist, <u>some of which</u> are quite distinctive, <u>such as</u> the symbol for
           C   **D**

    Mercedes-Benz and Jaguar. <u>No error</u>.
                                   E

DIRECTIONS: In each of the following sentences, some portion of the sentence is underlined. Under each sentence are five choices. The first choice has the same wording as the original. The other four choices are reworded. Sometimes the first choice containing the original wording is the best; sometimes one of the other choices is the best. Choose the letter of the best choice. Your choice should produce a sentence which is not ambiguous or awkward and which is correct, clear, and precise.

This is a test of correct and effective English expression. Keep in mind the standards of English usage, punctuation, grammar, word choice, and construction.

EXAMPLE:

When you listen to opera, <u>a person may not appreciate it.</u>

(A) a person may not appreciate it.

(B) it may not be appreciated by a person.

(C) which may not be appreciated by one.

(D) you may not appreciate it.

(E) appreciating it may be a problem for you.   Ⓐ Ⓑ © ● Ⓔ

11. <u>We saw many of, though not nearly all, the existing Roman ruins</u> along the Mediterranean coastline of Africa.

   (A) We saw many of, though not nearly all, the existing Roman ruins

   (B) We saw many, though not nearly all, of the existing Roman ruins

   (C) Seeing many, though not nearly all, of the existing Roman ruins

   (D) Having seen many of, though not nearly all, the existing Roman ruins

   (E) Many of, though not nearly all, the existing Roman ruins we saw

12. Literary historians <u>cannot help but admit that they do not know</u> whether poetry or drama is the oldest form of literature.

   (A) cannot help but admit that they do not know

   (B) cannot admit that they do not admit to knowing

   (C) cannot help admitting that they do not know

   (D) cannot help but to admit that they do not know

   (E) cannot know but admit that they do not

13. In many of his works Tennessee Williams, <u>of whom much has been written,</u> has as main characters drifters, dreamers, and those who are crushed by having to deal with reality.

   (A) of whom much has been written

   (B) of who much has been written

   (C) of whom much has been written about

   (D) about him much having been written

   (E) much having been written about him

14. The world history students wanted to know <u>where the Dead Sea was at and what it was famous for</u>.

   (A) where the Dead Sea was at and what it was famous for.

(B) where the Dead Sea is at and for what it is famous.

(C) where the Dead Sea is located and why it is famous.

(D) at where the Dead Sea was located and what it was famous for.

(E) the location of the Dead Sea and what it is famous for.

15. At this time <u>it is difficult for me agreeing with your plan of having everyone</u> in the club working on the same project.

(A) it is difficult for me agreeing with your plan of having everyone

(B) I find it difficult to agree to your plan of having everyone

(C) for my agreement with your plan is difficult for everyone

(D) an agreement to your plan seems difficult for everyone

(E) finding it difficult for me to agree to your plan of having everyone

16. When the Whites hired a contractor to do remodeling on their home, he <u>promised to completely finish the work inside of three months</u>.

(A) promised to completely finish the work inside of three months.

(B) promised to complete the work within three months.

(C) completely promised to finish the work inside of three months' time span.

(D) promising to completely finish the work in three months.

(E) completely finished the work within three months.

17. <u>Seeing as how the plane is late</u>, wouldn't you prefer to wait for a while on the observation deck?

(A) Seeing as how the plane is late,

(B) When the plane comes in,

(C) Since the plane is late,

(D) Being as the plane is late,

(E) While the plane is landing,

18. Only with careful environmental planning can we protect the <u>world we live in</u>.

    (A) world we live in.

    (B) world in which we live in.

    (C) living in this world.

    (D) world's living.

    (E) world in which we live.

19. <u>Being that you bring home more money than I do</u>, it is only fitting you should pay proportionately more rent.

    (A) Being that you bring home more money than I do,

    (B) Bringing home the more money of the two of us,

    (C) When more money is made by you than by me,

    (D) Because you bring home more money than I do,

    (E) If your bringing home more money than me,

20. Flooding abated and the river waters receded as the <u>rainfall finally let up</u>.

    (A) rainfall finally let up.

    (B) rain having let up.

    (C) letting up of the rainfall.

    (D) rainfall, when it finally let up.

    (E) raining finally letting up.

DIRECTIONS: The following passages are considered early draft efforts of a student. Some sentences need to be rewritten to make the ideas clearer and more precise.

Read each passage carefully and answer the questions that follow. Some of the questions are about particular sentences or parts of sentences and ask you to make decisions about sentence structure, diction, and usage. Some of the questions refer to the entire essay or parts of the essay and ask you to make decisions about organization, development, appropriateness of language, audience, and logic. Choose the answer that most effectively makes the intended meaning clear and follows the requirements of standard written English. After you have chosen your answer, fill in the corresponding oval on your answer sheet.

EXAMPLE:

(1) On the one hand, I think television is bad, But it also does some good things for all of us. (2) For instance, my little sister thought she wanted to be a policemen until she saw police shows on television.

Which of the following is the best revision of the underlined portion of sentence 1 below?

On the one hand, I think television <u>is bad, But it also</u> does some good things for all of us.

(A)   is bad; But it also

(B)   is bad. but is also

(C)   is bad, and it also

(D)   is bad, but it also

(E)   is bad because it also   Ⓐ Ⓑ Ⓒ ⬤ Ⓔ

QUESTIONS 21–26 are based on the following passage.

(1) A French composer, the bolero inspired Anton Ravel to create the ballet *Bolero*. (2) The sister of the legendary Russian dancer Vaslav Nijinsky choreographed the ballet created by Ravel. (3) A popular and well-known folk dance in Spain, the bolero as we know it is credited to Anton Bolsche and Sebastian Cerezo around the mid-1700s. (4) Although no one has actually seen the ballet, the music from *Bolero* has

retained immense popularity and is performed on a regular basis throughout the world.

(5) The center and driving force of it is a snare drum. (6) The percussionist begins by playing a rhythmic pattern lasting two measures and six beats, the rhythm of the bolero dance, as quietly as possible. (7) At the beginning, other instruments pick up the rhythm as the frenzy builds. (8) The first flute then introduces the melody, the second important part of *Bolero*; different instruments play individual parts, such as the clarinet, bassoon, and piccolo. (9) The buildup of the music occurs in two ways: the individual musicians play their instrument louder and louder, and more and more instruments beginning to play together. (10) For most of the 15 to 17 minutes of the performance, *Bolero* is played in a relenting harmony of C Major. (11) The end is signaled by a brief shift to E Major and then a strong return to C Major.

21. Which of the following revisions would best improve sentence 1?

   (A) The bolero inspired Anton Ravel to create the ballet *Bolero*, a French composer.

   (B) The bolero, a French composer, inspired Anton Ravel to create the ballet *Bolero*.

   (C) The bolero inspired Anton Ravel, a French composer, to create the ballet *Bolero*.

   (D) The bolero inspired Anton Ravel to create the ballet, a French composer, *Bolero*.

   (E) Best as it is.

22. Which of the following would best replace "it" in sentence 5?

   (A) this musical composition

   (B) the folk dance

   (C) them

   (D) Anton Bolsche and Sebastian Cerezo

   (E) None of these.

23. Which of the following best improves the underlined portion of sentence 8?

The first flute then introduces the melody, the second important part of *Bolero*; underline different instruments play individual parts, such as the clarinet, bassoon, and piccolo.

(A) the clarinet, bassoon and piccolo and other different instruments play individual parts.

(B) different instruments, such as the clarinet, bassoon and piccolo, play individual parts.

(C) individual parts are played by the clarinet, bassoon and piccolo, as well as other different instruments.

(D) different instruments play different parts, like the clarinet, bassoon and piccolo.

(E) Best as it is.

24. Which of the following verbs is used incorrectly?

(A) "inspired" in sentence 1

(B) "credited" in sentence 3

(C) "pick up" in sentence 7

(D) "beginning" in sentence 9

(E) "signaled" in sentence 11

25. Which of the following corrections should be made?

(A) Change "choreographed" to "composed" in sentence 2.

(B) Change "retained" to "remained" in sentence 4.

(C) Change "individual" to "total" in sentence 9.

(D) Change "relenting" to "unrelenting" in sentence 10.

(E) None of these.

26. Which of the following would be the best way to punctuate sentence 11?

(A) The end, is signaled by a brief shift, to E Major and then a strong return to C Major.

(B)   The end is signaled, by a brief shift to E Major, and then a
       strong return, to C Major.

(C)   The end is signaled by a brief shift to E Major, and then a
       strong return to C Major.

(D)   The end is signaled by a brief shift, to E Major, and then a
       strong return, to C Major.

(E)   Best as it is.

QUESTIONS 27–32 are based on the following passage.

(1) Dena may die soon. (2) For 21 years, all Dena has ever known is
captivity. (3) How would you like to spend your entire life in captivity?
(4) Even though Dena is not a human, but an orca, a killer whale, like in
the movie *Orca*, don't you think Dena deserves to be released from her
natural habitat? (5) Orcas are much too intelligent and too delicate to be
confined in tanks. (6) Dena's owners claim that she is displaying geriatric
signs normal for an orca 25 years old, Sea Habitat, Inc. (7) Orcas are not
meant to be caged, no matter how kind the jailer who holding the keys.

(8) We don't know enough about orcas and how they interact. (9) Who
are we to confine a species that may be as intelligent as humans? (10)
True, Dena may be rejected by her original pod, members of which stayed
together for life. (11) Maybe she is too old to live much longer. (12)
However, we should at least allow Dena to die with dignity in her natural
surroundings. (13) And, if Dena succeeds in surviving in the wild, maybe
we can pressure other zoos and marine institutions around the world to
release these beautiful animals back to the wild, where they can live
longer, healthier lives. (14) I urge everyone to write a letter to their local
senator and congressman demanding the return of all orcas to the oceans
of the earth.

27.   Which of the following phrases is unnecessary and should be elimi-
       nated?

(A)   "For 21 years" in sentence 2

(B)   "like in the movie *Orca*" in sentence 4

(C)   "may be as intelligent as humans" in sentence 9

(D)   "to the oceans of the earth" in sentence 14

(E)   None of these.

28. Which of the following corrects the underlined portion of sentence 4?

    Even though Dena is not a human, but an orca, a killer whale, like in the movie *Orca*, don't you think <u>Dena deserves to be released from her natural habitat?</u>

    (A) Dena deserved to be released from her natural habitat?

    (B) Dena deserves from her natural habitat to be released?

    (C) Dena deserves to be released under her natural habitat?

    (D) Dena deserves to be released into her natural habitat?

    (E) None of these.

29. Which of the following best corrects sentence 6?

    (A) Dena's owners, Sea Habitat, Inc., claim she is displaying geriatric signs normal for an orca 25 years old.

    (B) Since they are Dena's owners, Sea Habitat, Inc. claim she is displaying geriatric signs normal for an orca 25 years old.

    (C) Sea Habitat, Inc., Dena's owners, claim she is displaying geriatric signs normal for an orca 25 years old.

    (D) Choices (A), (B), and (C).

    (E) Choices (A) and (C) only.

30. Which of the following, if used between sentences 10 and 11, best develops the main idea of the second paragraph?

    (A) Another problem to be overcome is training Dena to hunt live fish, instead of depending on being fed dead fish by her human captors.

    (B) As a matter of fact, it is now against the law to capture orcas in the wild and sell them to zoos.

    (C) As we all know, the breeding of captive orcas has not been successful.

    (D) This issue has recently been made famous by the movie *Free Willy*.

    (E) Since orcas live an average of 20–30 years, Dena should not be released because she is clearly too old to adapt to the wild.

31. Which of the following verbs are used incorrectly?

   (A) "deserves" in sentence 4

   (B) "holding" in sentence 7

   (C) "stayed" in sentence 10

   (D) Choices (B) and (C) only.

   (E) Choices (A), (B), and (C).

32. Which of the following best punctuates sentence 8?

   (A) We don't know enough, about orcas, and how they interact.

   (B) We don't know enough, about orcas and how they interact!

   (C) We don't know enough about orcas, and how they interact.

   (D) We don't know enough: about orcas and how they interact.

   (E) Best as is.

QUESTIONS 33–38 are based on the following passage.

   (1) Polar bears, so named because they lived near the North Pole, are called "Nanook" by the Eskimo. (2) Living along the cold waters and ice floes of the Arctic Ocean, some polar bears spend time along the coastal areas of northern Canada, Alaska, Norway, Siberia, and Greenland, although some bears live on the islands of the Arctic Ocean and never come close to the mainland. (3) Most of these areas lie north of the Arctic circle and about 85% of Greenland is always covered with ice. (4) To protect them from the arctic cold and ice, polar bears have water-repellant fur and a pad of dense, stiff fur on the soles of their snowshoe-like feet. (5) In addition, the bears have such a thick layer of fat that infrared photos show no detectable heat, except for their breath.

   (6) Polar bears are the largest land-based carnivores. (7) Because their fur is white with a tinge of yellow, they are difficult to spot on ice floes, their favorite hunting ground. (8) Polar bears have a small head, a long neck, and a long body, so they make efficient swimmers. (9) Polar bears have no natural enemy except man. (10) Increased human activity in the Arctic region has put pressure on polar bear populations. (11) The Polar Bear Specialist Group was formed to conserve and manage this unique animal. (12) An increase in the number of polar bears is due to cooperation between five nations. (13) In 1965, there were 8,000 to 10,000 bears reported, but that population is estimated at 25,000 at the present.

33. Which of the following best expresses the author's intentions in the first paragraph?

    (A) To celebrate his/her fondness for polar bears

    (B) To describe some of the wildlife of Alaska

    (C) To provide a basic account of some of the polar bear's primary habits

    (D) To prove that mammals can live comfortably in unfavorable conditions

    (E) To show why polar bears are not suited to the Arctic region

34. Which of the following verbs is used in an inappropriate tense?

    (A) "lived" in sentence 1   (D) "conserve" in sentence 11

    (B) "Living" in sentence 2   (E) None of these.

    (C) "is covered" in sentence 3

35. Which of the following sentences is not necessary to the first paragraph, and would be best eliminated?

    (A) Sentence 1   (D) Sentence 4

    (B) Sentence 2   (E) Sentence 5

    (C) Sentence 3

36. Which of the following would be the best way to improve the structure of sentence 5?

    (A) In addition, except for their breath, the bears have such a thick layer of fat that infrared photos show no detectable heat.

    (B) The bears have such a thick layer of fat that, in addition, infrared photos show no detectable heat except for their breath.

    (C) Except for their breath, infrared photos show no detectable heat, the bears have such a thick layer of fat.

    (D) The bears have, in addition, such a thick layer of fat that, except for their breath, infrared photos show no detectable heat.

    (E) Best as it is.

37. Which of the following sentences would best fit the writer's plan of development, and would fit between sentences 6 and 7?

   (A) Full-grown polar bears may be about nine feet long and weigh between 1,000 and 1,600 pounds.

   (B) These bears have keen eyesight and are not sensitive to snow blindness.

   (C) In the winter the female polar bear enters a cave in an iceberg and gives birth to one or two cubs.

   (D) Polar bears can swim great distances with a speed of approximately six miles an hour.

   (E) Polar bears are often a popular attraction in city zoos; even Atlanta boasts a healthy polar bear.

38. Which of the following is the best way to combine sentences 9, 10, and 11?

   (A) Polar bears have no natural enemy, except man: increased human activity in the Arctic region has put pressure on polar bear populations, while the Polar Bear Specialist Group was formed to conserve and manage this unique animal.

   (B) Since polar bears have no natural enemy except man, the Polar Bear Specialist Group has formed to conserve and manage this unique animal because increased human activity in the Arctic region has put pressure on polar bear populations.

   (C) Polar bears have no natural enemy except man, and though increased human activity in the Arctic region has put pressure on polar bear populations, the Polar Bear Specialist Group was formed to conserve and manage this unique animal.

   (D) Polar bears have no natural enemy except man, and since increased human activity in the Arctic region has put pressure on polar bear populations, the Polar Bear Specialist Group was formed to conserve and manage this unique animal.

   (E) None of these.

QUESTIONS 39–44 are based on the following passage.

(1) In the poem "The Raven" by Edgar Allen Poe, a man has nodded off in his study after reading "many a quaint and curious volume of forgotten lore." (2) His mood is melancholy. (3) He is full of sorrow. (4) He is grieving for "the lost Lenore."

(5) When he hears the tapping at his window, he lets in a raven. (6) The raven perches on the bust of Pallas Athena, a goddess often depicted with a bird on her head by the Greeks who believed that birds were heralds from the dead. (7) At first, the man thinks the bird might be a friend but one who would leave soon, but the raven says, "Nevermore," an affirmation which makes the man smile. (8) However, the bird's repetition of "Nevermore" leads the speaker to the realization that Lenore will never return, the bird becomes an omen of doom and is called "evil" by the mournful speaker. (9) He becomes frantic, imploring the raven to let him know if there is comfort for him or if he will ever again hold close the sainted Lenore. (10) To both questions, the bird replies, "Nevermore." (11) Shrieking with anguish, the bird is ordered to leave, but it replies, "Nevermore." (12) At the end of the poem, the man's soul is trapped in the Raven's shadow "that lies floating on the floor" and "shall be lifted— nevermore."

(13) Thus, the bird evolves into an ominous bird of ill omen. (14) Some argue that the bird deliberately drives the speaker insane. (15) While others feel the bird is innocent of any premeditated wrong doing, and I think the bird doesn't do anything but repeat one word. (16) One thing is certain, however. (17) The poem's haunting refrain is familiar, one which students of American literature will memorize and forget "nevermore."

39. Which of the following is the best way to combine sentences 2, 3, and 4?

    (A) He is melancholy and sorrowful and grieving for "the lost Lenore."

    (B) He is grieving for "the lost Lenore," full of melancholy and sorrow.

    (C) Melancholy and sorrowful, he is grieving for "the lost Lenore."

    (D) Melancholy and full of sorrow, he is grieving for "the lost Lenore."

    (E) Full of a melancholy mood and sorrow, he is grieving for "the lost Lenore."

40. Which of the following is the best revision of the underlined portion of sentence 8 below?

However, the bird's repetition of "Nevermore" leads the speaker to the realization that Lenore will never return, the bird becomes an omen of doom and is called "evil" by the mournful speaker.

(A) realize the following—Lenore will never return, the bird is evil and an omen of doom.

(B) the realization of Lenore's failure to return, the evil and omen of doom of the bird.

(C) realize that Lenore will never return, so the bird, called "evil" by the mournful speaker, becomes an omen of doom.

(D) the realization that Lenore will never return, the bird becomes an omen of doom and is called "evil" by the mournful speaker.

(E) the Lenore will never return, that the bird is an omen of doom, and that the bird should be called "evil."

41. Which is the best revision of the underlined portion of sentence 11 below?

Shrieking with anguish, the bird is ordered to leave, but it replies, "Nevermore."

(A) the bird is ordered to leave but

(B) the man orders the bird to leave, but it

(C) the order is given for the bird to leave, but it

(D) the bird, ordered to leave,

(E) the man orders the bird to leave and

42. In relation to the passage as a whole, which of the following best describes the writer's intention in the second paragraph?

(A) To show specific examples of supernatural effects

(B) To argue that the bird has evil intent

(C) To convince the reader to read the poem

(D) To analyze the progression of ideas in the literature

(E) To describe the appearance of the bird

43. In the context of the sentences preceding and following sentence 15, which of the following is the best revision of sentence 15?

   (A) Only repeating one word, others feel the bird is innocent of any premeditated wrongdoing.

   (B) Innocent and not doing anything, the bird repeats one word.

   (C) Innocent of any premeditated wrongdoing, the bird does not do anything.

   (D) One may argue that, innocent of any premeditated wrongdoing, the bird does not do anything but repeat one word.

   (E) Others feel the bird is innocent of any premeditated wrongdoing because it does not do anything but repeat one word.

44. Which of the following would be a better way to end the passage, combining sentences 16 and 17?

   (A) One thing is certain, however: the poem's haunting refrain is a familiar one which students of American literature will memorize and forget "nevermore."

   (B) One thing is certain, however, that the poem's haunting refrain is familiar, one which students of American literature will memorize and forget "nevermore."

   (C) One thing is certain, however; the poem's haunting refrain is familiar, one which students of American literature will memorize and forget "nevermore."

   (D) One thing is certain, however: the poem's haunting refrain is familiar, one which students of American literature will memorize and forget "nevermore."

   (E) One thing that is certain is that the poem's haunting refrain is familiar, one which students of American literature will memorize and forget "nevermore."

DIRECTIONS: For each question, find the correct answer and fill in the appropriate oval on the answer sheet.

---

45. Sources published in the European medieval period would be most appropriate for a research paper on

    (A) classical music.

    (B) the history of medicine.

    (C) Native American societies.

    (D) foreign-language education.

    (E) biochemistry.

46. The correct spacing for a research paper is

    (A) single spacing throughout.

    (B) double spacing for the main text, single spacing for long quotes, footnotes (if any), and bibliography.

    (C) double spacing for the main text and bibliography, single spacing for all other materials.

    (D) double spacing for all text except for the bibliography, which should be single-spaced.

    (E) double spacing throughout.

47. The title for a research paper must appear

    (A) in all capital letters and underlined.

    (B) in quotation marks.

    (C) on a separate page.

    (D) on the first page of the paper.

    (E) on each page of the paper.

48. Which is true of a research paper?

    (A) Every page must have the title of the paper.

    (B) Every page must have the writer's name.

    (C) Magazine titles must be in quotes.

(D) Magazine article titles must be underlined.

(E) Book titles must be underlined.

49. Quotations of five lines or more should not be

(A) in quotation marks.

(B) in poetry format.

(C) indented from the main text.

(D) preceded by a colon.

(E) followed by a new paragraph.

50. Which of the following should be in quotation marks?

(A) The title of a short poem

(B) The name of a television program

(C) The rifle of a one-act play

(D) The name of a magazine

(E) The name of a painting

51. If the same author has written two of the books in a research paper, the text citation for a quote from either book, if no source material is given in the text, should include the

(A) author and page number of the source.

(B) title and page number of the source.

(C) author and title of the source.

(D) author, title, and page number for the source.

(E) author, title, page number, city of publication, publisher, and date for the source.

52. Pack, Robert, and Jay Parini, eds. *The Bread Loaf Anthology of Contemporary American Essays.* "Penelope—The Sequel: Some Uses of Mythology in Contemporary Poetry" by Linda Pastan. Hanover, New Hampshire: University Press of New England, 1989, pp. 273–285.

The bibliography entry above is incorrect because

(A) the editor's first name should appear first.

(B) the editors should not be listed.

(C) "eds." should be spelled out.

(D) the author and title of the essay should appear first.

(E) the page numbers should immediately follow the essay title.

53. Le Guin, Ursula K. *Dancing at the Edge of the World: Thoughts on Words, Women, Places.* New York: Grove Press, 1989.

_____. *Orsinian Tales.* New York: Harper & Row, 1976.

_____. *The Left Hand of Darkness.* New York: Ace, 1969.

The bibliography segment above is incorrect because

(A) the author's name should be given each time.

(B) the book titles should appear first.

(C) a different publisher is listed for each book.

(D) the text after the colon in the first book title should not be included.

(E) the word "the" in the third book title should be ignored when alphabetizing that entry.

54. The topic most appropriate for a ten-page research paper for a college-level education class is

(A) foreign-language education.

(B) history education in the United States.

(C) gender differences in third-grade map-reading test scores.

(D) bilingual Japanese-English teacher-training courses in Oregon colleges.

(E) teacher-training courses for gifted education students in the United States.

55. An abstract from a journal article is most useful for

(A) finding other articles on the same topic.

(B) checking the author's sources.

(C) deciding if the article would be helpful.

(D) deciding if the article data is reliable.

(E) looking over table and charts from the article.

Section II

TIME: 45 Minutes
          45 Questions

> **DIRECTIONS**: The following questions test your ability to recognize the content, form, and style of a passage as well as the writer's purpose. After reading each passage or poem, choose the best answer to each question and fill in the corresponding oval on the answer sheet.

QUESTIONS 56–62 are based on the following passage.

It is too little to call man a little world; except God, man is dimunitive to nothing. Man consists of more pieces, more parts, than the world; than the world doth, nay, than the world is. And if these pieces were extended and
5   stretched out in man as they are in the world, man would be the giant and the world the dwarf; the world but the map, and the man the world. If all the veins in our bodies were extended to rivers, and all the sinews to veins of mines, and all the muscles that lie upon one another to hills, and all the
10 bones to quarries of stones, and all the other pieces to the proportion of those which correspond to them in the world, the air would be too little for this orb of man to move in, the firmament would be but enough for this star. For as the whole world hath nothing to which something in man doth
15 not answer, so hath man many pieces of which the whole world hath no representation. Enlarge this meditation upon this great world, man, so far as to consider the immensity of the creatures this world produces. Our creatures are our thoughts, creatures that are born giants, that reach from east
20 to west, from earth to heaven, that do not only bestride all the sea and land, but span the sun and firmament at once: my thoughts reach all, comprehend all.
        Inexplicable mystery! I their creator am in a close prison, in a sick bed, anywhere, and any one of my crea-
25 tures, my thoughts, is with the sun, and beyond the sun, overtakes the sun, and overgoes the sun in one pace, one step, everywhere. And then as the other world produces serpents and vipers, malignant and venomous creatures,

and worms and caterpillars, that endeavor to devour that
30   world which produces them, and monsters compiled and
complicated of divers parents and kinds, so this world, our
selves, produces all these in us, producing diseases and
sicknesses of all those sorts; venomous and infectious diseases, feeding and consuming diseases, and manifold and
35   entangles diseases made up of many several ones. And can
the other world name so many venomous, so many consuming, so many monstrous creatures, as we can diseases,
of all these kinds? O miserable abundance, O beggarly
riches! How much do we lack of having remedies for every
40   disease when as yet we have not names for them?

By John Donne

56.   The central metaphor in the first paragraph is a comparison of

    (A) Man and God.

    (B) Earth and heaven.

    (C) Man and the world.

    (D) Man's mental and physical attributes.

    (E) God and nature.

57.   Which of the following can best be substituted for "answer" (line 15) without changing the author's meaning?

    (A) Surpass   (D) Repudiate

    (B) Correspond   (E) Aspire

    (C) Correct

58.   Which of the following statements most nearly expresses the main idea of the first paragraph?

    (A) Man is God-like.

    (B) Man is a macrocosm.

    (C) Man imitates small worlds.

    (D) Man is a microcosm.

    (E) Man is small and insignificant.

59. The "other world" (line 36) refers to

    (A) hell.

    (B) man's inner self.

    (C) the firmament.

    (D) the world of nature.

    (E) the Garden of Eden.

60. "Miserable abundance" (line 38) refers to

    (A) human diseases.

    (B) man's flawed intellect.

    (C) monstrous creatures in nature.

    (D) temptations that lead to excess.

    (E) the richness and limitations of language.

61. In lines 38–39, "beggarly riches" is an example of

    (A) apostrophe.

    (B) invocation.

    (C) dead metaphor.

    (D) synecdoche.

    (E) paradox.

62. The author's metaphor in the second paragraph suggests that sickness and malignant creatures are alike chiefly in that both

    (A) are unpleasant and unexpected presences.

    (B) violate the natural order of things.

    (C) are complex and difficult to understand.

    (D) dangerous but necessary aspects of the natural world.

    (E) destroy that which produces them.

QUESTIONS 63–71 are based on the following poem.

IMMORTAL AUTUMN

I speak this poem now with grave and level voice
In praise of autumn of the far-horn-winding fall
I praise the flower-barren fields the clouds the tall
Unanswering branches where the wind makes sullen noise

5   I praise the fall it is the human season now
No more the foreign sun does meddle at our earth
Enforce the green and thaw the frozen soil to birth
Nor winter yet weigh all with silence the pine bough

But now in autumn with the black and outcast crows
10   Share we the spacious world the whispering year is gone
There is more room to live now the once secret dawn
Comes late by daylight and the dark unguarded goes

Between the mutinous brave burning of the leaves
And winter's covering of our hearts with his deep snow
15   We are alone there are no evening birds we know
The naked moon the tame stars circle at our eaves

It is the human season on this sterile air
Do words outcarry breath the sound goes on and on
I hear a dead man's cry from autumn long since gone

20   I cry to you beyond this bitter air.

By Archibald MacLeish

63.   The title and the first line of this poem indicates that the poet intends to speak

(A)   in defense of autumn.

(B)   in praise of the passing of the seasons.

(C)   with reference to death.

(D)   with reference to the resurrection inherent in nature.

(E)   with sarcasm.

64.   The unpunctuated, run-on sentences the poet introduces in the first stanza are designed to

(A)   accommodate the long catalog of praiseworthy autumnal images.

(B)   approximate an ungrammatical and rustic country accent.

(C)   reinforce the images of tired nature the poet presents.

(D)   reflect the almost breathless excitement the season brings to the poet.

(E)   underscore the "nature in chaos" themes the poet advances.

65.   In the second stanza the poet surprises the reader most by

(A)   continuing to speak in the first person.

(B)   continuing to speak in unpunctuated, run-on sentences.

(C)   praising a season that is rarely praised.

(D)   expressing relief at the passage of summer.

(E)   expressing a dread of approaching winter.

66.   In identifying fall as "the human season" (line 17), the poet

(A)   personifies his delivery of autumn images.

(B)   indicates a shift in thematic intention.

(C)   places human life within a traditional natural framework.

(D)   makes an allusion to a famous Shakespearean sonnet.

(E)   indicates a continuation of his thematic intention.

67.   According to the speaker, the sun is "foreign" (line 6) because

(A)   it does not originate in the earth.

(B)   it destroys the "green" with its strong rays.

(C)   it throws the light of truth where it is better not to know.

(D)   it disturbs the "human season" by causing plants to grow.

(E)   its lessening strength brings on winter.

68.   In the third stanza, the poet implies that humans are similar to

(A)   the "spacious world" (line 10)

(B)   the "secret dawn" (line 11)

(C)   the passing of the "whispering year" (line 10)

(D)   the "dark unguarded" (line 12)

(E)   the "outcast crows" (line 9)

69. The phrase "There is more room to live now" (line 11) suggests that

  (A) the lack of leaves provides more room for human movement.

  (B) the late dawn provides a greater opportunity to view beauty.

  (C) the increasing darkness provides man with a more fitting world.

  (D) the fading year reminds humans that they have much left to accomplish.

  (E) harvest time provides man and crows both with sustenance.

70. In stanza four the speaker is doing which of the following?

  (A) Indicating that man is a destroyer of nature

  (B) Indicating that man is afraid of winter

  (C) Indicating that man is isolated in an unfamiliar world

  (D) Indicating that man is in communion with the universe

  (E) Indicating that man is helping the earth to prepare for winter

71. The phrase "It is the human season on this sterile air" (line 17) implies that

  (A) man's thoughts and creations are really barren of meaning.

  (B) man lives in a world which threatens his very existence.

  (C) autumn's air is crisp and beneficial to human health.

  (D) nature in autumn poses no interference to human wishes.

  (E) man lives in the sight of the other creatures of the universe.

QUESTIONS 72–78 are based on the following passage.

 The points that I particularly wish to make about Yeats' development are two. The first, on which I have already touched, is that to have accomplished what Yeats did in the middle and later years is a great and permanent example —
5 which poets-to-come should study with reverence — of what I have called Character of the Artist: a kind of moral, as well as intellectual, excellence. The second point, which follows naturally after what I have said in criticism of the

lack of complete emotional expression in his early work, is
that Yeats is preeminently the poet of middle age. By this I
am far from meaning that he is a poet only for middle-aged
readers: the attitude towards him to younger poets who
write in English, the world over, is enough evidence to the
contrary. Now, in theory, there is no reason why a poet's
inspiration or material should fail, in middle age or at any
time before senility. For a man who is capable of experience finds himself in a different world in every decade of
his life; as he sees it with different eyes, the material of his
art is continually renewed. But in fact, very few poets have
shown this capacity of adaptation to the years. It requires,
indeed, an exceptional honesty and courage to face the
change. Most men either cling to the experiences of youth,
so that their writing becomes an insincere mimicry of their
earlier work, or they leave their passing behind, and write
only from the head, with a hollow and wasted virtuosity.
There is another and even worse temptation: that of becoming dignified, or becoming public figures with only a public
existence — coatracks hung with decorations and distinc-
tions, doing, saying, and even thinking and feeling only
what they believe the public expects of them. Yeats was not
that kind of poet: and it is, perhaps, a reason why young
men should find his later poetry more acceptable than older
men easily can. For the young men can see him as a poet
who in his work remained in the best sense always young,
who even in one sense became young as he aged. But the
old, unless they are stirred to something of the honesty with
oneself expressed in the poetry, will be shocked by such a
revelation of what a man really is and remains. They will
refuse to believe that they are like that.

From "On Poetry and Poets," by T. S. Eliot

72.   According to Eliot, Yeats' achievements later in life

(A)   are a testament to the character of the artist.

(B)   are a testimony to his moral excellence.

(C)   are in contrast to the obscurity of his younger days.

(D)   are examples of intellectual and emotional excellence.

(E)   are important to middle-aged readers.

73. Eliot indicates that the poet Yeats

    (A) did not begin writing until later in life.

    (B) did not achieve fame until later in life.

    (C) did not enjoy his success until middle age.

    (D) did not achieve full poetic inspiration until middle age.

    (E) did not realize his potential until he began writing about middle age.

74. Which of the following best describes the function of the first sentence of the paragraph?

    (A) It simply states the main thesis of the paragraph.

    (B) It provides a transition statement from the last paragraph.

    (C) It establishes the credibility of the author as a noted critic.

    (D) It demonstrates that the author is aware his previous arguments may seem weak.

    (E) It provides a summing up of previously determined attitudes.

75. In context, the statement "Now, in theory, there is no reason why a poet's inspiration or material should fail, in middle age or at any time before senility" (lines 14–16) suggests which of the following?

    (A) Yeats and other poets used this theory as a defense against criticism.

    (B) Yeats used this theory as an excuse.

    (C) Eliot is praising Yeats for not having "failed."

    (D) Many poets' inspiration and material blossom in middle age.

    (E) Many poets' inspiration and material fail in middle age, and these poets use this observation to excuse their failure.

76. According to the passage, the key to retaining poetic inspiration lies in

    (A) remaining young at heart.

    (B) adapting well to the aging process.

    (C) leaving the "experiences of youth" behind.

(D) remaining "capable of experience."

(E) avoiding the trappings of a "public existence."

77. "Public figures" (line 27) are often "coatracks" (line 28) because they

(A) are public "skeletons" of their previous selves.

(B) are sensitive to contemporary poetic and public "fashion."

(C) are dignified, rigid, and uninspired.

(D) are only fit to remain in the "back rooms" of poetry's "house."

(E) are content to behave according to public whim.

78. Eliot determines that young men find Yeats' later poetry more acceptable than older men do because

(A) younger men have not yet achieved Yeats' level of emotional maturity.

(B) younger men see the older Yeats as a contemporary.

(C) Yeats was too far ahead of his time for his own generation to understand him.

(D) Yeats was emotionally immature.

(E) younger men relate to Yeats' disdain for the older writer.

DIRECTIONS: For each of the following questions, choose the best answer and fill in the correspondmg oval on the answer sheet.

---

79. The advisor to the treaty <u>mitigated</u> relations between the two warring nations in order to establish peace again.

Which of the following best captures the meaning of the underlined word?

(A) Degrade

(B) Soften

(C) Struggle endlessly with

(D) Attempt to mix

(E) Tirelessly continue

80. Her noticeably <u>pallid</u> complexion allowed the doctor to assume that her condition had worsened.

Which of the following substitutions best captures the meaning of the underlined word?

(A) lively   (D) pale

(B) ruddy   (E) haggard

(C) clear

81. Luisa <u>is careful to avoid excessive spending</u> when she travels during the summer.

Which of the following substitutions for the underlined words presents a most emphatically positive picture of Luisa?

(A) is frugal   (D) hates to spend

(B) is a pennypincher (E) saves a lot of money

(C) can't part with a dollar

82. Jamal told Lisa to meet him outside of the mall after 9:30 PM.

Which of the following is a correct revision of the ambiguous sentence above?

(A) "Be outside of the mall by 9:30 PM so I can meet you," said Jamal to Lisa.

(B) Jamal said to her that "Meet me outside of the mall after 9:30," he said to Lisa.

(C) "Meet me," said Jamal "outside of the mall after 9:30 PM, Lisa"

(D) "Lisa, meet me outside of the mall after 9:30 PM," said Jamal.

(E) "Outside of the mall by 9:30 PM, meet me," Jamal said to Lisa.

83. George bought an <u>annotated</u> version of the text in order to get a broadened perspective on the reading.

Which of the following best captures the meaning of the underlined word?

(A) Furnished with additional notes and comments

(B) Shortened and condensed

(C) Incomplete

(D) Larger sized

(E) Translated into English

84. The gleeful choir sang a hymn of <u>benediction</u> during the Christmas festivities at the church bazaar.

Which of the following substitutions best captures the meaning of the underlined word?

(A) reverence

(B) solemnity

(C) remembrance

(D) condolences

(E) praise

85. Nita's parents warned her not to stay out too late.

Which of the following is a correct revision of the ambiguous sentence above?

(A) "Nita," her parents said, "we ask you to not stay out too late."

(B) "Do not stay out too late we warn," said Nita's parents to her.

(C) "Nita, do not stay out too late," her parents warned.

(D) Her parents instructed her to not stay out too late with warning.

(E) "We warn you not to stay out too late," said her parents to Nita.

86. The <u>homogeneous</u> employee population within the corporation ensures a sense of commonality amongst them.

Which of the following best captures the meaning of the underlined word?

(A) Diversity among

(B) Belonging

(C) Uniformity

(D) Divisions between

(E) Unlikely

87. Ida maintains her innocence with <u>impenetrable</u> confidence.

Which of the following substitutions for the underlined word presents a most emphatically positive picture of Ida?

(A)   unbelievable   (D)   steadfast

(B)   stubborn   (E)   wavering

(C)   indignant

88.   The sudden <u>inflection</u> in the witness' voice indicated to the jury that the subject disturbed her.

Which of the following best captures the meaning of the underlined word?

(A)   Anger   (D)   Clarity

(B)   Sadness   (E)   Bewilderment

(C)   Change

89.   Karen hopes that tonight her lost puppy will return home before the sun sets.

Which of the following is a correct revision of the ambiguous sentence above?

(A)   Karen said, "Tonight I hope my lost puppy will return before the sun sets."

(B)   Hoped Karen tonight, "That my lost puppy will return before sunset."

(C)   "I hope that my lost puppy will return home before the sun sets tonight," said Karen

(D)   That the puppy which is lost will return home tonight, Karen hoped.

(E)   "I hope that the lost puppy will return tonight," said Karen, "before the sun sets."

90.   Mrs. Powers revealed her <u>taut</u> observance of rules through her strict enforcement of the grammar school's moral codes.

Which of the following substitutions best captures the meaning of the underlined word?

(A)   loose   (D)   rigid

(B)   ethical   (E)   obligatory

(C)   prudish

91. Mr. Oakes noted that in order to receive a quarterly raise, it was <u>imperative</u> that each employee pass a written skills test.

    Which of the following best captures the meaning of the underlined word?

    (A) Unfortunate circumstance   (D) Unjust demand

    (B) Necessary obligation   (E) Punitive gesture

    (C) Reasonable request

92. The happy recipient remarked that not many people get a chance to fulfill their wishes, unlike him.

    Which of the following is a correct revision of the ambiguous sentence above?

    (A) The recipient who was happy noted that it is not many people who get a chance to fulfill "their wishes" like him to.

    (B) "Not many people," unlike the happy recipient "get a chance to fulfill their dreams."

    (C) "Unlike me, not many people get a chance to fulfill their wishes," remarked the happy recipient.

    (D) "To fulfill their wishes, not many people get the chance," said the happy recipient, unlike him.

    (E) "Their wishes," according to the happy recipient, "are not always fulfilled because they don't get the chance like me."

93. The <u>fundamentals</u> of happiness are often not gained through money or fame.

    Which of the following best captures the meaning of the underlined word?

    (A) Credentials   (D) Ingredients

    (B) Objects   (E) Powers

    (C) Essentials

94. Julia's <u>remarkable intelligence</u> has often been a source of great pride for her parents.

    Which of the following substitutions for the underlined words present a most emphatically negative picture of Julia?

(A)   sheer genius

(D)   shrewdness

(B)   comprehension abilities

(E)   skillfulness

(C)   acute aptitude

QUESTIONS 95–97 refer to the following excerpts.

(A)   Nay, take my life and all. Pardon not that. You take my house when you do take the prop that doth sustain my house; you take my life when you do take the means whereby I live.

(B)   Ignorance is the parent of fear, and being completely non-plussed and confounded about the stranger, I confess I was as now much afraid of him as if it was the devil himself who had thus broken into my room at the dead of night.

(C)   The framers of the constitution established the separation of church and state, though it is up to each citizen to fight to insure that this separation continues, for otherwise, it would obliterate the freedom of religion that is the right of every American!

(D)   Begin today as if enlightenment is achieved, and start neigh-borhood improvement throughout the city, building golden towers that spiral to the sky, reaching to a land both tender and strong.

(E)   Women's suffrage was a social movement that was achieved in the early decades of the twentieth century, though it had behind it more than two centuries of political injustice and inequality.

95.   In which excerpt does the speaker's tone convey a sense of optimism?

(A)   (B)   (C)   (D)   (E)

96.   In which excerpt is there a fervent tone?

(A)   (B)   (C)   (D)   (E)

97.   In which excerpt can the speaker's tone be interpreted as defeated?

(A)   (B)   (C)   (D)   (E)

QUESTIONS 98–100 refer to the following excerpt.

During the Cold War, both the United States and the Soviet Union lived by the credo "In order to secure peace, one must prepare for war." This is evidenced by the proliferation of both countries nuclear arsenals, and by the proposal by the Americans for the Strategic Defense Initiative, or SDI. Historians have argued that while the Cold War averted military strife between the two countries, symbolic fighting was conducted in Grenada, Nicaragua, and other countries, with the United States and the Soviet Union supplying weapons to opposing forces.

98. The credo mentioned in the beginning of the excerpt is an example of a

    (A) hyperbole.   (D) paradox.

    (B) cliché.   (E) metaphor.

    (C) proverb.

99. It can be inferred from the excerpt that the author feels that the Cold War policies of the U.S.A. and U.S.S.R.

    (A) were a complete success in preventing war.

    (B) were the result of previous tension between the two countries.

    (C) brought both countries to the brink of military conflict.

    (D) failed completely in maintaining peace.

    (E) prevented military conflict between the two countries, but added to conflict in other countries of the world.

100. The term SDI used by the author in place of Strategic Defense Initiative is an example of a(n)

    (A) metaphor.   (D) acronym.

    (B) abbreviation.   (E) allusion.

    (C) paradox.

CLEP FRESHMAN COLLEGE COMPOSITION
TEST 3

ANSWER KEY

Section I

1.	(A)	15.	(B)	29.	(E)	43.	(E)
2.	(C)	16.	(B)	30.	(A)	44.	(D)
3.	(C)	17.	(C)	31.	(D)	45.	(B)
4.	(B)	18.	(E)	32.	(E)	46.	(E)
5.	(A)	19.	(D)	33.	(C)	47.	(D)
6.	(D)	20.	(A)	34.	(A)	48.	(E)
7.	(C)	21.	(C)	35.	(C)	49.	(A)
8.	(B)	22.	(A)	36.	(E)	50.	(A)
9.	(D)	23.	(B)	37.	(A)	51.	(D)
10.	(A)	24.	(D)	38.	(D)	52.	(D)
11.	(B)	25.	(D)	39.	(C)	53.	(E)
12.	(C)	26.	(C)	40.	(C)	54.	(E)
13.	(A)	27.	(B)	41.	(B)	55.	(C)
14.	(C)	28.	(D)	42.	(D)		

Section II

56.	(C)	68.	(E)	79.	(B)	90.	(D)
57.	(B)	69.	(C)	80.	(D)	91.	(B)
58.	(B)	70.	(C)	81.	(A)	92.	(C)
59.	(D)	71.	(B)	82.	(D)	93.	(C)
60.	(A)	72.	(D)	83.	(A)	94.	(D)
61.	(E)	73.	(D)	84.	(E)	95.	(D)
62.	(E)	74.	(B)	85.	(C)	96.	(C)
63.	(C)	75.	(E)	86.	(C)	97.	(A)
64.	(C)	76.	(D)	87.	(D)	98.	(D)
65.	(D)	77.	(E)	88.	(C)	99.	(E)
66.	(B)	78.	(B)	89.	(C)	100.	(B)
67.	(D)						

DETAILED EXPLANATIONS OF ANSWERS

TEST 3

Section I

1. **(A)** "Campus" is a singular noun; therefore, the pronoun referring to "campus" should be "its" so that the pronoun will agree with its antecedent. Choices (B), "findings of," and (C), "in which," both have prepositions appropriately used. Choice (D), "can," is a helping verb in the correct tense.

2. **(C)** Choice (C) should read, "could not care less." A person using this expression is indicating his total lack of interest in something; to say, "I could care less" indicates some interest, so the correct expression is "I could not care less." Choice (A) is the correct subject pronoun; choice (B), "good," is the adjective form used to follow the linking verb "be" and choice (D) is a gerund used as the object of a preposition.

3. **(C)** There is no antecedent for "it." Choice (A), "a person," is the subject to which "he" in choice (B) refers. "Never" in choice (D) is a correctly placed adverb. The sentence should include a phrase such as "a crime" to serve as the antecedent of "it," or the phrase "for it" could be deleted.

4. **(B)** The adverb "daily" is misplaced and should be placed with "is bringing," choice (A), or with "habit." Choice (C) is a prepositional phrase, and choice (D) is a subject pronoun for the subordinate clause.

5. **(A)** The adverb form, "frequently," should be used to modify the verb. Choices (B) and (C) are a correct subject-verb combination. The adjective form, "possible," of choice (D) follows the linking verb "is."

6. **(D)**   The expression should read, "renting (or buying) a tuxedo," in order to complete the parallelism following choice (B) "included": "hiring a limousine" and "buying gifts," choice (C). Choice (A) is a correct expression which can also be phrased, "more than he expected" if greater clarity is desired.

7. **(C)**   The object pronoun "us" should follow the preposition "of." In choice (A), "viewing" is a gerund used as the subject and therefore requires the possessive adjective "our." Choice (B) is the verb. Choice (D) is a correct idiom.

8. **(B)**   The modifier "only" is misplaced. To place this word before "stole" indicates that stealing is a minor problem; also, the meaning of the sentence clearly indicates Jules has stolen money one time, so the sentence should read, "stole money only once." Choice (A) is a correct preposition; choice (C) is a possessive pronoun modifying "conscience"; and choice (D) is an object pronoun as the object of "allow."

9. **(D)**   Sentences should not end with a preposition; the sentence should read, "an opinion with which everyone agreed." Choice (A) is a gerund as the object of a preposition. Choice (B) is an appropriate conjunction; and choice (C), "good," is the positive form of the adjective to follow the linking verb "tasted."

10. **(A)**   The expression should read, "as prevalent as" for the proper comparison. Choice (B) is a noun used as an adjective. Choice (C), "some of which," has clear reference to "ornaments." Choice (D), "such as," is correct to mean, "for example."

11. **(B)**   The interrupter, "though not nearly all," should be placed so as not to split important parts of the sentence. Choices (A), (D), and (E) are incorrect because the interrupter splits a preposition and its object. Choices (C) and (D) will produce a fragment because the subject "we" is missing.

12. **(C)**   The phrase "cannot help" should be followed by a gerund, not by "but." Choice (C) follows "cannot help" with the gerund "admitting." Choices (A) and (D) are incorrect because they follow "cannot help" with "but." The wording of choice (B), "cannot admit," and choice (E), "cannot know," twists the meaning of the sentence.

13. **(A)** Choice (A) correctly uses the object pronoun "whom" to follow the preposition "of." Choice (B) uses the wrong pronoun. Choice (C) inserts an extraneous preposition "about" that has no object. Choice (D) is awkward wording; choice (E) is also poor wording, especially with the pronoun "him" so far away from its antecedent.

14. **(C)** Choice (C) clearly and simply deals with the location and the fame of the Dead Sea. It is incorrect to use a preposition with no object in order to end a sentence. Choices (A), (D), and (E) are incorrect because they end with "famous for." Also, in the phrase, "where the Dead Sea is at," the word *at* is redundant; it is sufficient to write "where the Dead Sea is." Therefore, choices (A) and (B) are incorrect. Finally, since the Dead Sea still exists, the verbs must be in the present tense.

15. **(B)** Choice (B) plainly states the subject and the verb, "I find." Choices (A) and (E) have the subject in a prepositional phrase, "for me." Choice (E) produces a fragment. Choice (C), a fragment, has no subject because both potential subjects are in prepositional phases: "agreement" and "plan." Choices (C) and (D) imply "everyone" as the main subject.

16. **(B)** Choice (B) avoids the split infinitive and the incorrect expression, "inside of." Choices (A) and (D) split the infinitive "to finish" with the adverb "completely." Choice (C) uses "inside of," an expression that is incorrect to use because it is redundant ("of" should be deleted) and because it should not be used with measuring time. Choice (E) erroneously changes the idea and would employ two verbs in simple past tense: "hired" and "finished."

17. **(C)** "Since the plane is late" shows correct time sequence and good reasoning. Choice (A), "seeing as how," and choice (D), "being as," are poor wording. Choices (B), "when," and (E), "while," are the wrong time, logically, to be on the observation deck.

18. **(E)** Since a sentence should not end with a preposition, choices (A) and (B) are eliminated. Choices (C), "living in this world," and (D), "world's living," introduce new concepts.

19. **(D)** "Because" is the correct word to use in the cause-and-effect relationship in this sentence. Choice (A), "being that"; choice (E), "than me"; and choice (B), "the more," are not grammatically correct. Choice (C), "is made by you," is in the passive voice and not as direct as (D).

20.   **(A)**   Choice (A) produces a complete sentence: "rainfall" is the subject and "let up" is the verb. None of the other choices produces a complete sentence.

21.   **(C)**   The clause "a French composer" modifies Anton Ravel. In the original, it would appear to modify "the bolero." Choice (C) best corrects this ambiguity. Each of the other choices places the modifier in an incorrect place.

22.   **(A)**   "This musical composition" should replace "it" in sentence 5, since the paragraph should not start off with a pronoun that lacks a clear antecedent. Choice (B) ("the folk dance") may look right, but since the rest of the passage concerns the music and not the dance, it would be inappropriate. Choices (C) and (D) are clearly the wrong antecedents for "it" in this sentence.

23.   **(B)**   In the original, "clarinet, bassoon, and piccolo" would appear to modify "parts." Choice (B) best clears up this confusion by placing the clause so as to modify "instruments." Choices (A) and (C) are both technically correct, but are less clear in the structure of the sentence than choice (B). Choice (E) contains a misplaced modifier.

24.   **(D)**   The word "beginning" in sentence 9 is in the present progressive tense. It should be changed to "begin" to accord with the present tense used in the rest of the sentence and throughout the passage.

25.   **(D)**   The word "relenting," in this context, is wrong; if the harmony remains in the same key for 15 to 17 minutes, this is surely "unrelenting."

26.   **(C)**   Choice (C) separates the temporal relation of the shift in key nicely with a single comma, where the unpunctuated original was too jumbled. Choices (A), (B), and (D) all use too many commas in awkward positions.

27.   **(B)**   The phrase "like in the movie *Orca*" not only disrupts the rhythm of the sentence, but the allusion itself is gratuitous and is not necessary to the author's point in this sentence, which is to ask rhetorically whether or not this particular killer whale should be released from captivity.

28. **(D)** "From her natural habitat" is clearly an error, because what is being debated in this letter is the fact that Dena does not live in her natural habitat. Therefore, "into" is the best substitution for "from." "Under" in choice (C) makes no sense in this context. Choice (A) changes the verb to the past tense, which is clearly wrong, since what is being discussed is surely that Dena presently deserves to be released. Choice (B) makes a quasi-poetical inversion, which is unnecessarily stylized for such a letter, and more importantly, the sentence retains the incorrect preposition "from."

29. **(E)** In the original, the modifier "Sea Habitat, Inc." was in the wrong position to be modifying "owners." Both choices (A) and (C) correct this in acceptable ways. Only choice (B) is incorrect; "Since" emphasizes the incidental fact that "Sea Habitat, Inc." are Dena's owners, and creates a misleading logical relation.

30. **(A)** Choice (A) best follows sentence 10, as it continues the theme of obstacles toward Dena's release. Choice (E) is the next best choice, but it would make sentence 11 sound redundant and repetitive. Choices (B) and (C) set up misleading logical relations with the phrases "As a matter of fact" and "As we all know," and would not follow well from sentence 10. Choice (D) is as gratuitous and unnecessary as the *Orca* allusion in sentence 4.

31. **(D)** "Holding" in sentence 7 should either be "holds" or "is holding"; "stayed" in sentence 10 should be "stay" to agree with the present tense of the rest of the passage.

32. **(E)** Sentence 8 is simple in structure and direct in meaning, and is best with no punctuation. Choice (C) would also be a correct form, but does not improve the original any.

33. **(C)** The passage basically describes some of the polar bear's basic traits. Its tone is detached and factual, like an entry in an encyclopedia. Therefore, the writer's personal feeling is not the issue as in choice (A). The paragraph is describing one example of Alaskan wildlife, so (B) is insufficient. (D) is inaccurate because the passage does not seem to set out to "prove" anything. Choice (E) contradicts the focus of the entire passage.

34. **(A)** Polar bears continue to live near the North Pole, so the past tense is inappropriate.

35.   **(C)**   Sentence 3 digresses from the main topic, which is the polar bear and its habits, to a geological account of the Arctic region in general. This is irrelevant to the progression of this passage, and would best be eliminated.

36.   **(E)**   Sentence 5 is best as it is; the punctuation is correct and the modifiers are properly placed. (D) would be the next best choice; it is technically correct, though more clumsy than the original. (A), (B), and (C) all scramble the sense of an otherwise clear sentence.

37.   **(A)**   Choice (A) is best because it continues the physical description of the polar bear. (B) is not wholly irrelevant, as it deals with the bears' eyesight, but it would be best placed elsewhere. (C) and (E) introduces new subjects. (D), like (B), is somewhat relevant, but would be best placed elsewhere.

38.   **(D)**   Choice (D) combines the three sentences best using commas to separate the thoughts. Choice (A) introduces a colon which may work, if the end of the sentence were altered. "While" in the last portion of the sentence, though, is absolutely wrong. (B), as it stands, would best be changed back to two sentences. Choice (C) is similar to (A) insofar as "though" confuses the relationship between the two ideas.

39.   **(C)**   Choice (C) correctly and smoothly combines the two adjectives while providing sentence variety. Choice (A) is not parallel; "grieving" is not parallel with the other two adjectives. In choice (B), the adjectives appear to modify the dead Lenore. In choices (D) and (E), the ideas of melancholy and grief are not stated in concise parallel structure.

40.   **(C)**   Choice (C) is the most concise expression of the major ideas. Choice (A) is too abrupt and states that the bird "is evil" instead of being "called 'evil.'" Choice (B) contains awkward wording: "the realization of" and "the evil and omen of doom of the bird." The wording of choice (D) creates a run-on sentence. Choice (E) incorrectly twists the idea of evil.

41.   **(B)**   Choice (B) correctly identifies who is doing what. Choices (A) and (C) do not indicate the man as the subject. Choice (D) implies the bird is shrieking with anguish, and choice (E) implies the man is shrieking with anguish as well as replying.

42.   **(D)**   This essay is an analysis of Poe's narrative poem "The Raven," and as such shows the progression of ideas in that poem. Choices

(A) and (B) might be plausible, but there is too much ambiguity for the events to be classified as supernatural or the bird's intent as clearly evil. Choice (E) is not fully developed in the paper. Choice (C) might be a logical choice, but it is not the outstanding intent.

43.   **(E)**   Choice (E) correctly uses the cause-and-effect construction; in addition, this choice uses a transition word at the beginning of the sentence in order to indicate contrast of ideas. Choice (A) employs a misplaced modifier which implies the "others" are repeating the "one word." Choices (B) and (C) leave out a transition word and present as fact what is considered opinion. Choice (D) is too formal and also omits the transition word.

44.   **(D)**   The colon is the most appropriate way to unify the closing thoughts into a single sentence. (A) also utilizes the colon, but the elimination of the comma to create the phrase "is a familiar one" is more clumsy than the original. (B) adds a comma between the two sentences, which creates a run-on. (C) uses a semicolon which is inappropriate. (E), "that is certain is that," both loses the necessary sense of "however," as well as creates an unnecessarily long and convoluted sentence.

45.   **(B)**   Medieval sources would provide direct information on the scope of medical knowledge and use of medicines at that time. The classical music period began after the medieval period ended, so choice (A) is incorrect. Choice (C) is also wrong as Native American societies were unknown to Europeans in the medieval period. Foreign-language education was a very limited activity in that place and time, limited mostly to classical languages (and education limited to very few people), so choice (D) is inappropriate. Lastly, biochemistry as a subject of study did not exist then, so choice (E) is also wrong.

46.   **(E)**   All text in a research paper should be double spaced (except between elements such as the title and the first line of text) so it can be read easily. Choice (A) is incorrect as page after page of only single spacing would be extremely uncomfortable to read. Long quotes should have the same spacing (but different indentation) as the main text, and the same is true for any footnotes at the bottom of the page and for the bibliography at the end, so choice (B) is wrong. All text, without exception, should be double spaced, choice (C) is also incorrect. Therefore, choice (D) is wrong, as the bibliography should not be singled out from the rest of the text to be single-spaced.

47. **(D)** Regardless of the minor differences in styles among research papers, the paper's title must appear on the first page. The usual style for a research paper title (MLA style) is initial capital letters without underlining, not all capitals with underlining, making choice (A) incorrect. The entire title should never be in quotation marks, so choice (B) is wrong. Some styles call for a separate title page and some don't, so choice (C) is not the best answer. Choice (E) is wrong—although it may be helpful to have the title on each page, it is not required in most cases.

48. **(E)** Book titles must always be underlined, according to MLA style and most other research-paper styles. Some styles call for leaving the page number off certain pages such as the first page of the paper or the first page of a bibliography or works cited page, so choice (A) is inaccurate. It is useful, but not strictly necessary, to put the writer's name on every page, so choice (B) is not the best answer. Choice (C) is incorrect as magazine titles should be underlined, not in quotation marks. Choice (D) is also incorrect as magazine article titles should be in quotation marks and not underlined.

49. **(A)** Long quotations, of five lines or more, should not be in quotation marks—the proper way to set off long quotations is by indenting them. There is no rule against quotations in poetry format, so choice (B) is wrong. Choice (C) describes how long quotations *should* appear, so that choice is incorrect. Long quotations usually are preceded by a colon, so choice (D) is wrong. Lastly, starting a new paragraph after a long quote is common, so choice (E) is incorrect.

50. **(A)** The title of a short poem should always be in quotation marks. The name of a television program should be underlined, so choice (B) is incorrect. Choice (C) is wrong as the titles of all plays, including one-act plays, should be underlined. The name of a magazine, like the name of a book, should be underlined, not in quotation marks, making choice (D) wrong. Choice (E) is incorrect as the name of a painting should appear not in quotes but underlined.

51. **(D)** Since two books by the same author appear in the paper, any reference to either book must have the title of that book as well as the author's name and the page number, to distinguish between the two books. Choice (A) is wrong because without the book title, one couldn't tell which of the two books is the source. The name of the author should appear in the reference unless the author's name is mentioned with the quote, so choice (B) is not the best answer. The page number is a vital part

of the reference, so choice (C), which eliminates the page number, is incorrect. A full bibliographic-type reference such as the one described in choice (E) isn't necessary, so that answer is wrong.

52.   **(D)**   When only one item from an anthology is used, the author and title of that item should be listed first, not the editors and title of the anthology. In a bibliography the last name of the author or editor always appears first, making choice (A) incorrect. Editors' names should always be listed if they are available, so choice (B) is incorrect. Choice (C) is wrong as "eds" is the accepted abbreviation for "editors" in a bibliography. In bibliography entries for books, the page numbers should always appear after the publication date, so choice (E) is incorrect.

53.   **(E)**   In alphabetizing bibliography entries, the words "a," "an," and "the" are always ignored. Most official bibliography styles call for a repeated author name to be replaced by a long dash, making choice (A) incorrect. Author's names, not book titles, appear first in bibliographies, so choice (B) is wrong. Choice (C) is wrong as many authors have books published by more than one publisher. Choice (D) is incorrect as subtitles (which appear after the colon in a title) are a legitimate part of the title and should be included in the bibliography.

54.   **(E)**   This topic is specific enough to be a challenging, in-depth topic for a ten-page paper for an education class without being so specific that little information can be found on the subject. Foreign-language education is far too broad a topic for any college paper, so choice (A) is incorrect. Choice (B) provides a topic that is also too broad to be covered in detail in a ten-page paper. The detailed topic in choice (C) would probably be the subject of only one or two studies so there would be too little information for a ten-page paper. Choice (D) is inappropriate as it describes a highly specific topic that may not even be a subject of research or writing.

55.   **(C)**   An abstract is a summary of the main contents of a journal article, so a researcher could read it to find out if the article is relevant to the research topic and therefore worth reading in its entirety. Choice (A) is incorrect as an abstract will not include a bibliography or cross-references, the usual sources for other articles on the same topic. The author's sources will be listed in the bibliography at the end of the article, not in the abstract, so choice (B) is incorrect. Determining the article's reliability requires checking the author's credentials and sources, neither of which are given in an abstract, making choice (D) an inappropriate choice. The tables and charts in an article are not given in the abstract, so choice (E) is wrong.

Section II

56. **(C)** Donne's *Meditation* is built on the Renaissance notion of man as a microcosm (a little world), analogous to the big world outside (the macrocosm), except that Donne reverses the idea, temporarily arguing that man is the macrocosm and the world outside the microcosm. The first paragraph develops the comparison of man and the world, arguing that man is larger, more complete, than the world.

57. **(B)** The line means that the outside world does not contain anything to which some part of man does not correspond (put another way, some part of man corresponds to everything in the outside world).

58. **(B)** In the first paragraph, Donne plays with the idea that man is the macrocosm and the outside world the microcosm. See answer 56, above.

59. **(D)** Line 36 asks rhetorically whether the outside world (the world of nature) can produce as many monstrous, venomous creatures as man can produce diseases. In his comparison of man and the outside world, man's diseases correspond to the outside world's venomous creatures.

60. **(A)** Donne means that man himself produces an abundance of diseases, but it is an unwelcome abundance. Hence, "miserable abundance" refers to human diseases.

61. **(E)** A paradox is a statement that is seemingly contradictory or opposed to common sense but that is nonetheless true in context. How can riches be "beggarly"? Only in context can the paradox be explained: "riches" refers to the diseases man produces, and these diseases of course make him "poor" (hence the riches are only apparent).

62. **(E)** In the metaphor in the second paragraph, man's diseases are compared to the other world's "serpents and vipers, malignant and venomous creatures, and worms and caterpillars." The latter seek to devour the world that produces them, much as human diseases seek to destroy the humans who produce them.

63. **(C)** Mortality and other concerns of the "grave" will be the poet's concern. This is reinforced by the death-imagery of "flower-barren

fields'' (line 3) and perhaps even the "far-horn-winding fall" (line 2) — an allusion to a salutary funeral tune, or perhaps even "Taps."

64. **(C)** Run-ons, even in poetry, tend to make one "breathless," not in excitement, but in sheer fatigue. MacLeish's use of unpunctuated cataloguing here is intentional. Branches that don't answer, fields that have no flowers in them, and wind that makes only sullen noise are reflections of the tiredness of nature. Here, lack of punctuation reinforces theme.

65. **(D)** There are a number of surprises in the second stanza. Of the possibilities listed here, the poet's relief at the passage of summer (and spring) is perhaps the most surprising. Fall is not as often praised as spring, but its beauty is often the subject of poetry. The fact that the poet continues first person and unpunctuated sentences may be surprising, but the tone has already been set in the first stanza.

66. **(B)** The poet had begun by saying he would speak "In praise of autumn," and listed natural images to reinforce the point in the reader's mind. He continues cataloguing in the second stanza, but a dramatic shift in intent is indicated by his introduction of fall as "the human season." (line 5). He has played a trick on the reader. He is really talking about human life. It is unclear at this point if there is the kind of one-to-one metaphor demanded by personification.

67. **(D)** The poet's (and the "human's") world is almost the reverse of what would be expected in a typical seasonal poem. The sun brings "green" growth, and in doing so, disturbs the natural human season of fall.

68. **(E)** Humans share the world of autumn with the "outcast crows," implying that humans are similarly outcast in this crow and human season. There is some identification here with "whispering year" (line 10) and daylight as it fades, but the central parallel is a concentrated and haunting one between the unwanted birds and ourselves.

69. **(C)** The speaker provides an ominous hint here that man is a creature of the night — again, a reversal of what would be expected. The fall brings more room for humans not just because the leaves are off the trees, but also because there is less daytime.

70. **(C)** While a case could be made that burning leaves is an act of destruction, it would be mitigated by the fact that the leaves are already

dead and also by the poet's curious use of the laudatory word "brave." What is more evident here is that the human race is very alone and surrounded by an unfamiliar world ("there are no evening birds we know") (line 15). Even the moon is unexpectedly "naked." This image is reinforced by the notion of the previous stanza that man is somehow a creature of the night.

71.   **(B)**   "Sterile" refers to a "field" in which nothing lives but "sterile" also implies that man is a creature whose reproductive capabilities have been destroyed by his environment — by the same air that sustains him. Man draws his aerobic sustenance, then, from a gas which may eventually exterminate him. This foreboding is reinforced by the lines which follow.

72.   **(D)**   Eliot clearly states that he will make two points. The first — intellectual excellence — is to be expected. The second — a kind of emotional poetic maturity — is surprising because of the lack of this earlier in his career.

73.   **(D)**   Some readers may infer that Yeats did not find notoriety until later in life, but this is not the case. His first poems were published when he was 20, and soon after he began meeting the luminaries of his age. Eliot goes to great lengths to clarify his "middle age" comment — praising the poet for intellectual excellence early in life, but stating that he did not achieve "complete emotional expression" until later.

74.   **(B)**   While the first sentence provides a general direction for the paragraph (that there will be two points), the thesis statement is actually in the second sentence. What Eliot does in the first sentence is provide transition from the previous paragraph. If there was no need for a transition, he could have started with sentence two. In the second sentence he says that his first point had already been "touched" upon. Therefore, his mention of "the points that I particularly wish to make" directs the reader's mind to previous material at the same time as it is directed forward to the new second point.

75.   **(E)**   Eliot is implying not just that middle-aged poets often do "fail," but that they often use this common observation as an excuse, as if to say, "Of course I'm not as inspired as when I was younger. No one is." Eliot believes the opposite is true of Yeats.

76.   **(D)**   Syntactically as well as contextually, Eliot is clearly saying that any person short of senility can be able to retain poetic inspiration — by being "capable of experience." Capability, however, is not just defined by physical ability, but by a "capacity" to adapt — to find oneself in a "different world in every decade." One can grow older without being senile and still not be capable of experiencing this phenomenon.

77.   **(E)**   Eliot criticizes poetry's public figures not because they are sensitive to contemporary fashion, but because they are sensitive to it ONLY, and, in addition, are more than content to behave this way and to let this govern their writing, statements, acts, and thoughts as well.

78.   **(B)**   Eliot contends that younger men "can see him as a poet who in his work remained in the best sense always young." Young, as defined here, relates to honesty about oneself expressed in the poetry.

79.   **(B)**   Choice (B) is correct since it best captures the meaning of "mitigated." (A), (C), (D), and (E) are incorrect because they do not have the same meaning as the underlined word.

80.   **(D)**   Answer choice (D) is synonymous with "pallid," so it is correct. Choices (A), (B), (C), and (E) do not carry the same meaning as the underlined word.

81.   **(A)**   Answer choice (A) is correct because it conveys the same meaning as the underlined phrase in the most positive way. Choices (B), (C), and (D) are more negative ways of saying the same thing. Choice (E) does not have the same meaning. Saving money might lead one to assume that Luisa is frugal, but that's not necessarily so.

82.   **(D)**   Answer choice (D) is a correct revision of the sentence. Choices (A), (B), (C), and (E) are not clear in meaning.

83.   **(A)**   Answer choice (A) provides a definition of "annotated," so it is the correct choice. Choices (B), (C), (D), and (E) do not define the underlined word, so they are incorrect.

84.   **(E)**   Answer choice (E) is synonymous with the underlined word, so it is correct. Choices (A), (B), (C), and (D) fail to capture the intended meaning of "benediction."

85.   **(C)**   Answer choice (C) is a correct revision. Choices (A), (B), (D), and (E) are not clear revisions.

86.   **(C)**   Answer choice (C) is correct because it best defines "homogeneous," while choices (A), (B), (D), and (E) do not.

87.   **(D)**   Answer choice (D) is the correct answer since it portrays the most positive image. Choices (A), (B), (C), and (E) do not convey a positive picture, so they are incorrect.

88.   **(C)**   Answer choice (C) best captures the meaning of the underlined word. Choices (A), (B), (D), and (E) do not convey the same meaning as "inflection."

89.   **(C)**   Answer choice (C) is a correct revision of the sentence. Choices (A), (B), (D), and (E) are unclear sentences, and therefore are incorrect.

90.   **(D)**   Answer choice (D) is correct because it is a synonym for "taut." Choices (A), (B), (C), and (E) are not correct because they do not have the same meaning as the underlined word.

91.   **(B)**   Answer choice (B) best defines the underlined word, so it is correct. Choices (A), (C), (D), and (E) do not define "imperative," so they are incorrect.

92.   **(C)**   Answer choice (C) is a correct revision, while choices (A), (B), (D), and (E) are unclear sentences and therefore incorrect.

93.   **(C)**   Answer choice (C) best defines the underlined word. Choices (A), (B), (D), and (E) do not have the same meaning as "fundamentals."

94.   **(D)**   Answer choice (D) is correct because it conveys a negative picture. Choices (A), (B), (C), and (E) are not negative in meaning.

95.   **(D)**   Answer choice (D) is correct since it is the only optimistic statement. It is a call for improvement, which in itself is optimistic. Choices (A), (B), (C), and (E) are not optimistic in tone.

96.   **(C)**   Answer choice (C) is fervent in tone, so it is the right answer. It is a rally to fight to ensure the separation of church and state.

None of the other choices conveys rallying or fervent tone, so (A), (B), (D), and (E) are wrong.

97.   **(A)**   Answer choice (A) is correct because the speaker's comment "…take my life and all" is a direct statement of defeat. He has given up, so to speak. Choices (B), (C), (D), and (E) do not convey defeat.

98.   **(D)**   Answer choice (D) is the correct answer because the credo is a direct paradox. It is not a hyperbole, cliché, proverb, or metaphor, so choices (A), (B), (C), and (E) are wrong.

99.   **(E)**   Answer choice (E) is the right answer because the author states that even though the U.S. and the U.S.S.R. were never directly at war, they supplied weapons to warring nations. Choices (A), (B), (C), and (D) are not implied by the author, so they are wrong.

100. **(B)**   SDI is an abbreviation for Strategic Defense Initiative because it uses the first letter of each word to create a shortened version of a word, words, or phrase. Unlike an acronym, an abbreviation is not in itself a word and is not pronounceable; therefore, (B) is correct. SDI is not a metaphor, a paradox, an acronym, or an allusion, so (A), (C), (D), and (E) are incorrect.

ANSWER SHEETS

CLEP FRESHMAN COLLEGE
COMPOSITION – TEST 1

Section 1

1. Ⓐ Ⓑ Ⓒ Ⓓ Ⓔ
2. Ⓐ Ⓑ Ⓒ Ⓓ Ⓔ
3. Ⓐ Ⓑ Ⓒ Ⓓ Ⓔ
4. Ⓐ Ⓑ Ⓒ Ⓓ Ⓔ
5. Ⓐ Ⓑ Ⓒ Ⓓ Ⓔ
6. Ⓐ Ⓑ Ⓒ Ⓓ Ⓔ
7. Ⓐ Ⓑ Ⓒ Ⓓ Ⓔ
8. Ⓐ Ⓑ Ⓒ Ⓓ Ⓔ
9. Ⓐ Ⓑ Ⓒ Ⓓ Ⓔ
10. Ⓐ Ⓑ Ⓒ Ⓓ Ⓔ
11. Ⓐ Ⓑ Ⓒ Ⓓ Ⓔ
12. Ⓐ Ⓑ Ⓒ Ⓓ Ⓔ
13. Ⓐ Ⓑ Ⓒ Ⓓ Ⓔ
14. Ⓐ Ⓑ Ⓒ Ⓓ Ⓔ
15. Ⓐ Ⓑ Ⓒ Ⓓ Ⓔ
16. Ⓐ Ⓑ Ⓒ Ⓓ Ⓔ
17. Ⓐ Ⓑ Ⓒ Ⓓ Ⓔ
18. Ⓐ Ⓑ Ⓒ Ⓓ Ⓔ
19. Ⓐ Ⓑ Ⓒ Ⓓ Ⓔ
20. Ⓐ Ⓑ Ⓒ Ⓓ Ⓔ
21. Ⓐ Ⓑ Ⓒ Ⓓ Ⓔ
22. Ⓐ Ⓑ Ⓒ Ⓓ Ⓔ
23. Ⓐ Ⓑ Ⓒ Ⓓ Ⓔ
24. Ⓐ Ⓑ Ⓒ Ⓓ Ⓔ
25. Ⓐ Ⓑ Ⓒ Ⓓ Ⓔ
26. Ⓐ Ⓑ Ⓒ Ⓓ Ⓔ
27. Ⓐ Ⓑ Ⓒ Ⓓ Ⓔ
28. Ⓐ Ⓑ Ⓒ Ⓓ Ⓔ
29. Ⓐ Ⓑ Ⓒ Ⓓ Ⓔ
30. Ⓐ Ⓑ Ⓒ Ⓓ Ⓔ
31. Ⓐ Ⓑ Ⓒ Ⓓ Ⓔ
32. Ⓐ Ⓑ Ⓒ Ⓓ Ⓔ
33. Ⓐ Ⓑ Ⓒ Ⓓ Ⓔ
34. Ⓐ Ⓑ Ⓒ Ⓓ Ⓔ

35. Ⓐ Ⓑ Ⓒ Ⓓ Ⓔ
36. Ⓐ Ⓑ Ⓒ Ⓓ Ⓔ
37. Ⓐ Ⓑ Ⓒ Ⓓ Ⓔ
38. Ⓐ Ⓑ Ⓒ Ⓓ Ⓔ
39. Ⓐ Ⓑ Ⓒ Ⓓ Ⓔ
40. Ⓐ Ⓑ Ⓒ Ⓓ Ⓔ
41. Ⓐ Ⓑ Ⓒ Ⓓ Ⓔ
42. Ⓐ Ⓑ Ⓒ Ⓓ Ⓔ
43. Ⓐ Ⓑ Ⓒ Ⓓ Ⓔ
44. Ⓐ Ⓑ Ⓒ Ⓓ Ⓔ
45. Ⓐ Ⓑ Ⓒ Ⓓ Ⓔ
46. Ⓐ Ⓑ Ⓒ Ⓓ Ⓔ
47. Ⓐ Ⓑ Ⓒ Ⓓ Ⓔ
48. Ⓐ Ⓑ Ⓒ Ⓓ Ⓔ
49. Ⓐ Ⓑ Ⓒ Ⓓ Ⓔ
50. Ⓐ Ⓑ Ⓒ Ⓓ Ⓔ
51. Ⓐ Ⓑ Ⓒ Ⓓ Ⓔ
52. Ⓐ Ⓑ Ⓒ Ⓓ Ⓔ
53. Ⓐ Ⓑ Ⓒ Ⓓ Ⓔ
54. Ⓐ Ⓑ Ⓒ Ⓓ Ⓔ
55. Ⓐ Ⓑ Ⓒ Ⓓ Ⓔ

Section 2

56. Ⓐ Ⓑ Ⓒ Ⓓ Ⓔ
57. Ⓐ Ⓑ Ⓒ Ⓓ Ⓔ
58. Ⓐ Ⓑ Ⓒ Ⓓ Ⓔ
59. Ⓐ Ⓑ Ⓒ Ⓓ Ⓔ
60. Ⓐ Ⓑ Ⓒ Ⓓ Ⓔ
61. Ⓐ Ⓑ Ⓒ Ⓓ Ⓔ
62. Ⓐ Ⓑ Ⓒ Ⓓ Ⓔ
63. Ⓐ Ⓑ Ⓒ Ⓓ Ⓔ
64. Ⓐ Ⓑ Ⓒ Ⓓ Ⓔ
65. Ⓐ Ⓑ Ⓒ Ⓓ Ⓔ
66. Ⓐ Ⓑ Ⓒ Ⓓ Ⓔ

67. Ⓐ Ⓑ Ⓒ Ⓓ Ⓔ
68. Ⓐ Ⓑ Ⓒ Ⓓ Ⓔ
69. Ⓐ Ⓑ Ⓒ Ⓓ Ⓔ
70. Ⓐ Ⓑ Ⓒ Ⓓ Ⓔ
71. Ⓐ Ⓑ Ⓒ Ⓓ Ⓔ
72. Ⓐ Ⓑ Ⓒ Ⓓ Ⓔ
73. Ⓐ Ⓑ Ⓒ Ⓓ Ⓔ
74. Ⓐ Ⓑ Ⓒ Ⓓ Ⓔ
75. Ⓐ Ⓑ Ⓒ Ⓓ Ⓔ
76. Ⓐ Ⓑ Ⓒ Ⓓ Ⓔ
77. Ⓐ Ⓑ Ⓒ Ⓓ Ⓔ
78. Ⓐ Ⓑ Ⓒ Ⓓ Ⓔ
79. Ⓐ Ⓑ Ⓒ Ⓓ Ⓔ
80. Ⓐ Ⓑ Ⓒ Ⓓ Ⓔ
81. Ⓐ Ⓑ Ⓒ Ⓓ Ⓔ
82. Ⓐ Ⓑ Ⓒ Ⓓ Ⓔ
83. Ⓐ Ⓑ Ⓒ Ⓓ Ⓔ
84. Ⓐ Ⓑ Ⓒ Ⓓ Ⓔ
85. Ⓐ Ⓑ Ⓒ Ⓓ Ⓔ
86. Ⓐ Ⓑ Ⓒ Ⓓ Ⓔ
87. Ⓐ Ⓑ Ⓒ Ⓓ Ⓔ
88. Ⓐ Ⓑ Ⓒ Ⓓ Ⓔ
89. Ⓐ Ⓑ Ⓒ Ⓓ Ⓔ
90. Ⓐ Ⓑ Ⓒ Ⓓ Ⓔ
91. Ⓐ Ⓑ Ⓒ Ⓓ Ⓔ
92. Ⓐ Ⓑ Ⓒ Ⓓ Ⓔ
93. Ⓐ Ⓑ Ⓒ Ⓓ Ⓔ
94. Ⓐ Ⓑ Ⓒ Ⓓ Ⓔ
95. Ⓐ Ⓑ Ⓒ Ⓓ Ⓔ
96. Ⓐ Ⓑ Ⓒ Ⓓ Ⓔ
97. Ⓐ Ⓑ Ⓒ Ⓓ Ⓔ
98. Ⓐ Ⓑ Ⓒ Ⓓ Ⓔ
99. Ⓐ Ⓑ Ⓒ Ⓓ Ⓔ
100. Ⓐ Ⓑ Ⓒ Ⓓ Ⓔ

CLEP FRESHMAN COLLEGE
COMPOSITION – TEST 2

Section 1

1. Ⓐ Ⓑ Ⓒ Ⓓ Ⓔ
2. Ⓐ Ⓑ Ⓒ Ⓓ Ⓔ
3. Ⓐ Ⓑ Ⓒ Ⓓ Ⓔ
4. Ⓐ Ⓑ Ⓒ Ⓓ Ⓔ
5. Ⓐ Ⓑ Ⓒ Ⓓ Ⓔ
6. Ⓐ Ⓑ Ⓒ Ⓓ Ⓔ
7. Ⓐ Ⓑ Ⓒ Ⓓ Ⓔ
8. Ⓐ Ⓑ Ⓒ Ⓓ Ⓔ
9. Ⓐ Ⓑ Ⓒ Ⓓ Ⓔ
10. Ⓐ Ⓑ Ⓒ Ⓓ Ⓔ
11. Ⓐ Ⓑ Ⓒ Ⓓ Ⓔ
12. Ⓐ Ⓑ Ⓒ Ⓓ Ⓔ
13. Ⓐ Ⓑ Ⓒ Ⓓ Ⓔ
14. Ⓐ Ⓑ Ⓒ Ⓓ Ⓔ
15. Ⓐ Ⓑ Ⓒ Ⓓ Ⓔ
16. Ⓐ Ⓑ Ⓒ Ⓓ Ⓔ
17. Ⓐ Ⓑ Ⓒ Ⓓ Ⓔ
18. Ⓐ Ⓑ Ⓒ Ⓓ Ⓔ
19. Ⓐ Ⓑ Ⓒ Ⓓ Ⓔ
20. Ⓐ Ⓑ Ⓒ Ⓓ Ⓔ
21. Ⓐ Ⓑ Ⓒ Ⓓ Ⓔ
22. Ⓐ Ⓑ Ⓒ Ⓓ Ⓔ
23. Ⓐ Ⓑ Ⓒ Ⓓ Ⓔ
24. Ⓐ Ⓑ Ⓒ Ⓓ Ⓔ
25. Ⓐ Ⓑ Ⓒ Ⓓ Ⓔ
26. Ⓐ Ⓑ Ⓒ Ⓓ Ⓔ
27. Ⓐ Ⓑ Ⓒ Ⓓ Ⓔ
28. Ⓐ Ⓑ Ⓒ Ⓓ Ⓔ
29. Ⓐ Ⓑ Ⓒ Ⓓ Ⓔ
30. Ⓐ Ⓑ Ⓒ Ⓓ Ⓔ
31. Ⓐ Ⓑ Ⓒ Ⓓ Ⓔ
32. Ⓐ Ⓑ Ⓒ Ⓓ Ⓔ
33. Ⓐ Ⓑ Ⓒ Ⓓ Ⓔ
34. Ⓐ Ⓑ Ⓒ Ⓓ Ⓔ

35. Ⓐ Ⓑ Ⓒ Ⓓ Ⓔ
36. Ⓐ Ⓑ Ⓒ Ⓓ Ⓔ
37. Ⓐ Ⓑ Ⓒ Ⓓ Ⓔ
38. Ⓐ Ⓑ Ⓒ Ⓓ Ⓔ
39. Ⓐ Ⓑ Ⓒ Ⓓ Ⓔ
40. Ⓐ Ⓑ Ⓒ Ⓓ Ⓔ
41. Ⓐ Ⓑ Ⓒ Ⓓ Ⓔ
42. Ⓐ Ⓑ Ⓒ Ⓓ Ⓔ
43. Ⓐ Ⓑ Ⓒ Ⓓ Ⓔ
44. Ⓐ Ⓑ Ⓒ Ⓓ Ⓔ
45. Ⓐ Ⓑ Ⓒ Ⓓ Ⓔ
46. Ⓐ Ⓑ Ⓒ Ⓓ Ⓔ
47. Ⓐ Ⓑ Ⓒ Ⓓ Ⓔ
48. Ⓐ Ⓑ Ⓒ Ⓓ Ⓔ
49. Ⓐ Ⓑ Ⓒ Ⓓ Ⓔ
50. Ⓐ Ⓑ Ⓒ Ⓓ Ⓔ
51. Ⓐ Ⓑ Ⓒ Ⓓ Ⓔ
52. Ⓐ Ⓑ Ⓒ Ⓓ Ⓔ
53. Ⓐ Ⓑ Ⓒ Ⓓ Ⓔ
54. Ⓐ Ⓑ Ⓒ Ⓓ Ⓔ
55. Ⓐ Ⓑ Ⓒ Ⓓ Ⓔ

Section 2

56. Ⓐ Ⓑ Ⓒ Ⓓ Ⓔ
57. Ⓐ Ⓑ Ⓒ Ⓓ Ⓔ
58. Ⓐ Ⓑ Ⓒ Ⓓ Ⓔ
59. Ⓐ Ⓑ Ⓒ Ⓓ Ⓔ
60. Ⓐ Ⓑ Ⓒ Ⓓ Ⓔ
61. Ⓐ Ⓑ Ⓒ Ⓓ Ⓔ
62. Ⓐ Ⓑ Ⓒ Ⓓ Ⓔ
63. Ⓐ Ⓑ Ⓒ Ⓓ Ⓔ
64. Ⓐ Ⓑ Ⓒ Ⓓ Ⓔ
65. Ⓐ Ⓑ Ⓒ Ⓓ Ⓔ
66. Ⓐ Ⓑ Ⓒ Ⓓ Ⓔ

67. Ⓐ Ⓑ Ⓒ Ⓓ Ⓔ
68. Ⓐ Ⓑ Ⓒ Ⓓ Ⓔ
69. Ⓐ Ⓑ Ⓒ Ⓓ Ⓔ
70. Ⓐ Ⓑ Ⓒ Ⓓ Ⓔ
71. Ⓐ Ⓑ Ⓒ Ⓓ Ⓔ
72. Ⓐ Ⓑ Ⓒ Ⓓ Ⓔ
73. Ⓐ Ⓑ Ⓒ Ⓓ Ⓔ
74. Ⓐ Ⓑ Ⓒ Ⓓ Ⓔ
75. Ⓐ Ⓑ Ⓒ Ⓓ Ⓔ
76. Ⓐ Ⓑ Ⓒ Ⓓ Ⓔ
77. Ⓐ Ⓑ Ⓒ Ⓓ Ⓔ
78. Ⓐ Ⓑ Ⓒ Ⓓ Ⓔ
79. Ⓐ Ⓑ Ⓒ Ⓓ Ⓔ
80. Ⓐ Ⓑ Ⓒ Ⓓ Ⓔ
81. Ⓐ Ⓑ Ⓒ Ⓓ Ⓔ
82. Ⓐ Ⓑ Ⓒ Ⓓ Ⓔ
83. Ⓐ Ⓑ Ⓒ Ⓓ Ⓔ
84. Ⓐ Ⓑ Ⓒ Ⓓ Ⓔ
85. Ⓐ Ⓑ Ⓒ Ⓓ Ⓔ
86. Ⓐ Ⓑ Ⓒ Ⓓ Ⓔ
87. Ⓐ Ⓑ Ⓒ Ⓓ Ⓔ
88. Ⓐ Ⓑ Ⓒ Ⓓ Ⓔ
89. Ⓐ Ⓑ Ⓒ Ⓓ Ⓔ
90. Ⓐ Ⓑ Ⓒ Ⓓ Ⓔ
91. Ⓐ Ⓑ Ⓒ Ⓓ Ⓔ
92. Ⓐ Ⓑ Ⓒ Ⓓ Ⓔ
93. Ⓐ Ⓑ Ⓒ Ⓓ Ⓔ
94. Ⓐ Ⓑ Ⓒ Ⓓ Ⓔ
95. Ⓐ Ⓑ Ⓒ Ⓓ Ⓔ
96. Ⓐ Ⓑ Ⓒ Ⓓ Ⓔ
97. Ⓐ Ⓑ Ⓒ Ⓓ Ⓔ
98. Ⓐ Ⓑ Ⓒ Ⓓ Ⓔ
99. Ⓐ Ⓑ Ⓒ Ⓓ Ⓔ
100. Ⓐ Ⓑ Ⓒ Ⓓ Ⓔ

CLEP FRESHMAN COLLEGE COMPOSITION – TEST 3

Section 1

1. Ⓐ Ⓑ Ⓒ Ⓓ Ⓔ
2. Ⓐ Ⓑ Ⓒ Ⓓ Ⓔ
3. Ⓐ Ⓑ Ⓒ Ⓓ Ⓔ
4. Ⓐ Ⓑ Ⓒ Ⓓ Ⓔ
5. Ⓐ Ⓑ Ⓒ Ⓓ Ⓔ
6. Ⓐ Ⓑ Ⓒ Ⓓ Ⓔ
7. Ⓐ Ⓑ Ⓒ Ⓓ Ⓔ
8. Ⓐ Ⓑ Ⓒ Ⓓ Ⓔ
9. Ⓐ Ⓑ Ⓒ Ⓓ Ⓔ
10. Ⓐ Ⓑ Ⓒ Ⓓ Ⓔ
11. Ⓐ Ⓑ Ⓒ Ⓓ Ⓔ
12. Ⓐ Ⓑ Ⓒ Ⓓ Ⓔ
13. Ⓐ Ⓑ Ⓒ Ⓓ Ⓔ
14. Ⓐ Ⓑ Ⓒ Ⓓ Ⓔ
15. Ⓐ Ⓑ Ⓒ Ⓓ Ⓔ
16. Ⓐ Ⓑ Ⓒ Ⓓ Ⓔ
17. Ⓐ Ⓑ Ⓒ Ⓓ Ⓔ
18. Ⓐ Ⓑ Ⓒ Ⓓ Ⓔ
19. Ⓐ Ⓑ Ⓒ Ⓓ Ⓔ
20. Ⓐ Ⓑ Ⓒ Ⓓ Ⓔ
21. Ⓐ Ⓑ Ⓒ Ⓓ Ⓔ
22. Ⓐ Ⓑ Ⓒ Ⓓ Ⓔ
23. Ⓐ Ⓑ Ⓒ Ⓓ Ⓔ
24. Ⓐ Ⓑ Ⓒ Ⓓ Ⓔ
25. Ⓐ Ⓑ Ⓒ Ⓓ Ⓔ
26. Ⓐ Ⓑ Ⓒ Ⓓ Ⓔ
27. Ⓐ Ⓑ Ⓒ Ⓓ Ⓔ
28. Ⓐ Ⓑ Ⓒ Ⓓ Ⓔ
29. Ⓐ Ⓑ Ⓒ Ⓓ Ⓔ
30. Ⓐ Ⓑ Ⓒ Ⓓ Ⓔ
31. Ⓐ Ⓑ Ⓒ Ⓓ Ⓔ
32. Ⓐ Ⓑ Ⓒ Ⓓ Ⓔ
33. Ⓐ Ⓑ Ⓒ Ⓓ Ⓔ
34. Ⓐ Ⓑ Ⓒ Ⓓ Ⓔ

35. Ⓐ Ⓑ Ⓒ Ⓓ Ⓔ
36. Ⓐ Ⓑ Ⓒ Ⓓ Ⓔ
37. Ⓐ Ⓑ Ⓒ Ⓓ Ⓔ
38. Ⓐ Ⓑ Ⓒ Ⓓ Ⓔ
39. Ⓐ Ⓑ Ⓒ Ⓓ Ⓔ
40. Ⓐ Ⓑ Ⓒ Ⓓ Ⓔ
41. Ⓐ Ⓑ Ⓒ Ⓓ Ⓔ
42. Ⓐ Ⓑ Ⓒ Ⓓ Ⓔ
43. Ⓐ Ⓑ Ⓒ Ⓓ Ⓔ
44. Ⓐ Ⓑ Ⓒ Ⓓ Ⓔ
45. Ⓐ Ⓑ Ⓒ Ⓓ Ⓔ
46. Ⓐ Ⓑ Ⓒ Ⓓ Ⓔ
47. Ⓐ Ⓑ Ⓒ Ⓓ Ⓔ
48. Ⓐ Ⓑ Ⓒ Ⓓ Ⓔ
49. Ⓐ Ⓑ Ⓒ Ⓓ Ⓔ
50. Ⓐ Ⓑ Ⓒ Ⓓ Ⓔ
51. Ⓐ Ⓑ Ⓒ Ⓓ Ⓔ
52. Ⓐ Ⓑ Ⓒ Ⓓ Ⓔ
53. Ⓐ Ⓑ Ⓒ Ⓓ Ⓔ
54. Ⓐ Ⓑ Ⓒ Ⓓ Ⓔ
55. Ⓐ Ⓑ Ⓒ Ⓓ Ⓔ

Section 2

56. Ⓐ Ⓑ Ⓒ Ⓓ Ⓔ
57. Ⓐ Ⓑ Ⓒ Ⓓ Ⓔ
58. Ⓐ Ⓑ Ⓒ Ⓓ Ⓔ
59. Ⓐ Ⓑ Ⓒ Ⓓ Ⓔ
60. Ⓐ Ⓑ Ⓒ Ⓓ Ⓔ
61. Ⓐ Ⓑ Ⓒ Ⓓ Ⓔ
62. Ⓐ Ⓑ Ⓒ Ⓓ Ⓔ
63. Ⓐ Ⓑ Ⓒ Ⓓ Ⓔ
64. Ⓐ Ⓑ Ⓒ Ⓓ Ⓔ
65. Ⓐ Ⓑ Ⓒ Ⓓ Ⓔ
66. Ⓐ Ⓑ Ⓒ Ⓓ Ⓔ

67. Ⓐ Ⓑ Ⓒ Ⓓ Ⓔ
68. Ⓐ Ⓑ Ⓒ Ⓓ Ⓔ
69. Ⓐ Ⓑ Ⓒ Ⓓ Ⓔ
70. Ⓐ Ⓑ Ⓒ Ⓓ Ⓔ
71. Ⓐ Ⓑ Ⓒ Ⓓ Ⓔ
72. Ⓐ Ⓑ Ⓒ Ⓓ Ⓔ
73. Ⓐ Ⓑ Ⓒ Ⓓ Ⓔ
74. Ⓐ Ⓑ Ⓒ Ⓓ Ⓔ
75. Ⓐ Ⓑ Ⓒ Ⓓ Ⓔ
76. Ⓐ Ⓑ Ⓒ Ⓓ Ⓔ
77. Ⓐ Ⓑ Ⓒ Ⓓ Ⓔ
78. Ⓐ Ⓑ Ⓒ Ⓓ Ⓔ
79. Ⓐ Ⓑ Ⓒ Ⓓ Ⓔ
80. Ⓐ Ⓑ Ⓒ Ⓓ Ⓔ
81. Ⓐ Ⓑ Ⓒ Ⓓ Ⓔ
82. Ⓐ Ⓑ Ⓒ Ⓓ Ⓔ
83. Ⓐ Ⓑ Ⓒ Ⓓ Ⓔ
84. Ⓐ Ⓑ Ⓒ Ⓓ Ⓔ
85. Ⓐ Ⓑ Ⓒ Ⓓ Ⓔ
86. Ⓐ Ⓑ Ⓒ Ⓓ Ⓔ
87. Ⓐ Ⓑ Ⓒ Ⓓ Ⓔ
88. Ⓐ Ⓑ Ⓒ Ⓓ Ⓔ
89. Ⓐ Ⓑ Ⓒ Ⓓ Ⓔ
90. Ⓐ Ⓑ Ⓒ Ⓓ Ⓔ
91. Ⓐ Ⓑ Ⓒ Ⓓ Ⓔ
92. Ⓐ Ⓑ Ⓒ Ⓓ Ⓔ
93. Ⓐ Ⓑ Ⓒ Ⓓ Ⓔ
94. Ⓐ Ⓑ Ⓒ Ⓓ Ⓔ
95. Ⓐ Ⓑ Ⓒ Ⓓ Ⓔ
96. Ⓐ Ⓑ Ⓒ Ⓓ Ⓔ
97. Ⓐ Ⓑ Ⓒ Ⓓ Ⓔ
98. Ⓐ Ⓑ Ⓒ Ⓓ Ⓔ
99. Ⓐ Ⓑ Ⓒ Ⓓ Ⓔ
100. Ⓐ Ⓑ Ⓒ Ⓓ Ⓔ

REA's Test Prep Books Are The Best!

(a sample of the <u>hundreds of letters</u> REA receives each year)

(more on back page)

REA's Test Prep Books Are The Best!

(a sample of the <u>hundreds of letters</u> REA receives each year)

" Using REA's *Best Review for the CLEP General Exams*
with the companion book, *The Best Test Preparation for
the CLEP General Exams*, saved me from sitting in the classroom for a
whole semester. Provides sample tests, study tips — everything you
need to be successful. "

Student, Port Orchard, WA

" My students report your chapters of review as the most valuable single
resource they used for review and preparation. "

Teacher, American Fork, UT

" Your book was such a better value and was so much more complete than
anything your competition has produced — and I have them all! "

Teacher, Virginia Beach, VA

" Compared to the other books that my fellow students had, your book was
the most useful in helping me get a great score. "

Student, North Hollywood, CA

" Your book was responsible for my success on the exam, which helped me get
into the college of my choice... I will look for REA the next time I need help. "

Student, Chesterfield, MO

" Just a short note to say thanks for the great support your book gave me in
helping me pass the test... I'm on my way to a B.S. degree because of you! "

Student, Orlando, FL

(more on previous page)